MY ROCK-GARDEN

SAXIFRAGA LINGULATA

MY ROCK-GARDEN

BY

REGINALD FARRER

AUTHOR OF 'ALPINES AND BOG-PLANTS'
'IN A YORKSHIRE GARDEN,' 'IN OLD CEYLON,' ETC.

WITH ILLUSTRATIONS

EP Publishing Limited
1977

Reprinted from the 6th impression,
first published Edward Arnold,
London, 1920.

Republished 1977 by
EP Publishing Limited
East Ardsley, Wakefield
West Yorkshire, England

ISBN 0 7158 1222 X

British Library Cataloguing in Publication Data
Farrer, Reginald
    My rock-garden.
    1. Rock gardens – Great Britain   2. Rock
    plants
    I. Title
    635.9'672'0941   SB459
    ISBN 0–7158–1222–X

Please address all enquiries to EP Publishing Limited
(address as above)

Printed in Great Britain by
The Scolar Press Limited
Ilkley, West Yorkshire

PREFACE

NOWADAYS it is, indeed, becoming for a new 'gardening-book' to slink into the world under cover of an apology; and it had been my intention to plead, in excuse, that this volume of mine held no presumptuous notion of giving help to any rival gardener (for all true gardeners are rivals). I see, however, that such a plea would at once make publication a mere impertinence. Therefore I will frankly hope that some of my readers may consider this book's existence justified by the help it gives them. But if some are inclined to resent the appearance of yet another work on gardening, others may well cavil, I fear, at its confessed incompleteness and inadequacy. To these I plead that only the most stringent considerations of space could have compelled the many omissions that they will mark in my pages. I had originally dealt faithfully with all my plants, and if any reader now vainly search this book for a detailed treatment of Aethionema, Silene, Lychnis, Veronica, and many another treasure, let him blame not me, but the pitiless blue pencil that made such a massacre of the innocents. Faced by cruel alternatives, I chose rather to treat at length of the great races than cursorily and unsatisfactorily of all. As for spelling, some may be shocked by 'Himâlya' and 'Aeizoeides': my only aim in this was to help the proper pronunciation; it being quite as easy to say 'Aeizoeides,' which is right, as 'Aizoydes' or 'Aïzōïdes,' which are both wrong.

REGINALD FARRER.

CONTENTS

LIST OF PLATES

———————————

All the plates, except where otherwise stated, are from photographs
by Mr. HORNER, of Settle, Yorkshire.

MY ROCK-GARDEN

CHAPTER I

Of Making the Garden

FEW things are more annoying than dogmatism; and dogmatism is nowhere more misplaced than in horticulture. The wise gardener is he whom years of experience have succeeded in teaching that plants, no less than people, have perverse individualities of their own, and that, though general rules may be laid down, yet it is impossible ever to predict with any certainty that any given treatment is bound to secure success or failure. There are so many possibilities to be reckoned with, so many differences of soil, climate, and aspect. Then, when you have allowed for all these, remains the great stumping fact, that out of one seed-pod no two plants (any more than any two babies of a family) have precisely the same constitution or the same idiosyncrasies, so that what spells happiness for one may be misery to its brother. Even before grappling with this problem, the gardener is sternly confronted by the truth that what suits in Surrey is death in Westmorland; that what serves in Yorkshire loam is fatal in Suffolk sand; that what sunny Sussex favours, Cumberland's rainfall makes deadly—that, to sum up the huge uncertainties of gardening in one perspicuous instance, *Lilium candidum* will be a gorgeous weed in one cottage garden, and a blank rotten failure in another, divided only by a hedge, and identical in soil, culture, and

A

aspect. Therefore the gardener, and, above all, he who aspires to dealing with the perverse little people of the hills, must go very cautiously, and can base his rules only on the broadest general principles. He is for ever forbidden to dogmatise; and, in telling of his experiences, must remember that they are simply an individual's experiences, and must never be offered as any real basis of conduct to other individuals, but solely as an isolated chain of observations that may or may not be suggestive at the best.

I can talk about what has happened in my garden, and how and why it is that *Edraianthus pumilio* approves of me; but never let it be thought that I am promising anybody else that if he goes and does likewise *Edraianthus* will also approve of him. Very likely it will; I am inclined to think it will, of course; but Heaven forbid I should make any definite rule or promise, until I know that his soil, his rock, his air, his climate, his treatment are identical with mine. And, even so, there remains the idiosyncrasy of each individual *Edraianthus* itself to reckon with—a question quite beyond the calculation of man.

I am trying, by frank confession of that humility which must beset every gardener face to face with plant-nature, to disarm the criticisms of people cleverer or more lucky than I. All my aim is simply to take a few of the alpine plants that I grow, and give an honest account of whether I succeed or fail with them, and what may be the approximate causes of my success and failure. Beyond general hints and recommendations I can preach no definite gospel. There is no royal road to gardening; I myself have bought, with much failure, the joy of some success; the utmost that lies in my power is to tell my friends that I achieved the success, and to hope that they may avoid the failure, (although, if they

do, they will not really taste the full sweetness of success).
Even before I set out I am frightened in advance by the
thought of all those superior persons who have found
triumph where I have chronicled disaster. Will they
write me derisive letters, those gardeners—if any such
there be—who annually picnic on their mats of *Androsace
imbricata*, who play lawn-tennis over their courts of
Eritrichium nanum, who have had to buy a motor
mowing-machine to reap their yearly thickening jungles
of *Lilium Krameri*? 'If any such there be,' say I—let us
pray there be none such—let us even confess our belief
that there are none such, and that, on the contrary,
there may be many who will take an interest in hearing
of a mere average fellow-gardener's struggles, enthusiasms,
joys and sorrows. I speak of plants as I have found
them; nothing comes upon my page that has not lived
in my garden; nor shall any superstition prevent me
from owning to vegetable likes and dislikes, nor any
personal pride from confessing a failure. And so, with
all modesty, with all proper diffidence, I set forth.

First, as to the making of the rock-garden. Well,
now I must break my own rule, and dogmatise for a
minute or two. Otherwise I should be a traitor to my
own views and my own experience. But I will get it over
as quickly as may be. Also, remember, I am merely
talking of ideals. And where is the ideal to be found
on earth? If I discourse on what is best, that will not
hinder or discourage any one from having the best they
can get; nor must a discourse of the Perfect Rock-garden
be any sort of reproach to any beloved and cherished
strip of rock-work in villa or cottage border.

It is the grief of humanity that from one extreme of
error it must always sway back into another—from
crinoline to skin-tight vestments, from so-called Classic
to so-called Romantic. In gardening we are now

enduring the backwash of just such a terrific wave, whose
recession down the naked shingles of the world leaves our
horticultural future rather doubtful. The sixteenth and
seventeenth centuries knew what a real garden was; had
grasped, without extremes, the proper connection between
the pleasance and the house. Then follows the ghastly
period of Versailles and all that lath-and-plaster civilisa-
tion of le Roi Soleil, which is so faithfully reflected in
the pleasure-ground of the period—and Eden forgive one
for applying the name ' pleasure-ground ' to such gaunt
stretches as Lenôtre indulged his employers in! Then,
in a little, crash goes the whole fabric of taste all of a
sudden; the weathercock veers to the other pole. Now
we must have the Jardin Anglais—sham landscape,
sham wildness, sham ruins, wobbling walks, pagodas,
lakes, pools—you will find it all in *Headlong Hall* and
Sense and Sensibility; Lord Littlebrain's park is simply
a prophecy of Mr. Robinson, and Marianne Dashwood
anticipates Ruskin almost word for word. But the
effervescence of that romantic movement soon subsides,
with the subsidence of the great Revolutions. Peacock
gives place to Paxton, and Jane Austen to Felicia
Hemans, and the reign of uninspired comfort sets in,
bringing the grimmest, deadliest period ever struggled
through by art and horticulture. A fat, handsome
deadness seizes upon the popular taste like a great
cancer. Up come the crinoline and the peg-top trouser,
and the Victorian era, and the Crystal Palace, and carpet-
bedding, and such a crew of attendant horrors that one
shudders even in the second-hand reminiscence. Everywhere there is formality without beauty, extravagance
without value. The scarlet Pelargonium becomes the
national flower, and before its dread assessors, blue
Lobelia and yellow Calceolaria, all the gracious beautiful
flowers of long ago take flight like fairies at the approach

of trippers. The old gardens where Parkinson walked, where the great Tudor queens took their pleasure, are filled with dingy *Perilla* and *Alternanthera*; *Lilium candidum* and Daffodil and Crown Imperial are pitchforked over the wall on to the rubbish heap. Now indeed are we in the land of Egypt and the House of Bondage.

But suddenly there comes a Moses to our need. Out of the dense darkness arises the immortal Mr. Robinson, pointing the way to escape. He reminds us of beauties which we had almost forgotten, and leads us on to a land flowing with sweetness and delight. Yet all these emancipations have excesses (it is the law of their development); and, in their contempt for the abuses of the formal system, Mr. Robinson's successors and disciples have been driven into the foolish extreme of denying all value to form, of insisting on anarchy in the garden, of declaring that every restraint is hateful. Now we have nothing but weak lines in our gardens, vague, wibble-wobble curves that have no meaning nor explanation; our borders meander up and down and here and there like sheep that have no shepherd, our silly lawns erupt into silly little beds like pimples. All is uncertainty, formlessness—a vain, impotent striving after the so-called natural. Mr. Robinson, the great and good, with all the incalculable benefits that he has given, has given also, against his will, incalculable harm. For the prophet's words are always exaggerated and abused; and, in reacting violently against the heartless formalism of the eighteenth century, Mr. Robinson's creed has been used also against the large, orderly splendour of the sixteenth. Let us only hope and pray that people may not, by the fury with which walls and all bounding lines have been nowadays assailed, be swung back into another revulsion against the deliberate chaos into which garden design has at present been brought.

Truth, that unseizable thing, lies ever between two extremes; and, while the garden of multi-coloured gravel is an offence to the blessed sun, hardly less so is the amorphous foolishness that now makes our borders undulate and flounder so feebly. The garden proper, as seen from the house, is a part of the house, neither more nor less than the frame is part of the picture. From which it follows that the garden must be built on calm, firm lines—either straight, or intelligibly, strongly curved. It must have a definite scheme, coherence, unity—not be a mere reckless jumble of features. It must also make one individuality with the house it belongs to, harmonise with it, continue its plan, and carry out its intention. A garden is *not* a wild place—here is the great error of the extreme landscapists; therefore any attempt to make it so by incoherence and floppiness of line falls between the two stools and is doubly damned, being neither real Nature nor real art. Round the house, then, the garden must have a precise, definite plan. In that garden have all the lovely things you can grow, or that your heart desires to grow; and beyond it have as much real wild garden as you can manage. But don't try to combine incongruous elements.

Where does the rock-garden come in, then? Well, outside the real garden, please, if it can be arranged. In the wild garden, and if possible—this is only a beautiful ideal—out of sight of all formal and artificial surroundings. Let it crop naturally out from the fringe of a little shrubbery, perhaps, or make the brow of some small hill. Don't ever try to make your rock-garden among trees, in hollows of the wood. Don't let nurserymen pile you a Drunkard's Dream of noxious cement blocks, all volutes and exaggerated cavities. Don't build up a sham grotto of clinker-bricks on the lawn, and rig up nasturtiums over it to hide the places where your alpines have unanimously died. See that your site is at least clear, and clean, and open.

And then? The rock-garden stands to many people for the highest realisation of that shapeless, anarchic ideal held up for imitation by extremists of the Landscape school. They think that if any one invention on earth can be free from all element of design, that invention must be the rock-garden. But in the rock-garden rules, as a matter of fact, are more paramount than ever; for though it is built under different laws from those that govern the garden proper, those laws are in no way less stringent and stern than those that rule the borders; and it is the greatest mistake in the world to imagine that a good rock-garden can be made by throwing stones about in an incoherent heap. The rules of the garden itself are the rules of art: the rules of the rock-garden are the more awful rules of Nature herself. Nature is never haphazard or chaotic—she may seem so, but she never is; and the rock-garden which sincerely aims at following Nature must have Nature's own unity and decision of purpose.

The ideal rock-garden must have a plan. But there are three prevailing plans, none of which are good. The first is what I may call the Almond-pudding scheme, and obtains generally, especially in the north of England. You take a round bed; you pile it up with soil; you then choose out the spikiest pinnacles of limestone you can find, and you insert them thickly with their points in the air, until the general effect is that of a tipsy-cake stuck with almonds. In this vast petrified porcupine nothing will grow except Welsh Poppy, Ferns, and some of the uglier Sedums. The second style is that of the Dog's Grave. It marks a higher stage of horticulture, and is affected by many good growers of alpines. The pudding-shape is more or less the same in both, but the

stones are laid flat in the Dog's-Grave ideal.   Plants will
grow on this, but its scheme is so stodgy and so abhor-
rent to Nature that it should be discarded.   The third
style is that of the Devil's Lapful, and prevailed very
largely when alpines first began to be used out of doors.
The finest specimens of this style are to be seen in such
gardens as Glasnevin and Edinburgh.   The plan is simplicity itself.   You take a hundred or a thousand cart-
loads of bald square-faced boulders.   You next drop
them all about absolutely anyhow ; and you then plant
things amongst them.   The chaotic hideousness of the
result is something to be remembered with shudders ever
after.   Nurserymen still occasionally pursue this school,
which is another good reason among many why the
enthusiast should always insist on having his rock-garden
built under his own eye and on his own plans.   It is as
foolish to expect a nurseryman, untrained in design, to
build you a harmonious, genuine, schemed rock-garden,
as to ask a journeyman mason to make you a palace.
Rule and a knowledge of rule are as necessary to a rock-
garden as ever to an architect.   In fact, the builder of a
rockery must be, on his own different lines, as much of
an architect as any planner of houses.

And now, what *are* these rules that govern the ideal
rockery ?   Briefly, there is but one.   Have an idea, and
stick to it.   Let your rock-garden set out to be something definite, not a mere agglomeration of stones.   Let
it be a mountain gorge, if you like, or the stony slope of
a hill, or a rocky crest, or a peak.   But, whatever it be,
it must have definiteness of scheme.   It is, in effect, an
imitation of Nature, and, to be successful, must aim at
reproducing with fidelity some particular feature of
Nature—whichever you may choose.   Kew offers every
one a model which it would be impertinent to praise.
The Glen form is apt to be monotonous, perhaps, but

climatic conditions make it necessary at Kew, and in many other parts of England ; and Kew has triumphed over the problem of how to make a glen perpetually varied and interesting. At Warley, again, there is the Gorge-design to be studied—to my own personal taste, a trifle too violent to be altogether pleasant, but still a noble example of definite purpose definitely carried out. Of course the absolute masters of rock-garden, before whose names one must go helpless to one's knees in adoration, are the Japanese. Not to plunge into the bottomless sea of their mysticism and symbolism in design, the sight of a Japanese garden is enough to bring tears of ecstasy to the eyes of any garden-lover. No distortions, no abortion, no discords are there, but some corner of landscape—a rocky gully, a view among the islands—some famous corner of landscape carefully copied to scale, with a sense of harmony and perspective so perfect that in a cottage close four yards square you will seem to have half a mountain-side. Oh, those Japanese gardens! Nothing so tortures the mind with exquisite memories as my lost vision of the Koraku-en, or the Kencho-ji garden at Kamakura. But, perfected through a thousand generations as is their tact in dealing with rock, the Japanese care more for congruity of vegetation in the scheme, than for flowers as flowers. Here and there peeps out a wee rounded bush, or droops a gnarled aged pine a couple of feet high, but of alpine plants and the cultivation of them for their own sake the Japanese have no notion. The love of such mountain-treasures, indeed, is far more widely spread with us. Each rare Japanese species has its well-known popular name, it is true, but on their elaborate pondered pieces of rock-sculpture they have no wish to impose a second, perhaps distracting beauty, by luring one's mind away from the perfect balance of the design with the colours of the flowers that might grow on it. Therefore what the idealist cries hopelessly to high Heaven for is a Japanese garden stocked with European alpines ; and when I say Japanese garden, I don't mean a silly jungle of bamboos, with Tori, and a sham tea-house, and Irises, and a trellis—I mean a rocky glen, a pinnacled flank of mountain such as every other cottage in Kioto possesses, and has possessed, for half a dozen generations. (Oh, the beauty of the weather-worn, tormented fretted rock they use ; and oh, to see *Saxifraga burseriana* peering out of its crevices, or *Edraianthus serpyllifolius* showering down its great violet bells !) Some day, when the ship of my fancy comes home, I will have a Japanese build me one of his perfect gardens—no one in England knows yet what they are like—and then I will plant it with my own plants and be happy, unless, indeed, one beauty competes with the other, and both get spoiled.

And now, having soared through the Heaven of my ideals, I will drop thump to earth. My own rock-gardens are two in number and two in nature. The one is ill-built, ill-soiled, and a perpetual worry. Nothing except the commonest things will live or thrive, except with endless bother. There is some fatal canker in the soil, I fear, and besides, I made the garden many years ago, when, like Cleopatra, I was exceedingly green in judgment. Its situation is the best thing about it ; being a big semicircle in a sunny slope, whence, at one time, sand was quarried for the repairing of the house. That is to say, the whole bank is rubble and dust of an old moraine, absolutely devoid of nutriment, so that I have had to bring all the soil I needed from afar. On either side are shelving banks, and through one a gorge. In the centre lies a big pool, so shallow and ineffectually done—the result of many makeshifts—that, after years of worry, I am now renouncing it, and having it turned into a bed for *Iris*

Kaempferi. The rest of the space is taken up by masses
of rock-work, with two deep glens—one sunny, the other
shady—running on each side of a big mountain-mass.
The other garden is an unutterable joy, though younger
than the first. Whereas in the Old Garden, if you
planted a thing it either died or sulked or sat still, if you
plant anything in the New Garden on Saturday it seems
to have grown an inch by Monday, and a foot by Monday
week. And the cause of this difference is simply that the
New Garden is really an old disused kitchen-garden,
where the soil is rich and fat and full of hoarded nourishment. These alpines are such frauds; there is nothing
that they appreciate, I have found, like manure, as long,
of course, as it is not rank or recent. After all, why
shouldn't they, although they starve on rubble in the
Alps? Because a pauper-child exists and looks palely
pretty on kippers and gin, that is no reason why it
shouldn't, if the chance be given, grow fat and rosy on
buns. But, at first sight, it seems a little incongruous
that these austere little people of the hills, who live on
so meagre and ethereal a diet, should, when out on a
visit, as it were, take so kindly to the fleshpots of the
garden, and the somewhat material charms of manure.
However, the case is so; and therefore I will say to all
lovers of alpines, get, or make, a rich soil for your plants.
Not rough, coarse manure, but old well-rotted vegetable
ground, will please them thoroughly. There are only a
very few that will wax fat and kick. In other words,
there are only a very few plants which a rich soil will
make rank and leafy in growth. *Saxifraga oppositifolia*,
I find, is one ; so is *Arenaria gothica. Anemone pulsatilla*
is never so pretty as on its own barren downs. Besides,
certain species rather tender or very glacial, such as
Androsace lanuginosa and *Linaria alpina*, suffer more
from damp in winter if their soil be too fat. But on the

whole a general rule might almost be written in letters of gold, like the Chrysobulls of the Byzantine Emperors, 'the soil for your rock-garden cannot in reason be too fertile or rich'; and all rock-plants, remember, except the admitted shade-lovers, are as greedy of light as Little Nell.

Your soil must be free, too—neither excessively sandy, nor ponderous and podgy. Every one, here, must make his own mixture. And at this point I will not embark on the awful question of lime-lovers and peat-lovers. I will only go on to say that a pleasant loam, cool and moist in summer, porous and light in winter, is the ideal to be aimed at. Above all—drainage, drainage, drainage, is essential. More alpine plants are annually lost by defective drainage than by all the other fatalities of the garden put together (of course, I am now talking to those who, like me, have to cope with a wet winter-climate; but everywhere the rule holds good). Consider the slope of the Alps, the light, sharp grit in which the plants grow. Moisture is abundant, but it drains away with unfailing rapidity. Anything like clogging by damp or stagnant humidity in the soil is certainly fatal to mountain-plants. Even bog-species resent it bitterly. And no measure will go so far to ensure success as the laying of a good eight-inch bed of clinkers at the foundation of the rock-garden, before you build the erection itself. I have never had more triumph than out of compartments in the New Garden, where I took out the soil to two and a half feet, laid a drainage-bed of rough (they should be *rough*) broken burrs; then, atop of them, clods of coarse peat, with sharp-edged lumps of limestone or sandstone, and then old, old manure, leaf-soil in abundance, peat, sand, and good fibrous loam. This sharp drainage has done wonders, I find, for the difficult species which otherwise are liable to resent our damp winters. And the rule, together with that as to goodness of soil, is one of the few dogmas that are necessary to horticultural salvation.

The New Garden is not so well situated as the Old. It forms the lowest part of my Craven Nursery, and is a large square bounded on three sides by a wall. The odious formality of this was mitigated by sloping up banks of rock-work to the walls until they were hidden. These banks are diversified by ups and downs, beneath which the path wanders, skirting a big flat bog-garden, a glory of *Iris Kaempferi* in its time, on the farther side of which again lies a long pool occupied by Nymphaeas and by a corpulent elderly goldfish, whose mortal days, I fear, are drawing to a close, as he has recently blossomed out into a sort of grey fur. Across the pool are the two main ranges of rock-work, stately mountain piles, separated by a narrow gorge, where some of my chiefest jewels are growing—Saxifrages on the sunny cliff, Primulas and Ramondias on the other. Here and there are precipices built high, with beds on the top for things of special interest. The stone everywhere is the mountain limestone of the Craven Highlands, brought straight down from the fells of Ingleborough just above us. And this I recommend as the very best that can possibly be used for the rock-garden. It is soft, extremely beautiful in colour, and becomes fretted by air and water into the most varied wonderful shapes, of which you can make good use without following the Almond-pudding School. The rain of the hills sometimes even makes holes right through and through; and in the Old Garden I have some big boulders, lugged off the mountains, so pierced and riddled with hollows that all you have to do is to plant your plants, and there you have a miniature rock-garden ready-made, and one too that will thrive for years without attention. There is also about the weathering of these blocks a dignity and calm which somehow make them perfectly harmonious in the very best design of rock-garden building. Popular taste prefers the wilder conformations in them, stuck up on end to look like bears or old women or monsters; but the more refined, normal specimens may be used for any mass you wish to build, and will, if properly set up, weld together so as to look as if Creation had put them there exactly so. Where the track winds round the pool, past a dell carpeted with *Dryas, Primula farinosa,* and *Gentiana verna,* it debouches at last upon the main path. And there, jutting out into it, is my toy-garden, my baby moraine, the particular pet joy of my heart. And this is built of four big limestone blocks, arranged in a square, with a deep well in the middle. Drainage burrs were put at the bottom of the well, and then the whole filled up with mere rough blue limestone chips, with only the faintest possible dash of soil. And here do some of the most difficult plants go on and prosper in the most marvellous way. *Campanula Allioni*—yes, in limestone chips!—trots about like a cheerful weed, some of the rarest eastern Saxifrages live here, and *Diapensioeides* and *Omphalodes Luciliœ,* and many more that I will tell of in their time. Let me here most warmly urge all that can to build a real big moraine-garden. The débris of a slate quarry will do, and any rubble of rock, however small. Put only the tiniest sprinkling of loam. Arrange your bed to slide down between two great boulders in a fan-shape, exactly as detritus pours off a hillside. Then plant what you will, and however difficult the plants you choose, or however easy, you will have a wonderful permanent sight of beauty. For though the alpines, all except the very highest—the moraine plants—appreciate good fat soil, as I have said, yet very many of them appreciate the home-like barrenness of the moraine quite as much, while as for the moraine plants themselves—the difficult Campanulas, *Allioni*, *cenisia*, *excisa*, and so on, I believe, from my own experience, that there is no other certain way of making them perennial. My own moraine-garden is a perpetual pleasure to me, and, I think, to the plants that live in it; but I talk of it here simply as an illustration of our water-worn limestone, and its extraordinary decorative value. For those four blocks, set together and filled in, make the effect of one enormous boulder, into whose topmost crevices the plants have rooted.

No other formation has the same romantic quality as mountain limestone ; both granite and sandstone are apt to be too square, to offer monotonous slab-like faces, and, altogether, not to present those many varied surfaces that make a rock so much more attractive. Of course culturally the sandstone is rather more porous, moist and adhesive than the limestone, but the slight superiority it has in this way is so slight as to outweigh the far greater picturesqueness of the other. Mr. Wolley Dod took all the trouble to import mountain limestone to Edge, and though that marvellous garden of his made little claim to artistic construction (much of it being like three magnified and stony potato ridges), yet the beauty of the stone employed completed the attraction of those splendid plants of his. As for blocks of grit and sandstone, they never build properly, always look isolated, imported, artificial, and haphazard.

One thing to remember, whatever stone you may be dealing with, is always to set your rock with its largest surface to the ground. This is the natural arrangement ; Nature stratifies, Nature doesn't bristle her stones about like the quills of the porcupine, with their points sticking up in the air. As all stones may be taken to have two broad and four thin faces (infinitely modified, of course, but this stands for the usual conformation), the domino-shape, in fact, it is on the broadest surface that your domino should lie. And, supposing you are dealing with a bank, the effect of the stonework is vastly heightened by arranging the scheme in a series of inclined strata, with a steep slope falling away beneath, and here and there a fault, to break the line in a cliff or some bold feature. Boldness, no less than coherence, is usually too much lacking in the rock-garden. Within reasonable limits you cannot have too much of boldness, at least as long as you stop short of truculence, and are content with only one or two startling features. It is a good thing, I have always found, to meditate very carefully the lie of the ground before you set out to build your rock-garden ; then if you go about the business with a plan, further features and inevitable developments will impose themselves upon you as you go along. And I think this precept may be bravely given to every one. Of course it is only in the ideal garden that one will be ever able to have one's own untrammelled way ; in this world one has to make the best, more or less, of what circumstances offer or allow ; even as both my gardens, Old and New, have been hampered by circumstances, so that, with the best will in the world, I have not been able to carry out in either exactly, perfectly, what my heart desires, but have had to do what I could with the situation and stones at my command. Yet no shortcomings of reality should ever deter one from worshipping the ideal ; and so I will say that, though few have the money or the time or the taste to emulate Mr. Crispe's model Matterhorn, yet any garden, however little—yes, the merest little patch behind a cottage, or strip along a walk—should have a scheme and a unity of its own ; should be an individuality, that is to say, not a mere reckless jostle of stones, dropped there anyhow for Sedums and Campanulas to run about over.

Having got our drainage in, and our rock-scheme

ready, and then our soil in, now comes the final toil. Your banks and slopes will probably have pockets and compartments ; let the surface of them be not flat but sloping. Otherwise drainage will be inadequate, and the results disastrous. I have heard that even Kew suffered once from flat-surfaced pockets, and lost many treasures inexplicably, until it was discovered that a good raking slope was necessary to carry off the surplus moisture. Another precaution of the very greatest importance, and not always very easy to accomplish if you neglect it at first, is that every chink and cranny of the rocks be well packed with soil. Often, if one is not careful, an un-expected hollow is left behind some boulder. And you may pack the outer cracks with soil, but if there are cavities behind all your care will be unavailing. For the plant in that crevice will root blithely back into the soil you have inserted, until one fine day its root-fibres come upon the unsuspected hollow. It then languishes or expires. So I say again, see that every stone is well wadded up with soil at the start ; for, if you don't look to this while the garden is building, you will never be able to do so afterwards, but must always struggle on with deficiencies here and there. Few things are more exasperating than to try and stuff a hidden hole behind a big rock. You grope and poke and ram, and take all the skin off your hands most hideously, and even so the job is difficult to make good. And, if you don't make it good, first of all your plants will die in those cavities, and, in the second place, rats and mice and horrors will come and live in them.

Another thing. Always leave plenty of root-room in your crevices. Perennial plants generally have good roots, but the roots of alpine plants are phenomenal even among perennials. Take *Androsace helvetica* in a pin-wide crack of a boulder. If the rock is rotten and you can lift off the upper slab, you will see the roots of that *Androsace*, a tangled web of tiny thirsty silk threads, extending far, far back and out, fanwise, perhaps a yard or more into the rock. And the plant itself is not three inches high! As for the Primulas, special lovers of crannies, their yellow whip-lashes go delving deep, deep, deep into the living precipice. Rock and mountain plants, having none too much nourishment to hand, must needs go questing it much further than ordinary border plants, with fatness all around them. A rock-plant has to send his fibres far and wide to lick up every available scrap of food, and in the bright days of summer to absorb all the damp that lurks in the very heart of the cliff. Therefore it is useless to plant even the wee-est alpine, *Androsace*, *Draba*, or *Eritrichium*, unless its roots can have an ample run—a run that seems ridiculous by comparison with the squatty minuteness of the plant itself. No shallow hole is enough, no blind alley in the rock, no ill-drained cul-de-sac; they must be able to draw their food eighteen inches or so at least below the surface, with room beyond that again for all superfluous moisture to slip away.

As for aspect, I am inclined to think that soil and treatment is far more important, at all events in my climate, than aspect. At least, shade-loving plants will bear a good deal of sun with me; though sun-lovers, I must confess, won't tolerate shade. My manager believes that even the high mountain Saxifrages will prefer shade (of rock, of course; never, never, of trees) down here, where the sun's rays are so much fiercer than up on their native moraines. Of this I daren't be sure. Personally, I feel rather afraid of putting the rock Saxifrages of the Euaeizoön section out of the sun; and yet there is no doubt that the red species from Eastern Europe (and this is very curious, considering what the sun must be on

A Glen in the Old Garden

the Balkans in summer !)—*Frederici-Augusti, porophylla,
thessalica, Griesebachi,* and possibly even *Stribnryi,* are
inclined to resent summer baking in my garden, and to
turn faint and flag in the heat. The corrective of this
will always be efficient watering. So I need say no more
about aspects. In one climate one aspect will best suit ;
in another a different one ; just as soils and hardiness
vary for each plant in different places ; so that *Androsace
lanuginosa* is hardy in light loam, and tender in heavy
loam, in the same garden ; a sound perennial in one
place, soil and climate, but a miffy delicate untrustworthy
creature half a mile away, or perhaps even on the same
rock-work. And so, enough of the rock-garden and its
making.

CHAPTER II

Our English Alpines

BEFORE going afield for our treasures to adorn the rock-garden, let us, like charity, begin at home, and first reckon up what beauties we have ready to hand in England, among our own native wildings. I do not mean so much things common and beautiful and rampageous, like Stitchwort or Germander, but the rarer people who haunt our northern rocks and fells. No one, I imagine, would take a great deal of trouble to plant Stitchwort or Germander, least of all in a little or select garden. They are as lovely as anything could well be, and, if they were newly imported from Thibet and sold at seven and six, our sycophantic souls would probably grow into ecstasies over them at the Temple Show. Be the cynical truth what it may, the fact remains that the rock-gardener must exercise some selection; and while, if he has a large garden, he may allow pretty weeds a little rambling room (I admit Germander and Harebell wherever I can, though there come bitter moments, even in my large, diverse gardens, when I have to be pitiless and turn them out), he cannot be for ever exercising a ruinous charity at the expense of rare treasures.

And now the vast thorny subject immediately surges up before us—what *is* an alpine, for gardening purposes? Well, my own definition includes everything that will look well in a rock-garden. The definition, therefore, is the loosest possible, for all depends on the size of your ground. On a big bold bank Bamboos and *Lilium auratum* and Japanese Cherries have their place, and look superb. In a small garden their very notion is disproportionate. Thus every one must choose his plants and draw his line exactly where his own taste orders. I myself would only plead for the absolute exclusion of all Double flowers, except the Double Orange Welsh Poppy, from the rock-garden, and of all Annuals, only admitting a few of tiny nature and special beauty. It is possible to cram a bare rock-garden with Godetias and annual Linums and *Eschscholtzia*—you may even get a pretty, dazzling effect. But the effect is bastard art, illegitimate, ungenuine. It is no more right or appropriate than to put the prettiest of French picture-hats on the Venus of Milo. The rock-garden is a place sacred to the brave little perennials of the mountains; therefore to contrast their antlike perseverance with the grasshopper frivolity of an annual is to perpetrate a crying discord.

The path of definitions is a strait and perilous tight-rope. I know that mine are loose and lax; I make no claim to tread the tight-rope accurately. But I think my general rule is sound; it must be elastically treated, of course, and translated according to every one's common sense. But even when you have excluded Annuals, and reckoned with your available space, the question of what constitutes fitness for the rock-garden still remains. All plants of the rock-garden are by no means mountain or rock-species—who would do without *Anemone robinsoniana* or *Iris gracilipes*? Nor are all rock-plants by any means eligible for cultivation—who wants to be bothered with the ugly little glacial Camomiles or Plantains? Therefore all one can say is: be guided by rough-cast rules for a general principle, and by your own personal taste for particulars. For instance, I myself have a great love for our native *Viola lutea*, and an incurable coldness towards all the Drabas; therefore I cherish the one and exclude the other, though the Viola is not really a rock-plant, and the Drabas very distinctly are.

Nor shall I indulge myself with any prejudices as to keeping aliens in separate compatriot colonies. If *Ourisia* from Chili will thrive in one corner, there he shall go; and if I so please, he shall have the Japanese *Lilium rubellum* underground, and the Siberian Columbine on his left, and the Canadian Phlox on his right. Yes, and at the back there shall be Chinese Bamboos, and Himâlyan Rhododendrons, and American Azaleas, tangled up with big border plants like Delphinium and Helenium and the tall Asters. Nothing perennial comes amiss to me—if only it is pretty and suited to its place in size and habit. As for the pious-sounding objection that no plant is ugly—this I regard as a specious heresy. Many plants—yes, and many alpines—are dowdy and plain. It is of no use to deny it. They are. And their ugliness only adds to the beauty of their better-favoured relatives. And besides this again, there are the beauties that convince one's eye without convincing one's affection. There are many plants that I know to be splendid, but which I can never admire half as much as something else that I know and clearly perceive to be nothing like as magnificent. Certain flowers hold out the hand of comradeship at once to certain people; and others, again, have a different set of admirers. *Lilium rubellum* and *Aquilegia alpina* always make me feel quite gulpy; so do the Real Crocuses (not the fat Dutch kinds). On the other hand, I stand in front of the frilled, enormous Begonias that are now so admired, and experience nothing more than that *morne étonnement* which Swift is said to inspire in the French mind. There they are, gorgeous and bloated, like splendidly made-up ancient ladies with elaborate frisures. And their colours are unspeakably beautiful, and so is their texture. Yet they say nothing to me, absolutely nothing, though my mind realises that their glory triumphs insolently, arrogantly over anything that the Lily or the Columbine may have to show. But there, if the truth must out, I have an unconquerable distaste for doubled-artificial-looking flowers. The Rose, the Carnation, and the Chrysanthemum must stand excepted, though even of this last I love the single varieties best. But the Rose and the Carnation are, in their very conception, double flowers; the mention of Rose or Carnation calls up at once the image of a full-packed mass of petals. They don't really belong any more to *Rosa* or *Dianthus*. Years and years of cultivation have set them apart from the single-flowered races that they sprung from originally.

As for the rock-garden—far off, far off, please, all garden-roses and Carnations and Paeonies. Enter gladly, and be very welcome, single Paeonies, Rosa, Dianthus; Chrysanthemum, riot about if you will on upper slopes, though the Chrysanthemum more almost than any other flower suffers from that megalomania which is the British gardener's sole ideal of beauty. All he cares for is to get a thing large; farewell colour, fragrance, elegance, grace, so long as you have a vast draggled head that looks like a moulting mop dipped in stale lobster-sauce. The result is a show Chrysanthemum. Once I lectured to an enthusiastic roomful of gardeners on Japanese horticulture. Humbly and reverently I tried to unfold to them the unspeakable perfection to which the Japanese have brought their craft. And at the end a patriotic soul rose up and questioned me. 'Surely,' he said, ' we have at least improved the Chrysanthemum?' I am afraid I astonished that man. Oh, to

compare the exaggerated lumpishness of our show Chry-
santhemums with the flowers that Japanese taste has
loved and made perfect through five hundred years!—the
idea was a rank blasphemy when one remembered Dango-
zaka, and the exquisite, delicate glory of the Japanese
Chrysanthemum. We are indeed a brutish rather than
a sensitive race where beauty is concerned; size and show
are all our study—witness the unutterable horrors of obese
Calceolarias; of squatty, monotonous Chinese Primulas,
with neither elegance nor individuality; of Chrysan-
themums bloated out of all their proper loveliness, that
fortnightly defile our exhibitions, and really appeal to the
average working gardener a great deal more than any
delicate, charming, tiny creature of the rock or marsh.
There is hardly a flowering weed beneath the man's foot
as he goes back from work that is not more beautiful
than the nightmare exaggerations which to him repre-
sent floriculture at its finest. Therefore the Chrysanthemum, too, is best banished from the neighbourhood of
the rock-garden, and its exile must be shared by those
dreadful inventions, the Bedding Hyacinths and Tulips.
O *Hyacinthus orientalis*, O *Tulipa gesneriana*, that these
lumpish dwarfs should be sprung of your blood and
kindred, should dare to bear the same name!

Having done my best to purify my visionary garden,
like my real, from discordant elements, I will deal with
our own natives as far as they are suitable for our purposes. And I will not take the common species, nor will
I dwell on the obvious beauties that our mountains share
with the great mountain-chains of Europe. The Harebell, for instance, is among the dearest of plants, but no
one needs to be advised about it; while, on the other
hand, *Gentiana verna* is so universally famous that it is
better left till we come to deal with the whole group of
Gentiana. I shall take, then, just the rather rare and

less known natives in this chapter—plants whose rarity
may be estimated by the way they fluctuate on the edge
of having or lacking an English name.

And here I must pause yet again to enter an inevitable
caution. It is absolutely useless to ask any gardener to
spare you Latin names, for the excellent reason that nine
out of ten alpine plants haven't got any English name.
Even our native alpines are very often as badly off as the
newest Himâlyan in that respect. They have no names
except by the grace of science. It is not as in Japan,
where popular taste and love so go out to every little
plant of hill or valley that it invariably has a popular
name, be it the rarest of species or the highest of
alpines. (Where *Schizocodon* is the Mirror of the
Rocks, 'Iwakagami'; *Conandron*, 'Rock Tobacco'; *Androsace*, Rock-cherry, 'Iwazakura.') No, English peasants
don't know *Saxifraga oppositifolia*, or even *Gentiana
verna*; of all the vast race of Saxifrages only very few
have any title in English, and the preciosity of Ruskin's
'Rockfoil' has luckily not 'caught on,' besides being
quite inadequate. So the reader must accommodate
himself to the only names available. And this is really
not such a trial as people imagine, for botanical names
are generally more euphonious and invariably more descriptive than any English equivalent, where it exists.
Stitchwort must certainly yield the palm of beauty and
relevance to *Stellaria*, and Lousewort is certainly less
pretty than the more decent obscurity of *Pedicularis*.
At the same time, to be candid, there are *some* botanical
names that are teasers. Where Polish discoverers or
Russian explorers come upon the scene the result is apt
to be an appalling jangle of horrors. Michaux, Stribnry,
Przewalszky, Tchihatchew are responsible for some real
jawbreakers; and when it comes to *Michauxia Tchihatchewi*,
exhausted humanity gives up in despair. However, there

is no help for it but to persevere. You cannot talk of
these plants by any other name, because they haven't got
any other name; so all you can do is to shut your eyes,
blow your nose violently three times, and hope that you
have sufficiently expressed that you mean *Tchihatchewi*.
However, we have our own guilt to contend against and
make us humble. There once was a plant—a stove-
plant, I am thankful to say—called *Ohigginsia*. It is
true that it was ashamed of itself, and soon changed to
Hoffmannia, but even *Hoffmannia* isn't a great improvement. Let us then be thankful that the rock-garden
contains no *Ohigginsia*; and go valiantly on, contending
where we must with Przewalszky and Tchihatchew, con-
gratulating ourselves the while on the fact that botanical
names are, as a rule, so much more pretty and expressive
than their few and awful exceptions.

Arenaria gothica justly heads the list of our alpines.
Of all our English natives, this is, I think, the rarest.
It has only one certain locality—here and there on the
limestone levels round the eastern base of Ingleborough.
Unless it was imported years since in ballast (as some do
vainly and impiously talk), it is a survival of the great
glaciers that once covered all this country. Reported
from Sutherland, *Arenaria gothica* does not occur again
until you get to Gothland and Iceland. It was first
seen about the station yard at Ribblehead; then on
broken ground by the baby Ribble; soon it was discovered by Dr. Sylvanus Thompson on loose stone round
Helln Pot. After that begins my connection with the
plant, for I found it first on the highest point of the
limestone plateau, near Sulber Nick, a vast amphitheatre
of white precipices. Thence I tracked it patch by patch,
here and there, along the course of the fells, never far
from the path, and never anywhere but among broken
limestone *débris*. Last of all I found one extraordinary

station for it, quite isolated, about five hundred feet lower down. *Arenaria gothica* seems by all accounts to be spreading and increasing everywhere, and soon it may be recorded for the western side of Ingleborough—all its habitats, so far, having been restricted to the eastern. It is a typical Arctic rather than Alpine plant, frail, weak, and trailing, with inch-long stems and ovate, opposite dark-green little glossy leaves, and then flowers which are large for the plant, and of a most brilliant, pure, glistening white. In cultivation, like so many Arctic plants, it is rather inclined to forget itself—the stems grow erecter, the leaves paler and less solid, the flower smaller, and thinner, and poorer. It requires the moraine garden, and a soil all chips and sterile stone-dust, if it is to keep its pretty, independent character.

Arenaria verna is such a dear little alpine that it is a perpetual marvel to me why it is not more grown. It is of very general occurrence as soon as you are two thousand feet or so above the sea; and in mountainous countries like ours it often comes down to lower levels, though never to the valleys. It makes a neat, compact cushion like fine emerald-green fur, which in winter is as cheerful a sight as you could wish to see. Then in early summer (need I mention, by the way, that all plants mentioned in this book flower in early summer, except where otherwise stated?) up rise very airy, wiry little stems with abundance of delightful pure white flowers. It is a very easy plant to grow on the rock-garden, and I think it is one of the prettiest little mountaineers. There is a rather delicate double form which achieves the miracle of being as pretty as the type, and also in certain stations, as for instance near old lead-mines about here, the whole plant hypertrophies into a greatly magnified version of its own neat, brilliant self.

Now for the Campanulas. Well, the ordinary Harebell

is far too exquisite to be weeded out except for very special reasons. However, the Harebell plants itself quite gratuitously everywhere. But England gives us another magnificent Bell-flower which must only be used with great caution. *Campanula latifolia* is a gorgeous, tall-growing, rampageous person, who pervades the whole sub-alpine region, and luxuriates in moist ditches and opener places of our North-country woods. You see it at its best in the hedges and ditches where, in July, it sends up a great leafy spire, with very large pale purple bells. *Latifolia*, if you have a damp, out of the way, copsy corner, is one of the most valuable things you can use. But be careful how you admit it into choicer quarters. The other Campanulas which are found in these islands are not mountain-plants, and shall be treated with the rest of their family. As for *Convallaria maialis*, I only mention the Lily of the Valley to do it homage. It is too invasive for the rock-garden, but must certainly be put in any shady place near by. Though found here and there all England over, *Convallaria* is a true mountain-plant, and haunts the whole of this country, growing close up to the limestone cliffs at the top of every little hill-coppice. More than this, it shows the original character of the district, and is a visible memory of the great vanished forest that once clothed the lower flanks of the mountains. For you will find it here and there on the open moors, by the pot-holes, and, stranger still, in and out of the rifts between the blocks of flat scar limestone that crown the upper levels in a white pavement, and make the pedestal for the great gritstone masses of Ingleborough, Whernside, and Penyghent. Here, deep down in the darkness where no wind ruffles it, the *Convallaria* still abundantly survives, though I believe it never flowers now, or very rarely, at these bleak elevations where copses once ranged.

On this scar limestone are found some other very interesting and seldom cultivated alpines. The first is *Polygonatum officinale*, the mountain Solomon's Seal, which, like the Lily of the Valley, is a plant of the hill-jungles, pervading the whole district. This is a very attractive little species, absurdly neglected by gardeners. It is only about a quarter of the size of *Polygonatum multiflorum*, the big rampant species of the borders, and its sturdy little stems—about a foot high—carry large, important-looking, solid leaves, and only a brace, perhaps, of big, waxy bells, half the number and double the size of *multiflorum's*. And *officinale* never ramps, but grows happily, quietly, in any fair soil, making a modest, delightful patch, but not becoming obstreperous or greedy.

The next important plant of the Upper Scar-limestone is the very rare *Actaea spicata*, which rejoices in no fewer than two common names : being called Baneberry (it is very poisonous), or Herb Christopher. *Actaea* is a curious plant. He has American and Austrian cousins. But in Great Britain his distribution is extremely limited. He is confined, I believe, to this district, and haunts the rockiest places, high up. I have seen him very sparingly in copses about Malham, and I know a certain region of the flat limestone pavement under Ingleborough, about one thousand feet above the sea, and fifteen hundred or so below the summit, where *Actaea* is abundant, deep down in the sheltered crevices between the boulders, where no wind ever troubles him, and the soil is fat and good with the rottenness of ten thousand years. *Actaea* grows about two feet high, and remains almost the same in cultivation. He has a branching stem, large divided, lax leaves, like those of an Elder, and spikes of fluffy white flowers recalling those of a *Spiraea*, which are followed in autumn by venomous

blue-black berries (red in one form and white in another).
As a wild plant he has the attraction of his great rarity;
in gardens, where he thrives in any decent border, I have
never been able to muster any great passion for him.

Another of the scar-limestone plants is *Potentilla verna*,
a singularly lovely creature who, about here, only occurs
in isolated specimens. When you have found a *Convallaria* or an *Actaea*, you may rely on finding a dozen more
in five minutes. But in a day's journey on Ingleborough
you will be lucky if you see *Potentilla verna* twice. She
clings to the white cliff-face, and from far off you see a
splash of bright gold on the greyness, and wonder what
in the world it can be. Our *Potentilla verna* makes a
great tuft, which in June is hidden by innumerable dazzling yellow flowers rather larger than a shilling. In
cultivation I have always found her perfectly easy-going
and pleasant; nor does she in any way deteriorate, into
whatever corner you may poke her. In Teesdale lives a
still larger form, *alpestris*, which I have had and lost
and never replaced.

Geranium sanguineum is another of the scar-limestone
plants—a valuable rock-garden plant, with his bush of fine
leaves, and his big magenta-crimson flowers on thread-like, tossing stems. However, *Geranium sanguineum* is
not essentially a mountain- but a limestone-plant, for he
follows the limestone cliffs right down to the sea-level at
Cartmel and Grange, and though he is very useful, I say,
I must confess that his colour annoys. Now his albino
form, though a native of Wigtownshire, I believe, is perfectly exquisite—the flower-stems are longer and airier,
the flowers larger, and of the purest, most splendid white.

And here I must obviously treat of *Geranium lancastriense*, a supposed form of *sanguineum*. The plant,
whatever its origin, must have a very interesting history,
and be of enormous age. In the whole known world

Geranium lancastriense has only one home. It is restricted
to the Isle of Walney, a tongue of land lying off Barrow-
in-Furness. There, on a flat grassy down along by the
sea, lives *Geranium lancastriense*, running about among
the stunted lawn-like grasses. Further down the beach
Convolvulus Soldanella weaves his garlands of pink
trumpets over the shingle, and within a mile or so the
glaucous blue *Mertensia maritima* trails twinkling azure
eyes over the sand, within reach of the highest tides.
The Geranium, in June, makes a truly wonderful sight.
It is an absolutely prostrate plant that always creeps and
crawls, never, by any chance, stands up and walks; and
the flat tangle of it is covered with big florin-wide flowers
of a gentle rosy white, veined and lined all over with
ruby-red. In cultivation it is as easy as any daisy; put
it anywhere in fair, light loam and sunshine, and it will
be as happy as the day is long. And a more perfectly
dainty, exquisite creature doesn't live—no, not in the
wilds of Thibet or China. And there is an interesting
thing to note, as you see it wild on Walney. For
sanguineum grows among it. And *sanguineum* too has
become prostrate in the course of ages, beneath the pitiless
lash of the sea-winds. And if at some far-distant
date the rosy-veined *lancastriense* sprang suddenly, completely, like the armed Athena, into existence, then, in
the subsequent ages, parent and child must have hybridised. For the lawn is crowded with intermediate forms
between *sanguineum* and *lancastriense*, in which the
hybrid blood is clearly evident. They have an extraordinary range of colour, these mules—from a soft pure
pink, not far from *lancastriense* itself, to an ardent rich
carmine, far better than any true *sanguineum*. And
they, too, remain creepers in the rock-garden.

And now, to return to the mountain-country of West
Yorkshire. The essential glory of our district is, of

course, *Cypripedium Calceolus*. Wickednesses untold have
been perpetrated upon this plant, but, even so, it lingers
still unsuspected in the high hill valleys, nestling into
the steep copses under the cliff.   Only last year a clump
was discovered in its old station in the Arncliffe valley
under Penyghent, and was duly chronicled even by the
Strand Magazine.   A few seasons earlier, an innocent
factory-girl out for a treat near Thirsk came back to tea
with a big bunch of water forget-me-not, in the middle
of which were two blooms of the *Cypripedium*.   But
neither she, nor the child who found another plant, some
years later, as she came down into school at Settle, was
ever able to point out the plant whence she had picked
the flowers.   The Lady's Slipper is the Grand Duke of
all our native alpines.   A member of one of the noblest
great families in the noblest race of plants, *Cypripedium
Calceolus* has his tropical cousins, his priceless hybrid
cousins, and his hardy beautiful cousins of Siberia, Japan,
and North America.   He himself ranges over the alpine
woods of Europe, sometimes in isolated specimens, and
sometimes in abundance, as, here and there, between
Toblach and Cortina.   In England he has been known
for years uncountable, always confined to Yorkshire and
Durham, occurring rarely in the highest woodlands of the
mountain-country.   Being conspicuously beautiful—his
petals and sepals are yellow, his swollen lip of a brown
purple, and his flower very large and fragrant—he has
suffered, as I said, most terribly at the hands of the
despoiler.   No one, seeing him, could possibly ignore
him ; and the only alternative, to many minds, is to
mutilate and uproot.   Even in the days when gorgeous
Elizabeth was going down in gloom to the grave, Parkinson tells how the ' *Calceolus Mariae* ' abounded in the
' Helks Wood by Ingleton, under Ingleborough, the
highest hill in England,' and had often (Oh shame !) been

sent up to him, root and all, by Mistress Tomasin Tunstall, 'a worthy Gentlewoman, and a great lover of these delights, who dwelleth at Bull Bank, nigh unto Hornby Castle in those parts.' A worthy gentlewoman, indeed! O Mistress Tomasin, if only you had loved these delights a little less ruinously for future generations! Do you sleep quiet, you worthy gentlewoman, in Tunstall Church, or does your uneasy sprite still haunt the Helks Wood in vain longing to undo the wrong you did? And after Mistress Tomasin had long been as dead as the Cypripediums she sent up to Parkinson, there came a market-gardener, a base soul, animated only by love of lucre (and thus damned to a far lower Hell than the worthy if over-zealous gentlewoman), who grubbed up all the Cypripediums that she had left, and potted them up for sale. The Helks Wood, now, is an oyster for ever robbed of its pearl—unless, unless in some unsuspected nook somewhere, one gold-and-purple flower is yearly mocking at the memories of Mistress Tomasin and the wicked gardener both. For I do heartily believe, and nothing shall make me give chapter or verse, that in and out among the tangled thickets up under the rocks, the faithful seeker may yet be rewarded. One man swears to having seen the Cypripedium of late years under Ingleborough, and, for all I know, there may be others. Of late, too, rumour has it that the plant has been recorded from woods above Windermere.

In the Arncliffe valley the history of the Lady's Slipper has been even darker. The Arncliffe valley is a very narrow mountain glen, with steep fells rising through woods on either side towards the great moorlands overhead. It runs up due north of Skipton, and ends, a blind alley, under the eastern slope of Penyghent far above and out of sight. Here, in these mountain copses, ever since the time of Withering, the Cypripedium has been known. And one old vicar kept careful watch over it, and went every year to pluck the flowers and so keep the plant safe, for without the flower you might, if uninstructed, take the plant for a Lily of the Valley. Then one year he fell ill. The plant was allowed to blossom; was discovered and uprooted without mercy, and there was an end of him. And worse is to follow: for a professor from the north—I will not unfold whether it were Edinburgh, or Glasgow, or Aberdeen, or none of these, that produced this monster of men—put a price on the head of the Cypripedium, and offered the inhabitants so much for every rooted plant they sent him. The valley accordingly was swept bare, and, until the patient plant was rediscovered last year, there was nothing left to tell of the glen's ancient glory except one clump of the Cypripedium which, to keep it holy, had been removed to the vicarage garden, there to maintain, in a mournful but secure isolation, the bygone traditions of Arncliffe. As for the cultivation of the Lady's Slipper, I find it quite the easiest of the Orchids to grow. In any fair loam, whether exposed or sheltered, it makes good tufts and looks after itself, dying down and coming up again without any special attention at all.

Accursed for evermore, into the lowest of the Eight Hot Hells, be all reckless uprooters of rarities, from professors downwards (but the worthy gentlewoman, because she was worthy and a lover of these delights, must have a milder doom). However, the Arncliffe valley has yet another rarity—what the Japanese call a 'Meibuts'—an especial characteristic production. And that is the little form of *Dryas octopetala* which is called *minor*, and which occurs principally, if not solely, on Arncliffe Clouder, a high shoulder of limestone, far above the valley. There, on a very limited space, the rocks are covered with a dense carpet of tiny oak-like leaves, creeping and trailing about on wiry wooden branches, and then thousands upon thousands—a marvellous sight—of big creamy flowers like large golden-eyed Daisies on short stems. The commoner form is found in Teesdale, in Scotland and Ireland, and is very abundant in the Alps (I have been told of pink and double varieties), but in our parts the *Dryas* is, I fancy, only recorded from Arncliffe Clouder, where its form is the minute *minor*. No fear of this plant's being extinguished! It has a woody root that seems to ramble for miles, and it is sheer madness to attempt getting a plant of any *Dryas*, unless you can find a year-old seedling. Seed is the only way to obtain them; I have raised stocks of *octopetala* and *minor* from seed, and, though slow, the process is sure. Now in the Old Garden I have carpets of both, through which come perking the Spring Crocuses in the gayest way, and then die off long before the *Dryas* wants to flower. The flowering season, by the way, is long, so that you can have *Dryas* till fairly late in the summer. It is the easiest thing to grow, in any of its forms (Lanata only differs in being woolly in all its parts), if only you start with sound plants. And a mass of it is a perpetual joy in winter and summer. The other species, *Dryas Drummondi*, I have collected in the Rockies. It is quite as easy to grow, and flowers abundantly. The description arouses great eagerness, for the blossoms are 'golden yellow.' But, alas for mortal hopes, those flowers never open, simply hang in a half-shut condition all their lives. At least, this is my experience. 'Some may be Rooshians, and some may be Prooshans; it is their nature, and they must speak according.' All I can say is, I have seen millions of flowers in the Rockies, in all sorts of weather, and I never saw one fairly expanded, neither there nor anywhere else.

Primula farinosa is the 'Meibuts'' of North-Western

England, and the centre of its distribution is the mountain-mass of Ingleborough. From the days of my remotest childhood, when my anxiety was always whether I should return to the country in time to see it, *Primula farinosa* has been my best friend among English wildflowers. Such a gallant little gay thing it is, and so fragrant, and so dainty, and so altogether lovable. It is a thriving species, too, increasing by leaps and bounds, until places where ten years ago there wasn't a single plant are now stained purple with it in the spring. You cannot frequent this country without seeing it, for not only does it swarm on the mountains in places, but it covers the railway cuttings in the valley below, and here and there makes great patches of colour on the very highway sides, growing so stout and strong that you can scarcely believe that it is not some vigorous show Verbena, with solid round heads of blossom. All through the winter nothing is to be seen but a round, fat bud. Then, with spring, unfold the mealy little grey leaves, in themselves a joy. And then as June begins, up go the white stems, and out come the semi-globular trusses of lovely pink, golden-eyed flowers, looking so sweet and friendly there is no resisting them. A curious characteristic it has, too, which shows how it still remembers the alpine and glacial period. For in the high cool places it hurries eagerly into bloom, as early as it can, like a true alpine, anxious to get its flowering over safely in the brief flash of summer, before the glacial winter descends again; while in the valleys and on the rich railway cuttings it makes no such hurry, but takes its own time about blossoming. So that, while the Scars are pink with it, you will not find so much as a bud in the warm lands beneath, until the hill-plants have all withered and gone to seed. Ever since Parkinson's time the Pretty Bird E'en has laboured under a bad reputation in the garden.

'They will hardly bear any cultivation,' says Parkinson mournfully, and too many people have found it so ever since. Even Mr. Robinson gives such elaborate directions that the wary must needs feel that in buying *farinosa* they are embarking on a difficult plant. Now I can give no directions; but as a help I will tell my experience and give my theory. I find here that the plant grows anywhere and almost everywhere, thriving and seeding without any attention whatever. And I think that many people fail with it from a slight misunderstanding of its wants. *Primula farinosa* is a true bog-plant, and yet it does better, I believe, without bog treatment. I have found it all over the hills, and often in sopping wet places, but it is always on perfectly dry, exposed banks without any surface moisture that I find it at its best, in size, number, strength, and colour. This seems to show me that it depends on our climate rather than on situation. And our climate gives a parching spring and early summer, with a soaking autumn and winter. And the theory that I have therefore conceived and justified by experience is that the plant thrives best in a sticky, very heavy loam, kept fairly dry throughout the growing season, and almost incessantly wet throughout the resting and sleeping times. This treatment certainly gives the most wonderful results here; and I commend it to the consideration of those who have so far failed to establish *farinosa* with alpine or bog-culture.

Parkinson quotes also the albino form, and catalogues have occasionally offered it to me at high prices. But the so-called albinos always turned out to have the very faintest possible tinge of lilac, so that, after many years of disillusionment, I was inclined to give up *Primula farinosa alba* as a partial and inconstant variation. My views, however, were finally dissipated two years ago, when

Mistress Mary Saunders, 'a worthy gentlewoman and a great lover of these delights, who dwelleth at Wennington, nigh unto Hornby Castle in these parts,' discovered untold quantities of *Primula farinosa alba* in one field, all evidently from the same stock, as the plants were of every age, from seedlings to old clumps. And there was no doubt this time—no lilac tinge, however faint; nothing but the purest, most dazzling white with a golden eye, and in increased size of flower, and so on, answering precisely to Parkinson's admirable description of three hundred years ago. Few things are lovelier than this white Farinosa; though, even among the albinos from that blessed field, there are degrees of glory. For I have singled out one form with larger, broader, rounder flowers than the other, which seems, too, to be even more robust. For in vigour these white Farinosas are not, like so many albinos, at all behind their parent in vitality; their only peculiarity, and that may wear off, being a reluctance to set seed. So far my capsules have swollen and grown fat all right, but when opened are found to contain nothing but a sort of black soot. And Mrs. Saunders has the same tale to tell. And yet the plant must produce perfect seed, for it had evidently sown itself broadcast in that field.

Finally, I have a special love for the cheerful little Mountain Pansy (*Viola lutea*), which ranges all across the North of England. The yellow form grows under Penyghent, the pale blue, rarely, on the upper slopes; and in Teesdale whole miles of meadow, rich with Globe-flower and Geranium, are carpeted with millions of it, in every shade from butter-white to the densest Tyrian violet. In cultivation the plant grows happily anywhere in the sun, and makes a neat mass, soon hidden from sight by the profusion of its blossoms. I won't go so far as to compare it with *Viola calcarata* or *Viola cenisia*; the

PRIMULA FARINOSA ALBA

flowers are not so large nor the stems so dwarf. But the blooms are even more abundant, and in delicate beauty would enter into rivalry with any Pansy ever raised. It has a neatness of habit, too, which makes it desirable where one cannot admit the beautiful *papilio* hybrids. Yet I must be fair to *Viola cornuta papilio*; it is a plant not only of wonderful charm, but also of the most amazing generosity. From January to December that plant never ceases to flower, and in the bitterest days of winter exhilarates one with its great blue blossoms. And this is an amiable quality that it shares with *Viola calcarata*, though *calcarata* has it to a more moderate degree.

CHAPTER III

Ranunculus and Aquilegia

In talking about my plants the alphabetic arrangement of species would be too formal and pompous, especially as I shall only have space to deal with a very limited number of my treasures. Yet some sort of scheme is necessary; and with two big gardens I can't amble conversationally round them in the approved way, prattling about each plant as I come to it. The effect would be far too jumpy and disconnected. Therefore the least I can do is to begin at the beginning of the Botany books and work straight on as best I can.

And thus the invidious task of choosing a Genus to begin with is removed from any responsibility of mine. Botanists have decided that *Ranunculaceae* come first—I am sure I have no notion why. And so we will begin with *Ranunculaceae*. But botanists, having begun with *Ranunculaceae*, keep you fiddling about, for another unknown reason, with Clematis and Atragene, before they introduce you to the great race that gives its name to the family. We will have no such faulty precedence. Ranunculus shall stand at the head of his household, and after him we will treat of the others as fancy and a sense of fitness may dictate.

The Buttercups make up an imposing list of species, and the race is, roughly speaking, northern and temperate in disposition—some species loving full exposure, though, and others requiring shade and moisture. Hairy leaves mean sun-lovers; smooth ones damp- or shade-haunters.

Ranunculus aconitifolius is very abundant all over the Alps, in the lower region, extending to the upper pastures. He dwells always in very wet places, and in England, though of the easiest temper, is best treated as a true bog-plant. His habit is tall, stout, and branching, with big Monk's-Hoodish leaves, and a cloud of rather small pure white flowers. Horticulturally, *platanifolius* is almost identical; and while the form too often seen is a double one, the single type is a precious and delightful plant for any cool corner where it cannot overshadow anything choice.

Alpestris is the best of all the high-alpine Buttercups. He is a mighty climber, going up to the last edge of the moraines, and nothing is more cheering than to see his brilliant snowy cups glittering about among the dank, dripping rocks. *R. crenatus*, *Traunfellneri*, and *bilobus* must all be taken with *alpestris*; as, if not mere varieties, they are so close, in appearance and requirements, that they may be treated horticulturally under one heading. *Alpestris*, however, is with me the best plant of a good lot—finest, easiest, and most robust. The needs of all these very high-alpine Buttercups are astonishingly simple with me—a mere heavy, stony loam—and there is no more to be said. *Alpestris* soon makes itself at home in any quite ordinary corner, and forms clumps that go bravely on for ever, whether in sun or shade. Its leaves are three-lobed, crenate, beautiful light glossy green; the abundant, shilling-wide flowers are dazzling white with a golden eye. In cultivation, as in nature, the plant is generally about six inches in height, and blooms all the summer through—a miracle of generosity and charm.

I will not linger over the varieties of *bulbosus*, the common Buttercup. I grow (and faintly dislike) a double form; and also a certain pale-yellow variety, called *F. M. Burton*, which is not, in itself, very thrilling, but which makes an exquisite contrast if put side by side with *Aquilegia coerulea*. The ordinary Celandine, *R. ficaria*, has a magnified form which must be pretty, though I have never grown it; as for *R. repens*, a more deadly pernicious weed never found its way into any garden.

So much for our British Buttercups, unless I make mention of the rare, splendid *Lingua*, with its even larger *major* form, two glories of the bog.

The next I come to is *R. gramineus*, another of that delightful section headed by *amplexicaulis*, whose crowning merit is that they require no attention, but luxuriate in any cool light loam. *Gramineus* belongs to the Southern Alps. I collected him in October, by his decaying leaves, above St. Martin Vesubie. These mountain Buttercups dwell only on the high pastures of the upper Alps—bloom in a splendid mass, and then die down out of the way. *Gramineus* has blue-grey, grassy leaves, and large, lemon-yellow flowers on tall stems. Hardly distinguishable except in the flower and habitat is *R. Pyrenaeus*, which, in defiance of its name, you will find very abundant in the highest grassy Alps above Arolla on the western side. *Pyrenaeus* has the same glaucous grassy leaves as *gramineus*; but he is a trifle smaller, I fancy, in habit, and his lovely flowers are milk-white. And yet another Pyrenean is *amplexicaulis*, which is quite beautiful. He has broad, stem-clasping leaves of a lovely glaucous blue, and very large, milk-white blossoms. All he asks is an airy, fully-exposed place in any cool border-loam, in which he will continue to prosper easily, for these Alp-buttercups are without a fault in cultivation.

R. glacialis is the very highest of all European alpines, being found almost to the summit of the Finsteraarhorn

(whither, I must hasten to add, I have never pursued it).
You will not, as a rule, see a sign of *R. glacialis* until
you are almost beyond the region of flowers. Even *R.
alpestris* is beginning to become rare when, all of a
sudden, in the soaking shingle of the moraine, you are
startled by what you think at first is an *alpestris* swollen
out of all recognition. This is *R. glacialis*, and if any
one cavils at my description I must warn them that, so
far, I have principally seen the white form. For *R.
glacialis* as figured, and as often found, is rosy-red in
blossom. But though I have often collected the red type,
I have far more affection for the white form, and, as a
matter of fact, have seen more of it. The two merge
into each other, of course, and the white, when fertilised,
has a way of fading pink. *Glacialis* only grows about
six or eight inches in height, and forms huge clumps,
covered with blossom, and composed of hundreds of
fleshy-rooted, separable plants, each shoot being an independent individual. As far as I know, it dwells only
in the very wettest places, where water is perpetually
running through it or dripping over the rocks around it.
And yet this plant, which looks as if it ought to be so
exceedingly hard to cultivate, is the easiest and most
robust of all the very high alpines. I give it a sticky,
stony loam, and there *glacialis* thrives happily. The
leaves are very succulent (though downy in one form,
which is cobwebbed all over), palmate, and deeply incised,
dark metallic grey, and very attractive; the flowers are
enormous—as wide as a florin, or wider, of a brilliant
snow-white, or of a dull rose-red. *R. Seguieri* is so near
as to be probably only a variety.

R. Lyalli is—to make a bad matter short—a failure
here. It has large round, glossy leaves, and great white
flowers as large and as white as *Anemone japonica*. It is
a true alpine, a New Zealander, and may possibly thrive

elsewhere in England. But I imagine that most people find it rather intractable. It is indifferent, from what I hear of its native quarters, to any amount of cold and snow in winter, and of wet in spring. But it seems to insist on an absolutely torrid summer. And, in default of that, it fails to ripen, languishes, and becomes unable to resist even an English winter, contemptible as an English winter must be by comparison with the rigours of the New Zealand Alps.

R. nyssanus I imported from Servia, and am inclined to love. It is like a glorified edition of an English Buttercup, with three-lobed hairy leaves, very handsome, and all a sheen of silver beneath; the large flowers are of a brilliant golden-yellow. It likes a dry, sunny corner, and there will run about as freely as the dreadful *repens*, and soon take up the whole space.

R. parnassifolius is another very high alpine, from damp places near the everlasting snows. It abounds, so they tell me, about the Gemmi, but though I have hunted ardently I have never happed upon it there. It is small of stature, and rather dumpy of appearance, making a tuft of heart-shaped, very dark glossy green leaves, in a goodly little tuft; and the flowers, two or three to a short stem, are large and milky-white. It is a limestone plant, and I find it quite happy in heavy loam like the other wet-loving high-alpines of its kindred. There is a *major* form, too, which is rather larger, and quite as good.

Last of those alpines, but by no means least, comes *R. rutaefolius*, sometimes called *Callianthemum rutae-folium*. And well indeed may it be called the Rue-leaved Beauty-flower. A prettier flower, or a more ruelike leaf, no one ever beheld. And the leaf, too, is of the loveliest blue-grey, as succulent and even more glaucous than that of *R. glacialis*. And the flowers—large and bold—are bright, pure white. (Nicholson says 'yellow,' but he is wrong; they were bright white, with golden anthers.) *Rutaefolius* is a rare plant, occurring, like all this section, in damp places very high up, here and there, beginning with a station on the mountain between Lungern and Sarnen on the Brünig, and ranging locally through the Eastern and the Pennine Alps. It is an extraordinarily charming plant, and, after the paradoxical habit of its kind, extremely easy to grow.

Now that *Ranunculus* has been dealt with, *Aquilegia* clearly takes the next place, and for beauty might have had the first. The Columbines are a glorious proud family. But I wish they kept their pedigree in better order. More confusion, more inextricable and awful, reigns among Aquilegias than among any other race of alpines, until we reach Campanula and the Aeizoön Saxifrages. The Columbines seed with plebeian fecundity, and cross with one another to such an extent that there is no keeping a strain pure if there be any other kind of Columbine living within a ten-mile radius. Therefore it is always a speculation to buy seed, and a very risky speculation too, unless the seller is a man you know and trust. Even so, poor soul, neither he nor you can tell what may come of it. Again and again I have got seed of innumerable rare, valuable, interesting sorts; and you should see the dingy weeds that have resulted. Then I was told that *olympica* and *longi-calcarata* never lost their purity, so that seed from them could be relied upon. Eagerly I bought some ; it germinated, like all Columbine seed, so thickly that one didn't know how to deal with it. However, the babies were potted up reverently, with an immense outlay in time and pots, and nice, carefully mixed soil. And, when they flowered, they were all very inferior forms of *vulgaris*! For this reason then I shall not be able to tell you of any genuine experiences with these two species, with *leptoceras*, with *arctica*, with many another promising, exciting Columbine that one reads about and faithfully buys seed of, hoping against hope until the flowers have actually opened. Nor are grown plants always safe; for some gardeners have dwarf consciences; and I have seen a rather poor purple variety of *vulgaris* being shown at the Temple Show as *A. alpina.*

The Columbines, as a race, belong to the lower, lighter scrub of Alpine woods all along the great mountain-chains of the northern world. In cultivation the rarer ones are confessedly a little difficult. The essential is to give them perfect, quick drainage, and then a soil both rich and light. They dislike, too, being battered by winds and weather while they are coming up. The best that we can do is to remember how they lodge and dodge behind bushes on their native hills when they can, and give them some such similar protection in the garden.

A. alpina (the true *alpina*) is unquestionably the most beautiful plant of the European Alps. When after long search I first sighted it among the brushwood on the Vorder Wellhorn, I gave a loud cry and fell prone. The loveliness of it simply takes you between the eyes and knocks you dizzy. The flowers, dancing high on airy stems, are of enormous size, most exquisitely, daintily balanced, and of a soft, melting blue quite impossible to describe—a colour deep yet gentle, brilliant yet modest, perfectly clear and yet not flaunting. Sometimes the centre is white, but even this cannot increase the beauty of the blossom. *A. alpina* pervades the Alpine woods, always rare, but rather less so as you get towards the southern and eastern ranges. I believe that the Wellhorn is almost its only Oberland habitat, but I have seen it peering pleasantly at me from many copses on the eastern slope of the Arolla valley. In cultivation it wants a moderate amount of care—probably more in the South

of England than in this Alpine air and climate of Craven
—but is by no means to be reckoned among the most difficult species. Collected seed from the Alps is safe; but
the true species is by no means easy to get hold of, even
in gardens whose catalogues boldly advertise it. As for
A. pyrenaica, this is virtually a tiny form of *alpina*.

Haenkeana and *einseleana* have been sent me by
trustworthy people, and seem to answer, afar off, to their
description. All I can say is, I don't care for them.
I see in them little distinctness or superiority for gardening purposes. *A. coerulea* is perhaps the queen of the
family, and I will not tire any one with hunting out
epithets for this glorious plant, with its great delicate
pale blue flowers, long-spurred, carried erect, with a centre
of creamy white. *Coerulea* gives a pink form (and a
white of which I have seed), and some lovely hybrids
with Chrysantha, but is, itself, of no very brilliant constitution, if the truth is to be told. It is ' miffy '—a little
hard to reckon with—and not always to be counted on
for two successive seasons. But sound seed of it can
easily be got; and the plant is a thousand times worth
growing, even if it has to be treated as a biennial. There
is a quaint spurless form, like a wee Clematis, called
stellata ; but this, though charming, quite pales before
coerulea itself.

A. glandulosa, the Siberian Columbine, is another
gorgeous great blue creature with white centre. He
carries his flowers half-pendent, and is rather less fairy-
like and more solidly splendid than *coerulea*. And, like
coerulea, he has a bad reputation—indeed, a worse one
than the Rocky Mountain Columbine. At Forres, in
Scotland, in Mr. Wiseman's garden, he grows and ramps
about amazingly in a moist, cool, peaty soil, most creamy
and delicious to the touch. But in dry southerly
gardens he is very emphatically what a woman I know

calls a 'Mimp.' You may say of him, as the short-
sighted say of human life, 'here to-day and gone to-
morrow.' With me he grows well; and now I have a
bed full of seedlings which seem wonderfully vigorous.
From them I hope great things; seedlings being so much
more vigorous than bought plants, as from their birth
they are busy adapting themselves to the place they grow
in, instead of, like a poor bought plant, making vain
efforts to take up the broken strand of life, and forget the
place they came from.

A. flabellata is a queer, charming little Japanese, small
in growth, with bright pale green leaves and fat, waxy
flowers, either creamy white or pale blue with white
centre. It blooms very early, and takes kindly to any
cool garden soil. Another Japanese plant, from Saghalin
and Hokkaido, is the spurless, dark *A. ecalcarata.* My
stock looks very thriving and brilliant, but, until it
flowers, I had better say no more, lest Nemesis hear me
rashly boasting, and I find that all my ecalcaratas are
really *vulgaris.* *A. chrysantha*, the common golden-
spurred Columbine, needs neither recommendation nor
description. This and its numerous hybrids are good-
tempered, delightful, and lovely plants for any garden,
and for almost any part of it. Nor can I leave out the
rare native plant, the single deep blue *A. vulgaris*, which
peeps, here and there, from our Craven copses under the
cliffs. The other forms, pink and purple and so forth,
are not worth a place in the choice rock-garden; and as
for the double forms, *horresco referens*, they are ineffably
frightful, denying every single beauty in which the
Columbines are pre-eminent—lightness, daintiness, form,
and colour, and carriage. *A. vulgaris nivea* is not far, on
the other hand, from being the loveliest of all white
Columbines, and *A. vulgaris wittmaniana* is one of the
parents of *A. Stuarti.* *A. Stuarti* has for its other parent

glandulosa, and the result is a singularly beautiful little Columbine, as large as *glandulosa* in the flower, but rather smaller in growth. In habit and disposition it comes intermediate. It is more trustworthy and healthy than *glandulosa*, but less so than *vulgaris*. Lovely and vigorous as it is, for my own part I still prefer *glandulosa*, the species, to any raised garden-hybrid except *Helenae*.

The Globe-flowers are represented in England by our own native *Trollius europaeus*, who occurs freely in the high alpine meadows under Ingleborough, and abundantly round the High Force in Teesdale. Who does not know his fine dark-green palmate leaves, and the golden orbs of his blossom ? All the rest are, roughly speaking, variants on *europaeus*. I grow *asiaticus, japonicus, japonicus excelsior*, T. Smith, Orange Globe and Fire Globe. *Europaeus* itself varies extensively; *albidus* is a very pale form, and *napellifolius* the handsomest. *Asiaticus* and *japonicus* are a trifle less globular, and of a deeper orange. The various 'Globes' are of artificial raising or selection, and are glorified versions of *europaeus* and *asiaticus*— brilliant alike in vigour, size, and colour. Fire Globe, being the newest and the dearest, is therefore considered at present the best, until somebody else introduces a new one called Blazing Globe and charges a guinea for it. But, in point of fact, all the Trolliuses—it really isn't possible to say Trollii—are so thrifty and so splendid that it is very difficult to feel any preference for any one variety, though, I must say, Fire Globe at its best is a truly wonderful sight. The Globe-flowers only ask for plenty of root-room in a fairly moist, good loam, and then they will go on for ever, and make perpetually-increasing masses.

The Marsh Marigold or Kingcup of our bogs has a double form that you may admit, if you like ; but a very different person is *Caltha polysepala*, newly introduced, and now selling for about a guinea a plant. This, to describe it briefly, is the ordinary Marsh Marigold, multiplied by three—in all its parts, leaf, flower, stem—a tropical-looking aquatic of unequalled glory. The plant has a curious history, which may or may not be legendary. Report says that an Italian peasant found it in some unknown corner of the country, and, in consideration of its marvellous size, brought it to Rome and laid it at the feet of Pope Leo. The old Pope benignly accepted the offering, and *Caltha polysepala* established itself in one of the fountains of the Vatican garden. But the Pope would never let any one else possess bud or seed or baby of it. And there year after year it wasted its sweetness on the desert air, being seen by nobody except an aged gentleman who, presumably, had other things to think about. This policy survived Pope Leo, and continued until an English gardener (all honour to his name ; he is a male Antigone, daring a formal sin to secure the Higher Holiness) resolved that such a scandal should no longer endure. So he took with him into the Vatican gardens a covey of his sisters and his cousins and his aunts, and while they engaged the custodian in a conversation on Renaissance Art, our hero hooked out a root or two of *Caltha* with his umbrella. And now, Pope Pius is none the poorer, and the whole world is the richer. I cannot but think or dimly hope that horticulture has a code of ethics to itself. Why should a friend's seed-pod fall neglected, or a prey to slugs, when one has a pocket ready to receive it ? However, I hasten to reassure all my acquaintances ; my own spirit is far too meek for such adventures ; I merely admire the law-breaker from afar. I cannot steal, though to beg I am by no means ashamed.

CHAPTER IV

Anemone

WITH one exception, the Anemones are not exactly
rock plants, but there is no right-minded gardener who
would feel his joy complete if he did not possess a
fair collection of them. The race falls into three great
divisions—the woodlanders, of which our own *A. nemorosa* is the readiest type; the Hepaticas; and the open-
space group, which *pulsatilla* represents in the middling
lands, *fulgens* in the south, and *alpina* on the great
mountain-ranges. Leaving out of sight for a time the
nemorosa and the *Hepatica* sections, the most striking
feature of the third and largest group is its love for full
sun and light. All over the most torrid banks of the
Levant go *A. stellata* and *A. coronaria*—οὐρεσίφοιτα
κρίνα—all over the higher grassy Alps go *A. alpina*
and *A. sulfurea*. Their generic name—the Flower of the
Wind—so often cavilled at, is essentially true. They
may not sway and balance as one sense of Windflower
would have it; but they do require the incessant encouragement of every wind that blows to keep them
happy. They are true mountain-plants, though not, as
a rule, rock-plants in the accepted sense. They belong
to the high meadows where the light and air are pure;
though *alpina* and *sulfurea* do sometimes climb to higher
levels, yet it is the upper pastures of the Alps that are
their preferred dwelling, and mark the highest limit of

their race. In cultivation they are nearly all of the very easiest—provided you get seedlings or well-treated plants to start with. In that case a good and very deep loam in some open unshaded spot is all they need—for though some of them (none of the South-Europeans, of course) will thrive in shade, yet in such conditions they run towards rankness of leaf and poverty of bloom. But, as I hinted, the difficulty is to make a good start with them; and it is for lack of this that so many people have suffered trouble and disappointment with their Alpine Anemones. For all the mountain Anemones make the most terrific woody rootstocks, which it would tax Herakles himself to get up intact. Therefore too many of the imported plants that enthusiastic tourists grub up and bring home are mere mutilated stumps, that can but dwindle and die. Accordingly seed only should be collected; and, even as to the best time of sowing seed, a controversy rages. For my own part, I believe in autumn rather than in spring sowing; and my idea is that the seed of the mountain Anemone is quite short-lived, so that disaster and disillusionment are too apt to follow any expectations from stale shop-bought packets. With fresh collected heads I have raised hundreds and thousands of all the alpine species without the slightest difficulty, and I am sure that the only sound way to get a stock of these Anemones is not to try the vain chance of getting up roots, but to collect the great fluffy heads, and sow them as soon as possible. This is not a very quick method, of course, for these perennial Anemones live to a great age, and must therefore take time to mature their development and form established clumps; but their glory is such that few will grudge the years spent in watching a healthy little seedling grow and grow into a great spreading mass with dozens of flowers.

The joy and splendour of the limestone Alps is, of

course, *A. alpina*. It grows from six inches to a foot or more, has clouds of ferny foliage, and big white starry flowers, that, in my form, are of a lovely pale blue on the outer side. I have never had any trouble with it anywhere, so long as it has plenty of root-room. It is a plant of singular charm, and I myself prefer it, I *think*— though it is a rash thing to compare two such beauties— to its yellow form, the more famous *A. sulfurea*. This, too, is wonderfully beautiful—rather larger, in all ways, than *alpina*, with flowers of a clear pale yellow. Although *sulfurea* is only the granitic form of *alpina*, no two plants could well be more distinct for gardening purposes; and yet, I am glad to say, *sulfurea*, despite its natural love of granite, is no more exacting than *alpina* as to soil, but thrives even more robustly in any cool very deep loam in any garden in the kingdom.

A. baldensis is found originally, or abundantly, I suppose, on that illustrious Monte Baldo which I have never visited yet, but which must be the rock-gardener's Mecca —judging from the number of beautiful things whose specific name is *baldensis*. And the Monte Baldo Anemone is not unworthy of its name. A dearer little plant I don't know. It is—to make a conversational description—rather like a pure white *stellata*, and, in habit, stands midway between the *nemorosa* and the *alpina* sections. If you search piously in and out among those ghastly white boulders that make the top of the Gemmi such an abomination of desolation (if it were not for the flowers all about), there, in cracks and crannies, will you at last discover *A. baldensis*. The flower, carried on a slender, six-inch stem, reminds one of a very fine, delicate, single Chrysanthemum with a golden centre, and a pale pink reverse to the petals. Instead of the broad sepals of the Alpinas, *baldensis* makes itself daisy-like (after the fashion of *apennina*, *blanda*, and *stellata*) with

eight or ten narrow ones. It comes upon one suddenly
—at least it came on me—as a gracious surprise. I had
no suspicion at all that it dwelt on the Gemmi, and I
was already vexed and bored with the tedious mountain
Camomiles and things that swarm in high places. Then,
when my tin was heavy with plants, on came a scud of
rain, and I took shelter under the ledge of a great overhanging rock. My fingers idly wandered along a ledge,
for something to do—and there, all of a sudden, was that
dear little Anemone, in seed, it is true, but quite unmistakable. Nor is it hard to collect. Instead of a woody
stock, it makes a small concise mat of fibres, so that I
was able delicately to hook out two or three plants along
the ledge, here and there. And now, thank goodness,
those cherished people are as comfortable on my rock-
garden as ever they were on the Gemmi. *A. baldensis* is
a fairly willing little soul in cultivation. But it wants
more rock than most, and it likes, I find, peat. Give it
a peaty crevice, and *A. baldensis* will be happy—and so
will you.

A. apennina.—Is there any one who does not know this
common but ineffably precious little species? It is
daisy-like as *baldensis*, but blue and brilliant and heartening beyond words. It is a South-European woodlander
(naturalised here and there, says report, in England and
Ireland). No plant is more precious for naturalising—
deliberate naturalising. In grass, in copse, in garden, it
is equally invaluable—neat in root and habit, and dying
down with discreet promptitude the moment its flowers
are over. There is also a white form, no less vigorous
and charming. And it has a little cousin, *A. blanda*,
with tuberous black knobs for root-stock, and flowers
exactly like those of *apennina*, but larger, and either
bluer or paler. *Blanda* is a Greek and Levantine; a
choice dainty creature, more admissible into small gardens

ALPINE ANEMONES IN THE OLD GARDEN. (ALPINA AND NARCISSIFLORA)

than *apennina*, because rarer, less invasive, and more justifiably cherishable. You cannot cherish a plant, however beautiful, if it runs about like a weed. But *A. blanda* is much quieter in temperament. It must have a warm, sunny corner, not a shady, anyhow place, such as one pokes *apennina* into. And then, in its sunny, warm corner, *A. blanda* will grow and flower gloriously, but without spreading into any vast mass. There are many colour forms, from white to pink, and a high-priced *blanda scythinica*, white internally, with a blue reverse, which I have often and often flowered anonymously out of importations of the typical plant. Imported bulbs will give you an enormous variety of colours, and not one of them will be anything but dainty and delightful.

Man, says Montaigne, is undulating and diverse. He didn't know the ways of horticultural nomenclature, lucky Montaigne—for anything more undulating and diverse than these no mind could conceive. *A. dichotoma* is *A. pennsylvanica*, take note, and *A. pennsylvanica* is identical with *A. dichotoma*. I collected *Anemone* ——, whichever you like to call it, in the Rockies, where it grows in open glades of woodland, and I announce that I find it a perennial joy, though gardeners incline to ignore it, and even catalogues are tepid or silent about it. *A. dichotoma* (Nicholson, I see, awards it a star of merit, so it has had some recognition at least) grows to about eighteen inches, has a tall, forked stem, a peculiarly graceful carriage, and a quantity of fairly large, five-sepalled white flowers with a tinge of pink on the reverse, borne each on a long dainty foot-stalk from a few-flowered, elongated umbel. I put it anywhere and everywhere, and it is always cheerful, and, indeed, is even threatening to prove a greedy ramper.

A. globosa I mention here only as a solemn warning. It is sometimes advertised in flaming terms. Beware!

It is faintly like a very much shrunken *A. dichotoma*, with all the grace eliminated, and tiny, ridiculously tiny, miserly-looking dull red flowers on stiff, erect stems. Its culture appears perfectly easy. But I don't think it worthy of garden-room. Nor am I at all happy about *A. cylindrica*; I rather think that, too, comes under the same condemnation. The worst of buying seed is that one has to speculate. One orders any new Anemone that can be got, and if one is to come early into the field, one has to buy these seeds, of course, with no description or guarantee. However, hope lingers on until the young plants flower, and you discover, to your grief, that even an Anemone can be dull and dingy. *A. magellanica*, as well as *albana*, *rupicola*, and *burseriana*, are other species which have a note of interrogation against them, in my mind. Others may grow them into fine and lovable things; to me they have always seemed obscure, indistinct, and of no great value. I have dropped them from my collection, considering them only poor cousins of far grander species, though *albana*, at least, has a distinct prettiness, like a small *alpina*.

A. narcissiflora has suffered to a deplorable extent —indeed all the less showy Anemones have suffered—from undeserved neglect. On every count I give the very highest praise to this charming person, robust of habit, unexacting of temper, and lovely in flower. *A. narcissiflora* grows on the lowest edge of the Alpine region, or so I have always found it, either on the upper and upmost pastures, or in light woodland just below. It is a sturdy perennial, with a tufted root quite easy to collect. The leaves are soft and velvety, cut into long rounded lobes; then up go stalwart flower-stems, perhaps a foot or a foot and a half in height, which carry, above the invariable Anemone-frill, a long-stalked umbel of charming flowers, in shape and size like apple-blossom, with the lovely apple-blossom pink staining the reverse of the sepals, and making the buds glow like living rubies. I find *A. narcissiflora* of the very easiest culture, any-where, anyhow, in any sound light loam. It might even be used as a border plant, though perhaps a little too delicate in charm to cope with more flaming beauties.

As for *A. nemorosa*, I so love our little common native woodland Anemone that I would put him everywhere where he does not matter. The double form (as a rule, I am afraid I hate doubles, and ' Fl. Pl.' in a catalogue gene-rally makes me pass on to the next article) is extremely charming, and so is a monstrosity called *bracteata*. As for *A. robinsoniana*—oh dear me, in what fit words can one describe the Quakerish loveliness of that soft pale blue, blushing to lavender, and fawn-coloured on the re-verse ? *A. robinsoniana* is worthily named, for its delicate, refined loveliness. And the shape of it, too, and the grace of it, and the dainty poise of it ! It is not with me an increaser—that is to say, it lives and thrives, and goes on very happily—but it doesn't run about usurping other people's ground in the way that *nemorosa* would, if one admitted it to any choice place. So that one need never hesitate to plant *robinsoniana* in any reserved pocket or select corner. There are several varieties of *nemorosa* —*coerulea*, *purpurea*, *Alleni*, and yet another (*cornubiense* I have discarded), Blue Bonnet, which is rare and slow of increase, but very beautiful, and with the added advan-tage of blooming when all the other Nemorosas are over. Blue Bonnet is rather larger in size and stouter in build and deeper in colour than *robinsoniana*. It cannot hope to surpass the sedate charm of *robinsoniana*, but it makes a brave effort.

A. palmata is a strange, brilliant person, from Northern Africa, which—contrary, I must admit, to my own expec-tations—thrives here and increases mightily, and flowers with perfect generosity. It is quite deciduous, and has fat-looking leaves, three- or five-lobed, vaguely recalling a Cyclamen's, and then, isolated on tall stems, great yellow flowers that glitter finely in the sun. It likes a sunny warm corner in deep cool peat, but I have seen yard-wide masses of it as a border plant in ordinary loam, so that it is clearly not particular. Its white form, too, is pretty and vigorous—the two, side by side, looking like giant white and golden daisies.

A. patens is a handsome, easily cultivated plant. But I don't care for it very much, nor for its variety, *nuttaliana*, nor for *pratensis*, its cousin-german. They are all of the *pulsatilla* group—that is to say, with large fluffy flowers of various deep and rather (to my taste) dingy purples. The dull-coloured Japanese *cernua* is the worst of this group, I think, but there is something sombre and repellent in nearly all of them. I want, however, to be grateful and respectful to *A. patens*, so I will repeat that it is very handsome, and easily grown, with big, purplish flowers (varying to yellow in one form, and to a winy-black in another). But oh, if I could only come across the real Purple Caesar of this group! He is sprung from the bones of dead Ming Emperors of China, and he roots down, down, between the flags of their graves, into the very vaults where they are lying. In that desolate great mountain-valley guarded by stone monsters, and full of an enormous everlasting silence, there was, when I saw it early in March, no sign of life at all, but only, in each dead sovereign's precinct, this Anemone blooming close down upon the flag-stones of the paved temple-courts. He was a cousin of *patens*, but there was no washiness or dowdiness about him! No; his great, many-sepalled silky flower was of the most ardent imperial violet, and his beauty was such that I skinned my fingers to the bone in vain hope to get even

one little plant of him. No such luck; his roots went
down into the tombs of the emperors, I verily believe.
Oh, would that some visitor in August would note his
great fluffy seed-heads, and collect me some! I cry
urbi et orbi!

A. pulsatilla is the eponymous hero of this section.
And *A. pulsatilla* (with the rare high-alpine *Halleri* of
the granitic ranges) is also, to my taste, the most
beautiful cultivated member of this group. He also
has faint claims to be treated among the British alpines,
except that he is not really British, and not at all
alpine. He is a Roman, staunch and indomitable as a
Roman should be. Wherever the Romans went, there,
with them, went *A. pulsatilla.* Why they should have
taken him I do not know; but, to this day, on old
Roman dykes and circumvallations, all South and Mid-
England through, there you have a very good chance
of finding *A. pulsatilla.* The Middle Ages used him to
dye the Easter eggs with. He stained them of a
beautiful tender green, and, either from that usage, or
from his blooming-season, he has the name of Pasque-
flower. I have seen him on the Devil's Dyke by New-
market—that solid ridge of Roman work that stretches
far across the country. And along and along it, up and
down, faithfully follows *A. pulsatilla,* the least changed
of all Rome's contributions to our island. Over that
wind-swept embankment the Anemone makes little tufts
of close carroty leaves, and on them lie the great violet
blossoms, with their golden central tassel, and the fine
silk that clothes them. On a windy March day the
startling beauty of this little creature in a sere world
seizes one by the throat. But *A. pulsatilla,* I regret to
say, is not quite a gentleman, in spite of his imposing
history. Prosperity turns his head and spoils him. In
cultivation he stands among the very few wild plants

who grow coarse and rank by comparison with their
beauty in a wild state. *Pulsatilla* is the easiest of plants
to cultivate, in any deep soil, but, alas! he is not quite so
daintily charming as in his stunted state on the bare down.
He can never be ugly, but he runs more to leaf and
growth, so that his flower, though not really smaller or
paler than in a wild state, manages to look both. But
when all is said and done, he remains a remarkably
lovely and delightful species, a lover of lime, chalk, sun,
and exposure. He has some pretty pinkish varieties, too,
and an untidy ragged - petalled one; but the albino
Pulsatilla is a fraud — like the ghost of a dead white
flower seen through a sea-mist.

Himâlyan Anemones are comparatively rare in our
gardens, and this in itself should predispose a romantic
mind to welcome *A. rivularis*, who, for the rest, needs no
introduction except his own beauty. There is no plant
of higher value for a cool corner in the bog-garden.
Dampness and even wet he must have, in most parts of
England, and even here I grow him in the bogs, although
he is very obliging and seeds all over the place—even on
quite dry banks. *A. rivularis* is deciduous and late to
appear: he grows about two feet high or more, and
throws up clouds of rather small white flowers, with
blue anthers, and blue reverse, making a most fascinating
picture. His abundant display of bloom comes, too, at
a most welcome time of the year, when all the other
Anemones—and, indeed, practically all the alpines, have
gone to rest. For *A. rivularis* blossoms in August, con-
temporaneously with the bog-lilies and *Gentiana asclepiadea*. Give him coolness and moisture, and he will
reward you richly, and look after himself. (As for *A.
vitifolia*, this rare Himâlyan is quite hardy here, without
any attention, but is only a tall magnificent version of
japonica.)

Let others tell of their triumphs with the Snowdrop
Anemone—*sylvestris*. It is a native of German woods,
and Mr. Robinson always talks of it in the most radiant
and encouraging way. My experience of it was miserable.
It grew—oh yes, it grew all right; but never, never
would it flower. Then, one fine day, I allowed myself to
be persuaded into buying a plant that called itself *A.
sylvestris major*. I planted it rather sceptically, and
nourished no false hopes. It at once began to spread,
however. No goutweed ever ramped so fast or so far.
'Aha,' thought I, 'the old story; only worse.' Next
season came, and that Anemone flowered fit to kill itself.
Never have I seen a more luxuriant spectacle of loveliness. And since then *A. sylvestris major*, planted all
over the garden, has been one of the most free-flowering
joys of my life. Not only does the angel bloom when
bloom is due, but also again in autumn, in the most
generous and uncalled-for way. And this Snowdrop
Anemone certainly is a jewel. It is just like a small,
rather refined form of *A. japonica*, with smaller, creamier
flowers, carried each by itself on a wiry little stem. The
plant grows about a foot or a little more, and must be
put where you can allow it to ramble, for it is a fearful
devourer of ground. I am already beginning to tremble
for some of my choicest Primulas in their crevices of the
New Garden. For I once, thinking no evil, planted *A.
sylvestris major* about three yards away. And now, in
the most improbable crannies and nooks come creeping
the shoots of that invasive plant—threatening even
Jankaea Heldreichi in its sacred isolation under the
cliff. As for the double form of *A. sylvestris*, I would
not possess it—no, not for all the gold of Asia—nor
encourage others to do so.

Last of all, we come to the one species of the race
which is really and truly a high Alpine. You don't

begin to see *A. vernalis* until you are very high on the
Alps, not far from the lower edge of the moraines. And
I almost wish now that I had not so openly owned my
love for the other Anemones. For I want superlatives
of affection for the Lady of the Snow. I first saw her
many years since on the little Scheideck. The winter
was hardly over on those heights, and the snow had
melted in patches here and there. And in those dank
grassy patches lay what looked like great pearly water-
lilies. I soon nipped out of the train to make a closer
inspection. It was *A. vernalis*. Two or three thin-
looking, carrot-like leaves, lying pressed to the ground;
then an inch or so of shaggy stem, all covered with the
most lovely bronzy-gold fur; then a fluffy cup of the
same; and then, goblet-shaped, sumptuous and splendid,
a magnolia-like flower, snow - white within and silky
without, a-shimmer with gold and purple, iridescent with
the most subtle sheen of lilac, fawn, and pearl-white,—
that is the Lady of the Snow, and her glistening cup is
brimming over with the golden foam of her stamens.
Then the stem lengthens, the blossom dies and fades
without falling, and soon it turns to a sere yellow, and
the seed-head begins to develop into a marvellous
glorified dandelion-clock that ultimately looks like an
aged, aged Struwwelpeter. I myself fall down and worship *A. vernalis*, but gardeners as a rule are inclined to
be cold about it. Nicholson even says that it is a
'curious rather than showy species.' Well, substitute
'exquisite' for 'curious' (that catalogue's euphemism for
'ugly'), and I am with you, Mr. Nicholson; but it is
as well that people should know how lightly so great a
Panjandrum prizes what I, in my humility, commend as
altogether beautiful. I wish I could say that the Snow
Anemone was quite as amiable as it is lovely. I myself
have never had trouble with it; but then my climate is

damp and mountainous. The Lady of the Snow very much dislikes being parched or scorched. She further insists on a cool, rather moist, peaty loam. But, with those precautions, I do not think that any one should have much bother with her—always remembering that what I have ventured about *A. alpina* applies even more forcibly to *A. vernalis*. It is almost hopeless to try mutilated imported roots. *Vernalis*, though so dwarf, has an awful deep woody stock, quite impossible to cope with; therefore it will always be with seedlings, no matter how small, that will lie the greatest chances of success and good sturdy plants.

CHAPTER V

Papaveraceae, Cruciferae, and Dianthus

THE Poppies are a gorgeous race, but for the most part unsuited to the rock-garden. I have a few forms of *Papaver orientale* in high bold places, and the new innumerable-flowered *tauricola* (like a coppery *Meconopsis*) looks promising, and *rupifragum* sows itself freely and rejoices every one in August with its abundant flowers of an unusual soft tawny orange. The habit of the plant is a little straggling, worse luck, and the blossoms not quite large enough to harmonise with the length of the stem that carries them. But, when all is said and done, there is something hearty and friendly about this Poppy which makes me feel rather a brute whenever stern necessity compels me to weed him up. He has married *orientale*, too, and gives a very valuable offspring in *P. Ruporient*, a splendid intermediate, of mild but vigorous habit, with graceful scarlet cups half - way between his parents in size.

But among Poppies, and, indeed, among Alpine plants in general, few are more precious than *P. alpinum*, a true mountain-plant, found on the high shingle of the moraines in his various forms. He has finely-divided, glaucous-grey little leaves, and then large Iceland Poppy-like flowers on a stem three or four inches high. There are several colour varieties, and one form with fringed petals. The White Alpine Poppy dwells in the limestone Alps; the pale yellow one in the eastern ranges, and is called *P. pyrenaicum*. There is also a most exquisite variety, with soft chamois-pink flowers, which is even lovelier than the others. *P. burserianum* seems another form of *alpinum*—and so, of course, is the Iceland Poppy itself. But this last is so absolutely different in its large, rollicking habit, as to be quite distinct, for gardening purposes, from the tiny, fairy-like beauty of *P. alpinum*. The Alpine Poppies often make bad perennials if grown in fat soil and low corners of the garden. I have had the greatest success with them on high, exposed points, in rather thin gravelly loam, where they form tight little bushes, and go on from year to year. They seed, too, with the usual Poppyish prodigality, and the only warning one need lay to heart about them is that, being tap-rooted, they dislike being transplanted, and that they very much resent excessive moisture in winter round the neck of the plant.

Passing hurriedly over *Meconopsis*, that race of glories which we are only just becoming acquainted with (*Aculeata*, the silky-blue Poppy, is so lovely that one's heart yearns over it), I come to the Cross-bearers, that vast family of weeds and vegetables. Among them are very few alpine treasures. *Petrocallis pyrenaica* is the first, a typical limestone plant, found, for instance, on Pilatus, in the *débris* of the cliffs. He makes dense, neat cushions, rather like a wee, wee *Saxifraga hypnoeides*, and then, sitting close upon them, come stalks of charming lilac-pinky flowers, with a strong sweet hawthorn scent. The plant is quite easy and good-tempered here, especially in the moraine-garden, where it luxuriates among the chips, and has a yearly top-dressing of lime-rubble. It is difficult to analyse the attraction of *Petrocallis*; it lies not so much, perhaps, in the brilliancy of his flowers, which are rather faint in tone, as in the general

E

neat, concise sturdiness of its growth, so hearty, yet so minute.

Next comes *Morisia hypogaea*, which is not only of front rank among Crucifers, but very high indeed upon the list of alpines in general. From rocks and shores of Sardinia, this most delightful person likes a shady, rather rich corner of my rock, and there runs about, making flat rosettes of long, narrow, pinnatifid leaves of a bright glossy green. Then come innumerable big golden flowers, sitting tight on the leaves, and continuing for several months. On a dull spring day he is about the most inspiriting thing the eye can light on, and is altogether excellent in beauty, temper, and constitution, which is rather strange, I think, considering where he comes from.

Iberidella makes the third in my trinity of loves among the Cross-bearers. *Iberidella* is a very high alpine indeed, whom you never sight until you are close on *Ranunculus glacialis*. It grows in the shingle, and has immense taproots very difficult to get up unless you find young plants. Once got up, however, *Iberidella* thrives in any ordinary garden in a most surprising way, by no means to be prophesied from its chosen dwelling in Nature. The plant makes small mats of dense, fleshy-leaved, dark-green or rusty-looking growths, covered with big heads of bright lilac flowers, that share with *Petrocallis* the very rare charm among high alpines of being deliciously fragrant. In spite of all these recommendations, though, of beauty, sweetness, and good temper, *Iberidella* is seldom grown. Let me cry aloud its charms to every one. I have it in the moraine-garden, where it thrives and seeds robustly and never makes itself a nuisance, either by not thriving or by thriving too rampageously. And here, as I don't like any of the Drabas (except *D. dicranoeides*), ends the glory of

the Cruciferae, there being no need to tell of *Aubrietia*, *Ionopsidion*, or lovely *Alyssum gemonense*.

The alpine Pinks are for the most part lovers of open sunny ground in high places, and as for their culture, all that my experience entitles me to say is that when they are good, like *Dianthus neglectus*, they are very, very good, and when they are bad, like *D. sylvestris*, they are perfectly horrid. But a beautiful family they are, and there is no mistaking it, nor is there any group of plants more devoted to rock-work and stony crevices. A certain amount of confusion reigns among their names, so I will make no attempt to deal with them alphabetically, but simply take them one by one, each with his nearest relations. All the species that thrive with me do so in full exposure in light loam among rocks; with a few exceptions the race dislikes fat, retentive soil, and damp and richness; rather arid, baked ground is what certainly appeals most to the mountain Pinks from Southern Europe.

D. alpinus is perhaps the best known—dwarf and very handsome, with glossy dark leaves and big, round, carmine flowers, dotted with crimson. The plant is a native of high pastures in the Eastern Alps, and I have always found it very easy to grow, but capricious; that is to say, for some years it would thrive eagerly, and then would come lean seasons of inexplicable decay. Of course, wireworm has to be looked after, but otherwise I do not really think *D. alpinus* has any special fad about soil. A fine specimen of him is a wonderful sight when in flower, for few garden-plants bloom with such prodigality. *D. alpinus*, being a pasture species, will not, of course, ask for the crevice that suits the rock-loving kinds; he likes a light sound loam and a quiet place to ramble about in and make a good tuft. Nor must he be parched or harassed by torrid sunshine. The albino which one

so long wanted has at last turned up, and proves yet
again how foolish one is always to want a flower to be of
a different colour from that by which we know it. How
we pant for blue roses or tulips, and always imagine that
the unknown must necessarily be the beautiful! As a
matter of fact, few colour-forms are better than their types.
Even of the Gentians no white is an improvement on its
blue parents; nor, indeed, is any quite as good as its
parent, except the white *asclepiadea*; while *D. alpinus
albus* is a blank disappointment to me. The whiteness is
all right, but the tone is not good, rather mean and
ungenerous; no brave, pure, rich white, but a starved-
looking, pining colour. As for the confusingly named
D. alpestris, this is quite distinct from *alpinus*, a brilliant
and apparently thrifty Pink, whom I have in a batch of
vigorous young plants.

　D. glacialis is the Eastern Granitic version of the lime-
stone-loving *alpinus*. It has much longer leaves, not shining, and curiously grasslike, with flowers of a uniform pink,
a little smaller and by no means so round in shape as those
of *D. alpinus*. *Glacialis* is rather a rare plant in gardens,
and has a bad reputation for ill-temper. And these
cross Mountain Pinks are very hard to deal with when
their tempers are bad. In a way they are incalculable,
and seem to cultivate a certain personal animosity against
their wretched purchaser. As a matter of fact, I have
always found here that *D. glacialis* is one of the species
that looks on lime as a thing devised by Satan. Peat
and grit it must have, no lime whatever; and a good
moist, cool corner (here again is a pasture-species, from
very high up), neither exposed nor parched nor sodden.
In such circumstances it will generally do fairly well. It
is, I must say, distinctly less beautiful than *alpinus*, but
all the same a brilliant and desirable plant. *D. Freyni*
is said to be a local form of it, very much more minute,

from mountains in Bosnia. This I have found to be rather more amenable than the type. But all these difficult Pinks have a trying way of disappearing after a season or two.

D. neglectus is certainly the glory of the Alpine section. It is the Oeillet Bleu (why ' Bleu,' Heaven alone knows!) of Dauphiné and the Maritime Alps. I have collected it in seed above St. Martin Vesubie in October. The plant makes tufts of narrow, wiry foliage, extraordinarily like grass, and then bears innumerable large flowers of the most dazzling carmine-pink, a magnificent, eye-piercing colour, with a very lovely wash of nankeen or buff over the reverse of the petals. But at the same time I must warn you *D. neglectus* has innumerable varieties, and it is never safe to buy the plant unless it is guaranteed a good form, or unless you see it in flower. For, while some plants have immense, cart-wheel-shaped blooms, luminously pink, others have poor, thin-petalled, ragged-looking flowers, sometimes dull and washy in tone. I have never had any trouble at all with the Glacier Pink. It even thrives out in the open border. But any good light soil, neither parched nor soaking, will probably suit it everywhere, and—I think this is rather a great point to remember—*D. neglectus*, like all the other alpines that make deep tufts, is very thankful for a top-dressing of helpful soil as soon as the denuding winter and the upheaving frosts are over. Frost and rain work all these tufted plants rather bare and desolate; just as the growing season begins they very much appreciate a fine sifting of light rich soil fretted gently in among their growths.

D. callizonus would have an even higher prize for beauty than *D. neglectus*, if only its moral character deserved it. Its flower is indeed a ' Beauty-girdle.' Figure a great round blossom, bigger than *D. alpinus* at

his very best, brilliant pink, with a belt of purple at the
base, peppered with white dots. The plant has broad,
blunt, greyish leaves, and is perfectly dwarf, with a tendency to run about ; and any one who has seen the great
specimen at Kew will go on his knees at any mention of
D. callizonus. But, alas, the plant is ' gey ill to live wi,'—
one of those horticultural riddles that one can never give
up, in spite of innumerable failures. I have come to the
conclusion that this Transylvanian dreads lime and sunshine. I have him now looking, so far, happy and
stalwart, in a cool, shady patch of rock-work, in loose,
spongy peat and leaf-mould, among rare Primulas with
Lilium Alexandrae below. What will happen, though,
I cannot tell. These Dianthuses have such a trying way
of looking so vigorous one day that no Life Insurance
would hesitate about them, and then, the next, temper
or wireworm has triumphed, and only a wizened mass
remains ; not to mention that slugs have a special passion
for *D. callizonus*.

D. sylvestris is a species you hardly ever see in gardens.
I used to wonder why. Now I know. The plant is of
fairly general occurrence, rather high up, and highest in
the Western Alps. I have collected it very rarely in the
Oberland, quite close to snow patches on the Vorder
Wellhorn ; and abundantly on sun-baked hillsides as you
go up from Evolena to Arolla. The plant is the loveliest creature, and looks as if any sort of treatment would
suit it. Just you try—and give me news, please. For I
have always found this vigorous-looking creature one of
the very worst doers of all my Alpine Pinks. I make no
pretence at understanding it. No amount of attention
seems to mollify it. In future I shall try slapping it in
the face with a little wholesome neglect. Then it will
probably take to thriving like Goutweed. *D. sylvestris*
(the name is a monumental fatuity ; the plant detesting

woods, and never being found except on high and perfectly open places : so let no Latinist be deluded) is not
a dwarf, but from a rather sparse, flat tuft of leaves sends
up a six-inch stem carrying one or two delicious rose-
pink flowers, large and fairly round, particularly attractive when you see it jewelling an arid hillside. And
from these conditions you would surely think the plant
ought to be easy. Perhaps it is, with other people.
Here it flowers once, then it miffs off without any
apparent reason, in any soil, in any aspect. The albino
form is very beautiful indeed, but quite as trying as the
type, if not more so.

D. caesius is one of the best all-round rock-plants.
You will find it hanging in sheets from the Cheddar
cliffs, where in all probability it is wild. In growth it is
vigorous, in leaf beautiful, and in flower a delight. The
grass is glaucous-grey, forming mats or cascades ; and the
flowers, on six-inch stems, are fringy, pink, and sweet-
scented. The Cheddar Pink is a true crevice plant, and
is not safely perennial in low, rich, or damp parts of the
garden. But ram a seedling into a cranny, or sow it on
a wall or in any crack, and it will be an increasing glory
for years uncounted. *D. arvernensis* is a tiny form of it,
growing in wee, compact masses, which have twice the
beauty of *Freyni* with twice the general usefulness. *D.
suavis* is, I think, very near *caesius* for garden purposes—
a little larger in all ways, more bushy and less matted,
with delightfully sweet pink flowers, which are very
generously borne. Nobody seems to know where *D.
suavis* comes from, but he is a charming, willing little
person.

Unlike the Alpine Pinks, the taller sorts are often inhabitants of wood and copse (except the sun-loving cluster-heads
like *Carthusianorum*, which I dislike), so that they will
apparently put up with less open positions. However, as a

race, they are easy enough almost anywhere, so that one need not be troubled by any such considerations. For most of them I cannot, I confess, muster any warmer feeling than a regret that I cannot love them more. (But my favourite is a nameless November-blooming treasure with big flowers, that I collected above St. Martin Vésubie). So many of them have such dreadfully untidy, floppy petals, all torn to rags, that they make me quite unhappy. I long to have them sewn up again, or ironed out by a competent maid. They do look so draggled and miserable. *D. aridus* (a false name), *monspessulanus*, *superbus*, its variety *nanus*, *plumarius*, *squarrosus*, are all more or less jagged (some, as I say, to so distressing a degree that not even their delicious fragrance can ever make me feel quite happy about them, or quite certain that they are really comfortable, or have any right to be comfortable, in such a Tilburina-state of dishevelment). As for cultivation, that offers no puzzle; almost any soil will please them, and for the most part they are sound, if not robust growers.

Far otherwise is it with the gorgeous *D. cinnabarinus* from Parnassus, with his wonderful flowers of fiery cinnabar-scarlet (and so many, if not all, the other pink Pinks, have chalk or magenta in their tones too !). Years ago I flowered *cinnabarinus*, and when he immediately died, exhausted by the effort, I ransacked the world for more. But not until last year was I able to get seed. Now, however, I have hundreds of dear stout little plants, and another couple of months will tell me whether I have really got my old friend again. He seems almost to have passed out of cultivation, and probably is inclined to be rather a miff (though I do know one plant of him that sits tight in an open border near London !) But I think he is a true sun- and crevice-lover, so my seedlings shall have no trouble, I promise them, with fat soil or

damp about their necks.   Yet, when all is said and done,
too many of these Pinks, though not biennial, have a
way of flowering themselves to death, and I rather fear
cinnabarinus may be of that vain and frivolous persuasion.
With him, attracted by their names, I got seed of two
Pinks called *pruinosus* and *cinnamomeus*.   They both
look very beautiful in leaf, and vigorous in growth, so
that I do hope their epithets may not have been as mis-
leading as specific names too often are.   Their seedlings,
like those of *cinnabarinus*, are being packed into close,
sunny corners of rock in light soil with yards of root-room
behind.   Take your seedling young enough, and wad him
in tight enough, and you will have far more chance of
success with him than with any bought or pot-reared
plant, to say nothing of the far less difficulty of planting
them.

Of the hybrids and race-parents I grow in odd corners
D. caryophyllus, that august but simple-looking person
who is the parent of the Carnations.   I found him growing in sheets all over Fountains Abbey, and look upon
him with the awe one feels for the obscure parent of a
royal line—a sort of Owen Tudor of a plant.   He forms
loose great glaucous sheets, and bears sweet, pink flowers,
and, altogether, is like an exaggerated *caesius*.   Then
there is the inevitable semi-double mule, *Napoleon III.*,
who is perfectly gorgeous in colour, but too fond of
flowering himself into his grave—such a vulgar and really
second-empire passion for display, that I cannot say he
wins either my affection or my respect.   Another pluto-
cratic snob of the same nature is the even more splendid
Atkinsonii, and I will admit that I could live my life
quite happily without either.   A plant so bent on
making a show of itself that it dies of the effort, cannot
have a nice mind or any sense of perspective.   Especially
as they don't even bear seed!   Nor do they make any

effort to atone by producing good grass. No, they are flaunting crimson glories quite devoid of good feeling. And so, though to a lesser extent, is that fat little dwarf, the double crimson Sweet William, whose notable name is *D. barbatus magnificus plenus.* He is distinctly stronger and healthier than the others, but I don't like him, and I can't like him, and never shall be able to like him, except quite platonically, as a mere splotch of colour. Whereas, of course, a well-bred alpine appeals to one primarily as a personality, an interesting, shy, rather proud character. Indeed some people who do not feel the sacred passion keenly, complain that the alpines are sometimes too lacking in those splotches of colour. The insulting words 'Minute' and 'Invisible' float in the air. Well, the lover of rock-plants loves his children for their individualities, their little ways, their personal appeal, not at all for any accident of gaudy colour or obviousness; and those others whose ideal of floral beauty is a triple border of Pelargonium, Calceolaria, and Lobelia, are just the people to appreciate these double crimson mule-Pinks, and as far as I am concerned they are welcome to monopolise them all, except my dear *D. striatiflorus* from Oxford, a hybrid of really solid habit with flowers that, in my form, are of a pure and exquisite pale pink, without any nasty flakes at all.

Nothing is lovelier than an old wall ablow with masses of Dianthus, Wallflower, Linaria, and Erinus; nor are the Pinks of the *caesius* and *caryophyllus* persuasion ever better suited than with an old mortared chink; but I now want to raise my inconsiderable voice against the excessive use of that unsatisfactory hybrid, 'the wall-garden.' One sees it far too often, and it sins against the cardinal rules of art and horticulture. For it aims at being two things at once—a wall and a garden, with the consequence that it is never wholly satisfactory

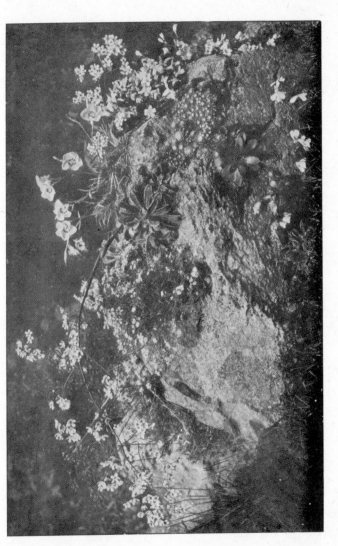

A BOULDER IN THE OLD GARDEN, PLANTED WITH PINKS, SAXIFRAGES, CAMPANULAS AND HOUSELEEKS

as either. The real, dignified wall-garden is that which
set out originally to be a wall, and a wall only, with no
arrière-pensée or ambition after frills of any kind. Such
are the great walls of St. John's at Oxford. The only
gardener that they know is Time, who sows them cun-
ningly, with the result that they end by being doubly
beautiful—a magnificent wall in the first place, and
essentially; and then, accidentally, a garden of pleasant
flowers. But the wall that is built for wall-gardening
has always to be built at a slant, instead of with the
stern straightness of the real thing. Thus it gives away
its duplicity of purpose at a glance, and as you look at it
leaning back against a bank, conveys an inevitable feeling of weakness. The poor creature looks as if it had
unfortunately got drunk, and could not stand without
support. It is of no use to try combining the artificial
with the natural, or the imitation of the natural. A
wall is, *ex hypothesi*, an artificial product, flop it about
as drunkenly as you will; while the rock-garden is, *ex
hypothesi*, an attempt to give the impression of Nature.
There the wall-garden is discord, naturally and invariably;
nor do I see, in spite of all that is said and written, that
it grows the plants any better than a well-set rockwork. It might be better, perhaps, if it were built more
frankly as a wall, with huge squared blocks like the
Lion Gate of Mykenai; then you might gain the effect
of an artificial creation made by Time to serve as
Nature's nursery. As taste now runs, though, the wall-
garden is generally made of small flat stones piled atop
of each other till the whole effect is as of a very ill-built,
toppling 'dyke,' altogether slipshod and undignified.
And 'this I say, and I can no other,' although I have
seen many of these dishevelled embankments well adorned
with tufts of blossom.

CHAPTER VI

Saxifraga: the Smaller Groups and the Mossies

From age to age, by every race, in every clime adored, the Family of the Saxifrages rules unquestioned, unquestionable sovereign of the rock-garden. Primula, perhaps, may reach a rather higher general average of beauty, but no group of plants combines so much charm, so much adaptability to cultivation, so much good humour, as the Saxifrages. Their clan is enormously large, and swelled by innumerable varieties, but its range seems practically restricted to Europe, North Africa, North America, and is divided up into several groups, for the most part well-marked, and bearing their cultural needs written well on their foliage and habit. Roughly speaking, the Saxifrages generally like a sunny but not too torrid place; while those of the Mossy and Miscopetalum sections prefer, as a rule, a damp and shady but not dank corner for their best development. In no great family is there more fearful confusion as to names : the invaluable Engler is hardly for general consumption, Nicholson is weak and inadequate, and some Oedipus is sadly needed to take the race in hand and unravel its riddles. *Fosteri, Zimmeteri, scardica, Malyi, Frederici-Augusti*, are all synonymous, not with the species whose names they falsely bear, but with the dire slackness and ignorance of the nurserymen who send them out.

And now I will gird up my loins and set forward,

terrified and yet undaunted, to my task, taking the smaller groups first, to prepare me gently for the three vast phratries of *Hypnoeides*, *Aeizoön*, and *Apiculata*.

The first section contains only one plant that I grow— only two or three altogether. *Saxifraga cymbalaria* is an annual, with glossy little tufts of foliage like a Toad-flax, and gay little yellow flowers; plant it in any cool moist place and it will never give you any trouble again, except in the way of weeding, for never did any plant seed itself so passionately all over the place. However, one cannot reject such a pleasant, generous visitor, and, after all, he is very easy to cope with, his plants being brittle and shallow-rooted.

S. hirculus gives its name to another tiny branch of the family, its brothers being *flagellaris*, and what I grow as *diversifolia*. *S. hirculus* is a very rare native, being found here and there in becks and bogs of Upper Tees-dale, where it makes sparse wandering branches, with two or three large, frail-stemmed, brilliant buttercup flowers. But he is not a very good garden plant—a shy thriver and a shy bloomer. His variety *hirculus major* is far finer, freer, and better. A very near relation, and not, I think, in general cultivation, so far as I know, is the high Arctic *S. flagellaris*. *S. diversifolia* is an obscure and doubtfully-named species. I grow under this title an extremely pretty plant which is out and away the best of the *hirculus* group, making good mats of deciduous foliage, with abundance of bright golden blossoms. I forget where, or with what authority, I got this plant. But in my memory floats a notion that the real thing claims to be a Himâlyan species; in any case, whereas the other *hirculus* species are difficult plants, requiring a bog and rather elaborate treatment, my *diversifolia* (which, I am afraid, is only an extra-good *hirculus major* after all) is very easy and thrifty in any cool damp corner, at the base of the rock-work, where nothing else would do.

The Boraphylla section contains some real Uglies—among the comparatively few real Uglies that the race affords; for, though by no means all Saxifrages are brilliant, yet very few Saxifrages lack charm. But, to my taste, the Boraphyllas do; *erosa* and *pennsylvanica* are fat giants, advertised in flaming terms. They make great rosettes of smooth, limp leaves, and you expect something splendid in the way of flower from such fine preparations. Then up comes a stout spike of pale greenish-looking dowdy blossoms, quite uninteresting and uninspiring. One can tell from the rank look of the plants that they love a stream-side in woodland, with shade and moisture; but no one is likely to care much what they want. *S. nivalis* is a rare native of the Lake Country, growing a few inches high and making tight rosettes of leaden-looking, leathery little leaves, extraordinarily like those of a Primula, with fat heads of closely packed, tiny white flowers, dotted with red. The plant is interesting, but not really attractive; I got utterly sick of it in the Rockies, where I was always being annoyed by what was either *nivalis* or a large twin of *nivalis* that occurred on every alpine slope. I grew *nivalis* here and there for a good many years; but now, I think, it has all died off, and I do not feel any great stirring within me to replace it. As for *stellaris*, this is the prettiest of the Boraphyllas, a plant of the sopping bog, with loose, frail clouds of white, pink-dotted blossoms. It occurs in alpine streams in England and Scotland fairly commonly; although reported from Ingleborough, and obviously suitable to Ingleborough, it is the only one of the reported Saxifrages that I have never yet found there.

The Miscopetalums contain one or two useful species,

most of which are deciduous woodlanders. *Rotundifolia* is a type-plant of the group—tall, herbaceous, with handsome rounded leaves and abundance of rather small white, pink-spotted flowers—very fine for an odd corner of the copse or bog in any cool soil. You find it everywhere in wet shady places in the sub-alpine woodland zone of the great ranges. Very near it are two Servians—*graeca* and *rhodopea*—which I imported a few seasons since, and have confused till I don't really know which is which. I know that one is distinctly handsomer than the other, with larger milk-white flowers ; and there my knowledge stops. Both species hugely disappointed me, on their arrival, for I had expected Silvers, of absolute novelty and extreme beauty. However, they are effective, very easy, and useful for any rank, unvalued dell. *S. Fortunei* is a singularly beautiful species, far too little cultivated. It has very handsome dark-green glossy leaves, and then, in October, when the garden is dying, large loose heads of brilliant white blossom. The plant has a splendid solidity and sanity of aspect, and turns out, though a Chinaman, perfectly hardy in any decent place. He deserves a good sheltered corner, of course, for the sake of his fleshy foliage and his season. *S. odontophylla* is an extremely rare Himâlyan species, with the usual beautiful leaves, downy and roughly heart-shaped this time (all the Miscopetalum Saxifrages run to handsome foliage), and large pink-and-gold flowers, very effective and charming. So far I have only treated him to pot-culture, but I see no sort of reason why he should not thrive in the open like *Primula megaseaefolia*. So out he shall go. About *taygetea* and *soldanellaefolia* I dare not speak with any certainty, they seem to be wrapped in such a mystery. Whatever my plants may really be, the one called *soldanellaefolia* has leaves exactly like a *Soldanella*—not that that proves much—and is very neat and pretty; so is the other species, *taygetea*, with clouds of white blossom. But my *taygetea* almost certainly belongs to the Umbrosa section, so, despite my affection for it, I look upon its name with suspicion. Both are quite easy in a cool corner.

The Umbrosa section has the London Pride, *S. umbrosa*, for its type, and contains some lovely things. First, London Pride itself; then its kidney-leaved cousin, *S. Geum*, from Killarney, where it clothes the hills. Then *serratifolia*, with long, conspicuously saw-edged leaves; *Andrewsi*, similar in appearance, with showers of pinky flowers; *guthrieana*, another cousin, who has a silver-and-gold-variegated variety, whose bedizened leaves contrast very daintily with its flesh-pale blossoms; and *Geum cochlearis*, a funny little squatty form of *Geum*. All these have pinkish pretty clouds of blossom, and are invaluable for shady ledges and pockets, remembering that *umbrosa* and *Geum* are far too rampant for a choice place. The finest delicacy of the group is the very rare true *Zimmeteri* (hardly to be got hold of, as a rule, for gardeners sell innumerable false forms of it, and it was only after years of effort that I got the genuine thing), a minute Alpine or Arctic species, with loose little clusters of white flowers hovering above a tiny rosette of glossy dark green. *S. Zimmeteri* rather frightens me, and I have not yet dared to plant it out. It looks as if it would resent any burning, torrid atmosphere, and would pine for cool moisture in air and soil alike. However, some day I must try. The other beauty of this group is a dear little rather unguaranteed person, whom I have grown for a long time as *S. primuloeides*. He makes fine dark-green rosettes, like a Primula, but even more like a small tidy form of *umbrosa*; and then carries delicate showers of the loveliest bright carmine-rose flowers, with orange stamens. He is a gay, brilliant little creature, very easy to grow in sun or shade, but never ramping you out of house and home like some others of his group, especially *Geum* and *umbrosa*. I forget whence I had him, but he is certainly a jewel. Last year I was given another plant called *primuloeides*, which is quite different—larger and laxer in growth, and with dull little pale flowers. The other good friends in this section are *Bucklandi*, a neat little *Geum*-cousin, and *cuneifolia infundibuliformis*, whose awful name is his one fault—a lovely common plant of Alpine woods, like a very modest, delicate little London Pride, and quite as easy to do with. Of the smaller groups (I don't grow any of the Nephrophyllums) only remains that of *S. oppositifolia*, all of whose cousins are prostrate dwarfs, with large purple or crimson flowers sitting more or less close upon the leaves. *Oppositifolia* itself is a native of our limestone cliffs about two thousand feet up, and forms great sheets of colour in early April on Ingleborough and Penyghent. It varies in depth of tone, and there is one most ardent crimson one who sits secure on an inaccessible precipice of Penyghent. In the Alps the plant goes high towards the snows, and even in July you will find it blooming near *Eritrichium*, close on the snow-level. There are in cultivation a big pale form, *pyrenaica*; a white form, with rather poor, meanly-built flowers, like a large Arenaria; and a most gorgeous but very frail-growing crimson, finer than even the advertised *splendens*, which I collected on Ingleborough, and think of as *splendidissima*. In ordinary cultivation *oppositifolia* will thrive anywhere in the sun, but must always have poor soil if you expect it to do itself justice in the matter of blossom. At least here I find that fat, rich ground makes it go to lush, leafy growth, at the expense of its proper floriferousness. Naturally it is one of the most generous of plants in the matter of blooming, and a mat of it on the hills is a splendid sight; for, though the colour is purplish, yet there is, luckily, just enough crimson in it to give the blossoms luminosity and brilliance.

S. retusa is a tiny, smooth-leaved cousin of *oppositifolia*, easy to grow, if let alone, and charming with its large crimson blooms, which come later in the season. *Kochii* and *biflora* are rare high-alpines seldom, I think, grown successfully for very long. At least I have not always been successful with either, though I have grown *biflora* from very perfectly rooted little plants that I collected from the grey glacier mud below the Col de Bertol. It is just possible that these two species need a good deal more well-drained moisture than I have given them yet. I must try them in the moraine. Their flowers are very large indeed for the size of the plant, and make a notable show. *S. rudolphiana* is a tiny *retusa*-like species, much more compact, and I must add my dire belief, more difficult to keep in health. The very high Alpine and glacial Oppositifolias do seem to need special treatment, and to be of frail, untrustworthy dispositions. *Wulfeniana* is near *retusa* also, and I am told (I have not yet tried it) fairly easy to deal with.

It is one of my life's innumerable ambitions to secure a hybrid between an *oppositifolia* and an *aeizoön*, so as to get big red flowers into the silver group. I don't see why this should be impossible; *mutata* and *aeizoeides* have crossed, so have *aretioeides* and *media*. Already I have a promising, odd little seedling of *S. media* crossed with *oppositifolia*. The seed was certainly that of *media*, and the growth of the seedling is certainly *not* pure *media*; so goodness knows what may be the result! But, where the drunken polypragmatic bee goes bumbling about, it is never possible to say that your parentage has not been vitiated by pollen from some other Saxifrage. I have whole pans of weird, improbable seedlings, of which I hope great things—and, at all events, great surprises—when their blooming days arrive. *Longifolia* X *mutata* may give a good thing. *Aeizoön* X *thessalica* (true) should give a very fine, sensational one, if it comes off. The seed is coming up thick and fast, but who knows what confusion the bees may have wrought!

The Mossy Saxifrages take high rank among rock-plants for general amiability and charm. They will grow almost anywhere, but hardly ever, I think, do they affect the very high open places beloved by the Silvers and the Kabschias. And, as a rule, the few high Alpine Saxifrages of the Mossy Section are neither easy nor very desirable. *Varians*, to my mind, is almost an ugly little creature, with abundance of greenery-yallery flowers; *Seguieri* follows the same tradition; *androsacea* is pretty with milk-white blooms, but not remarkably so, and I have always found it more or less of a miff; however, as far as I am concerned, it is not much missed or mourned.

One finds it hard to adjust one's rule as to worshipping rarity. It seems vulgar to spend years coping with an ugly little plant simply because it is rare; but, on the other hand, it seems cowardly, and makes one a mock to the more successful, if one lays oneself open to the charge of abandoning a rarity simply because it is difficult. As far as I have a principle, it is that beauty, and beauty alone, entitles a plant to a place in the garden, and makes it worthy of any attention it may exact. Beauty, of course, embraces charm—nothing should deprive me of *Astrantia minor*—and, where beauty or charm is found, no trouble is too great to take. But, for mere sheer rarity, undistinguished by any other quality, I have little taste left. So good-bye, *Saxifraga androsacea, aphylla, citrina, stenopetala, varians, sedoeides,* and all the other more or less synonymous dowdies of the Mossy Section.

The chosen homes of the best Mossies are the lower rocks, and, transferred from there, there is hardly a

cottage garden where most of them won't make dense
evergreen mats and cushions of green or red. They like
a stone to lean on, and they are sometimes liable to
brown in very hot sun and to rust in the centre during a
wet winter; otherwise they have no cultural fault and
are altogether desirable.

The type-plant is our own native Saxifrage *hypnoeides*, found, I believe, in the Mendips, and then abundantly all over the English mountain-chains, beginning
at a lower level than the other Alpine Saxifrages, and
climbing as high as any. Here you will find it among
the lower limestone copses, and it goes to the very
summit of Ingleborough, where it is one of the few
flowering plants to be found on that wind-swept plateau.
The needs of *S. hypnoeides* will do for all the others,
except where I have to deal with some rare or special
kind. It may be taken, then, that all the more ordinary
Mossies are tolerant of sun and shade alike, though they
don't want to be rotted with damp nor broiled to death.
A light, well-drained soil, and water during heavy
droughts, will keep them all green and happy. *Hypnoeides* has a variegated variety whose leaves are prettily
laced with silver. This must have very thin poor soil, or
it reverts to the common green form. Another form,
densa, occurs on Ingleborough, and is much neater and
tidier and prettier than the type. *S. caespitosa* is probably a fat-leaved high-Alpine variety of *hypnoeides*,
whose leaves have grown almost succulent to resist the
trying temperatures of the elevations where it lives; this
is a very rare native found on some Scottish mountains,
with white flowers like *hypnoeides* on tall firm stems,
but tighter and cosier-looking in growth. The common
Mossy, however, varies a great deal, and on Ingleborough
alone you may collect half a dozen divergent forms.
Some from other parts, especially from Ireland, have

been dignified with names to themselves ; and whether worthy of these or no, they are all interesting thrifty plants—*Sternbergi, decipiens, hirta, groenlandica,* and so forth, besides a red '*atropurpurea*' which is pretty. But here I must mention that a very delightful thing is just coming into cultivation called *decipiens hybrida grandiflora.* (It is so annoying when *grandiflora* is tacked on to so terrific a name ; surely the ' grand-floweringness ' might be allowed to speak for itself ? The epithet always allures me, I must own, but always exasperates me ; for I hope against hope that it may be just, and I know in my secret heart that it almost certainly isn't.) Anyhow, this *S. decipiens,* etc., is a large-growing, handsome-leaved Mossy, close to *caespitosa* in blood, very sturdy, and fine of flower. And those flowers are very variable in colour, and some are of a lovely pink—probably got from *Rhei.* I foretell for this Saxifrage a large and popular future.

Our other natives are *granulata* and *cernua.* Of *cernua* only a mournful tale can be told. The species is a very, very high Arctic and Alpine one, scattered rarely, here and there, over the northern mountain-chains. In Great Britain it has only one station—among rocks on the summit of Ben Lawers, where it lives from age to age, and very seldom flowers. *Granulata* is a lovely deciduous species, like a magnified *cernua*—or *cernua* after a course of Nauheim Baths, with the floppy weakness cured, and vigour restored. *Granulata* has handsome, succulent-looking leaves, and very large, pure white flowers collected on stems about a foot high. It makes little bulbs and multiplies at a prodigious rate. Round Malham Cove it occurs, and is very abundant in the meadows as you cross the Pass from Brough into Upper Teesdale. There is a double variety, which is quite pretty, though less so than the type, which is far too seldom seen in gardens; and then there is a close, but I think distinct, cousin, who interests me very much, because I collected him years ago, below Roquebrune, on my way from St. Raphael. To my astonishment this plant, from the level of the Mediterranean, has completely established itself here, and every year its little dark clustered leaves appear, and then showers of white flowers smaller and looselier borne than those of *granulata*, on taller stems. *Rivularis* is a near cousin of *cernua*, rather more vigorous, and more common in the one recorded British station for it—by stream-sides in the range of Lochnagar.

Of the minor Mossies it would be difficult and tedious to particularise their appearance. My favourites are *Allioni* and *nervosa*—wee, wee-growing things, like mats of the neatest possible moss. *Nervosa* is given by Nicholson as a synonym for *exarata*; my *nervosa* is certainly much farther away from my *exarata*, which ought to be the true plant, as I imported it from Servia under solemn guarantees of authenticity. *Exarata* is a fine neat-growing Mossy (with tufts of lovely green, and rather large sulphur-coloured flowers), that seems good at growing and good at seeding. *Iratiana* belongs to the *varians* division, but is prettier, with fine foliage and the usual greenish-yellow inconspicuous blooms. *Laevis* and *hirta* are larger, not very distinct, *hypnoeides* sorts; *corsica* is smaller, tidier, and more attractive. *Prostii* and *cuneata* are two very rare Spanish kinds, neither of which did I use to love, in spite of having purchased them at great expense and with the most flaming descriptions. *Prostii* I am still tepid about; it has too much leaf to too little flower—rather poor, small, and dull-white in colour. But *cuneata* seems to have taken a new lease of life lately, and in the last two years has leapt to a very high place among my Mossies. It has loose glossy dark leaves, rather like those of the common *ceratophylla*, but not curled up like a stag's antlers. The flowers are white, of course, but quite small, and carried in rather tall, very airy showers. Both *cuneata* and *Prostii* are rather pernickety people, and, as far as this garden goes, I have found that they die in cold wet winters unless planted high and dry where the damp will run away quickly, and where they will get every available ray of sun. Planted thus, in warm crevices, they go on quite happily and prove perfectly robust. It is interesting (and a sound general rule, I believe), that the Mossy Saxifrages, and indeed all alpines, except the woollies like *Androsace*, will tolerate more sun for the species whose leaves are dark and leathery, than for those with downy soft-looking green foliage. *Ceratophylla* with its splendid crisped foliage is another instance of this ; and then there follows a ruck of Mossies with whom it is almost impossible to deal, for every nurseryman sends them out with different names, and none of them are right. I will only mention *cervicornis, Willkomiana, canaliculata, palmata*—an exceedingly handsome plant with immense rosettes—*soldanellaefolia*—a ridiculous impostor with leaves like moss—*pedemontana, palmatifida*, and ever so many more, all mixed up and confused in the most hopeless manner.

S. palmata, I say, is a very good plant indeed, though, so remarkably splendid that I feel I did him an injustice in herding him with the crowd. In fact, I am inclined to say that he is the handsomest of all the Mossy Saxifrages —like a gigantic *Wallacei* rather. Nicholson calls him only a form of *hypnoeides* ; certainly my *palmata* is absolutely distinct and far superior. As for *pedemontana* he is reported (when you get him true, which I have done at last, after years of search) to be one of the very best—a sturdy grower, with great snowy panicles of blossom. I only hope my baby plants may prove this to be so. *Tricuspidata* is another youngling which I am just trying, and, of course, one goes on making perpetual experiments.

S. maweana is a rare, curious, North African in whom I have ceased to take very much stock. He seems to be almost a desert plant—at least for months he lies apparently brown and dead; then out break big apple-green leaves, and large snow-white flowers. Evidently special hot treatment is appreciated, but I don't consider *maweana* in the same field as far as attractiveness goes with common plants like *Camposii*.

S. Camposii is better known as *Wallacei*, under which name it stands supreme over the white-flowered Mossies; a rampant, thriving doer, and a bloomer so profuse as to look like a snowdrift, there is no more beautiful alpine anywhere in the lower reaches of the rock-garden. His only fault is a certain straggliness of growth which makes him difficult to exhibit in a solid block. *S. aquatica* is not far off, a very rare plant, though frequently offered in catalogues. But *aquatica* of catalogues is too seldom *aquatica* of stern fact. The real thing is a bog-plant with immense fat-looking foliage and big white flowers; I have only one specimen of it, which appears to be prospering in a marsh with the Glacial Buttercups, *alpestris*, *rutaefolius*, and *glacialis*.

As *exarata* stands for the few sulphury Mossies, and *Wallacei* for the whites, the dear little *muscoeides* takes place at the head of the crimsons. *Muscoeides* varies in depth of colour, and one form—the best—is called *atropurpurea*; but the type-plant is quite delightful enough, forming great close sheets of green-and-red foliage, rusting to crimson in autumn, with abundance of little pink blossoms on short stems. No neater, prettier species can be invented, nor any easier or more useful in growth.

S. Rhei is, to all intents and purposes, a *caespitosa* with flesh-pink blossoms—a very free, vigorous grower. Its flowers incline to grow paler in colour as they age, and in very hot sun they fade. But in a moderately shady corner the plant makes a spectacle of delightful refreshing delicacy amid the glare of other things—a demure, quiet beauty, full of satisfaction and charm. Its variety, *S. Rhei Guildford Seedling*, has been very much and deservedly trumpeted. It is simply *Rhei* with flowers deepened to carmine when young, and pink when old. The colour is wonderfully effective, but a doubt haunts one as to whether the thing is really a sport, or simply a selection from batches of pure *Rhei* seedlings. However, this question does not in the least affect the immense value of *S. Guildford Seedling* for gardening purposes. Both these plants make the most splendid indestructible masses of green, and are a perpetual pleasure in flower or out of it.

S. *Fergusoni* and *S. Stormonth Seedling* and *S. atropurpurea* are simply variants on *Rhei*, as far as I can see, all beautiful and all desirable. *Fergusoni* has the advantage of blooming at least ten days earlier than any other of the group, and *Stormonth's Seedling* is smaller, I fancy, and rather more brilliant than the others. *S. Wolley-Dod* has only just been given me. To be worthy of its name (as I suppose it is) the plant ought to be very beautiful, and it is evidently a Mossy, and evidently red-flowered and presumably of the *Rhei* persuasion; and I also have a self-sown seedling this year, a lovely *Rhei*-form, quite dwarf and cushiony. As for cultivation, all these are perfectly easy, but I always find that these red Saxifrages are certainly at their best when given a spot where they are protected from excessive sunshine. Not that they object to sun, but their colours remain purer and brighter if they are not scorched.

As much confusion reigns among the Mossies as in the other two great sections, but here the danger is not only of getting a false plant, but of getting an indistinct one.

For, in candour, one must acknowledge that the Mossies of each group have a very strong family resemblance, so that if one buys too much by faith one runs the risk of being cluttered up with obscure, indistinguishable forms of *hypnoeides*, and so forth. Even where genuine, the Mossies are too much alike for many of them to have any great value in the garden. They are far more alike than any even of the Aeizoöns, and of course less brilliant in effect. So that, for any one who does not set out to collect Saxifrages, it should be enough to grow *Wallacei*, *Rhei*, *Guildford Seedling*, *cuneata*, *palmata*, *muscoeides*, *pedemontana*, *aquatica*, and *exarata* (only let him be sure to have the true plants of these, not the wretched *hypnoeides*-forms too often sold under these names). My own case shows the peril of specialising. For years I have gone on acquiring Saxifrages, until I have now got together a collection which is said to be about the largest known. And this I say not in pride, but for an excuse; for such is the welter of spurious forms in which I lie entangled that I envy from afar the neat simplicity of those gardens that rest content with two or three unquestioned and distinct species. This daunting multitude of names, too, must be my plea in the next section, to which I tremblingly advance—the even more wildly chaotic Aeizoöns. But if once one sets out to specialise, as I have done, one has to accumulate every form, spurious or not, in order to collate false and true, and get some idea of the entire race; and then, when you have got to know the impostors, you never dare resist one of the great names if you see it in a catalogue, on the chance that it may really cover the plant it belongs to. And so the tale grows; and when you have all the innocent impostors filling frames and beds they are most of them so pretty, and all of them so innocent of intentional fraud, that no heart could find itself capable of

SAXIFRAGES IN THE OLD GARDEN

ejecting them into the outer darkness of the rubbish-
heap. I hate destroying, or throwing away—I can only
do it with coarse uglies and herbaceous stuff; and even
they have to be planted out in the wild garden at a vast
cost of time and trouble. But it does seem to me such
black ingratitude to kill a plant that has been at all the
trouble of growing and flowering. As for the Saxifrages,
I have never thrown away any yet, except *pennsylvanica*
and *erosa*, which were really too ugly to do with. It is
true I have neither mourned nor replaced *androsacea* and
varians, but to be calm about a guest's departure is quite
a different thing from hoofing him violently out.

Many of my illegitimates are possibly of mixed parentage; but I do possess some acknowledged crosses that
deserve a separate treatment. The Aeizoöns and the
Kabschias loom ahead, but *aegilops* is a useful, easy-
going mule — a quaint person, with blunted-looking
leaves and loose showers of blossom. The most sensational hybrid I have, however, I collected on Ingleborough
three years ago. On the western face the limestone
cliffs fall sheer to a very steep shale slope below, and
while over the cliff four Saxifrages grow—*hypnoeides*,
aeizoeides autumnalis, *oppositifolia*, and *tridactylites* (the
little annual), all over the slope beneath appear their
seedlings among *Cochlearia alpina* and *Arenaria verna*.
One day a baby struck my notice there, with strange
foliage. He had only made one pair of leaves, but that
pair belonged neither to *aeizoeides* nor to *hypnoeides*.
Accordingly I reverently dug him up and brought him
home, my first notion being that he might be a natural
hybrid between a belated *hypnoeides* and *aeizoeides*, or
the other way round. However, with the years, he has
developed into a most extraordinary little plant, with
wee rosettes on long withered stalks, and small white
flowers very abundantly produced. The latest and

soundest idea, accordingly, is that he is a mule between *hypnoeides* and *tridactylites*, to whom I give the provisional name of *cravoniensis* (Mr. Claridge Druce has recognised him as *Farreri*, which makes me justly proud). As soon as I have raised a good stock of him, I shall go back in state to the shale slope and there replant him for future generations.

People so often raise hands of horror over the collector's methods and morality, that I must stop here to vindicate myself. In the first place, no words are too bad for the devastator who sweeps a valley clean of all its rarities, or puts a price upon a plant's head. But, on the other hand, it is mere idle sentimentality that rhapsodises over a plant growing where no one but bees and butterflies ever see it. Parkinson sums up the proper point of view at the end of his chapters on *Tulipa*, where he says that being brought into cultivation, the Tulips give us more pleasure 'than ever to their own naturals.' Quite so. The 'own naturals' of alpines are stonechats and marmots, and unæsthetic bumble-bees. And in cultivation their powers of pleasure-giving are vastly enlarged. And, as the enlargement of pleasure-giving powers is highly beneficial to the moral nature, it follows that the plants are immensely improved, educated, and elevated by removal to our gardens, where they can practise generosity more extensively. Let us then, unabashed, continue to collect modestly and with consideration, respecting great rarities, and remembering that, of two specimens of a colour-variation or some such precious find, the one should be taken and the other left. To buy the bales that are offered for sale abroad is usually wicked, encouraging wholesale destruction to no good end. For of these poor plants, hardly one is likely to have a root or any fair hope of thriving. Therefore one should always do one's own collecting, and never do even that unless one has a garden at home to grow the things, and never unless one has a fair chance of securing sound roots. Anemones of the *alpina* section, *Trifolium alpinum*, the Phacas and Astragaluses, Rhododendrons, *Rhodothamnus*, *Pyrola*, should hardly be attempted. With the others dig the trowel *straight* down into the earth about five or six inches away from the plant, and lever up the whole thing in a mass, after which you may shake away the soil to any extent, for you will have got perfect roots, probably. Never put the trowel in at a slant, or close under the plant ; this will invariably destroy your roots, and is far too often done. A deep insertion at right angles, six inches away, and then similar ones all round, if necessary, is the only safe and certain method of proceeding. Few joys are greater than when a good clod comes easily up, and then you squat down fretting and shaking away the soil from a sound solid clump of *Androsace glacialis* or *Eritrichium nanum*. Even with woody-rooted things, too, this system answers, if only you are lucky enough to discover some baby plants or year-old seedlings.

As to packing, I have had such success with this that my experience may come in handy. In the first place, remember that nowhere, now, is there any prohibition against sending plants away by parcel post—*colis postal.* Sample post and letter post are useless, I believe, and now in the Maritime Alps, I fancy, all export is prohibited since a wicked collector devastated the valleys of St. Étienne du Tinay and St. Dalmas de Tende. But elsewhere, whatever hotel-keepers may, like the Pelagians, vainly talk, there is no sort of obstacle against the sending away of plants by the parcel post. Next, get hold of a biscuit-box—nothing else suits so well, the tin preserving the plants in cool moisture without evaporation, so that they will stand a journey of almost any length. I remember demanding a tin box at Nice once, and how the managers, after vast pondering, said they could contrive it in three days' time, if I would wait. How astounded they were when I mildly pointed out that biscuit-boxes were made of tin, and that all I required was a large old Huntley and Palmer! Then, having got your box, collect a quantity of moss, not wet, or even damp (this is exceedingly important), but only just fresh, with the faintest natural moisture in it —not parched or dry, of course. So, gather your plants together, having shaken them free of soil, into tight bundles, wrap the roots in moss, and pack them as close as you can get them—the closer the better—without brutality or bruising, naturally. And in this state they will emerge sound and well, from a month's hermetically sealed sojourn in that blessed tin box. Their foliage will blanch a little, but if your moss was not too damp, not even the leaves will have mouldered, and the roots will still be in perfect condition. Indeed, the state of the moss is really the most important consideration; for I have brought home a cargo from the Rockies wrapped in moss, but packed in wood, which arrived as fresh as the day they started; and I may say the same of the Japanese Alpines sent me across Canada from Yokohama, which don't seem to turn a hair despite the length of the journey, mossed up tight in half-open wooden cases.

CHAPTER VII

The Silver Saxifrages

Saxifraga aeizoön is, take it all round, the most valuable of all rock-garden plants. 'And if any one has anything to say contrairy to her character, which well I knows, afore her face, behind her back, or anywheres, is not to be impeaged, then they and I do not part as I could wish, but bearing malice in our 'earts.' But *S. aeizoön* labours under the same disadvantage as the admirable woman of whom those words were spoken. 'For I don't believe there's no sich a person.' At least I have never seen the real *S. aeizoön*. I have seen innumerable plants bearing the name, but all different, and my final conviction is that *S. aeizoön* is a sort of Platonic Idea—an abstraction possibly existing in some supra-mortal state, but represented on earth only by innumerable varieties or partial manifestations of its sacred essence. And those manifestations are legion. If I have suffered from an influx of Mossies, far, far worse have I suffered from accumulations of Aeizoöns, inasmuch as the Silvers always interest me more than the Mossies, and have always been my most special craze.

The appearance of the Silver Saxifrages does not need description. Every one knows their larger or smaller rosettes of grey and silver-edged leaves, their stiff sturdy stems, and their loose panicles of white, creamy, or pink-dotted flowers. The type may safely be called *aeizoön* ;

it is the first Alpine plant that hits one's notice in the mountains. Even as you climb the Brünig, you begin to see its neat grey mats rambling about among the stones, and the plant goes with you to within a fair distance of the moraines. The hard, resistent nature of all the Silver Saxifrages is foretold by their leaves, so leathery and firm and solid. Nothing comes amiss to them but excessive shade and moisture. In open ground they sometimes rot in winter, or burn in summer, but with stone to creep round, and fair soil, the Aeizoöns and all their cousins are the easiest, the most persistent, the least troublesome of any group in the garden.

To deal, in the first place, with the closest varieties of what is called *S. aeizoön*. The type has closeish panicles of white flowers on six- or eight-inch stems above the tumbling cushion of rosettes. But their whole growth and colouring varies in the most Protean manner. For my own part, I have collected three distinct forms—another, so far unproved, making a fourth. It was a very tall, large, loose-flowered variety, from bushes coming down the Gemmi. I was at a disadvantage that day; before I got well off the Gemmi itself my rucksack was full of *S. caesia*, and the weight of it was cutting my shoulders in two most pitifully. Never, never will I carry a rucksack again (my usual receptacle is a botanist's big tin vasculum, or two of them. They hurt cruelly when full, but nothing like so much as a rucksack). Then I failed to find *Ranunculus parnassifolius*, which I had heard abounded, and, altogether, was already weary when, before I had got across the last plain before you drop into Kandersteg, there burst over the mountains the most appalling, blazing, crashing thunderstorm, with a perfect Noah's Deluge of rain. I clutched the sack in my hands, and ran the whole way down to Kandersteg, a dripping jelly of anguish. But as I went I saw this great *aeizoön* peering at me through a bush, and stopped my headlong career to gather him. These bush forms sometimes prove constant, and this season I expect to see whether my Gemmi discovery will prove so. Of the other three, one is a fine, stout-rosetted form, incurved and neat, rather like one which is sold as *aeizoön rosularis*; the other is Engler's *elongata*, from a copse at Iseltwald—a very interesting plant, whose leaves are pale and etiolate, drawn and spidery, so that one thinks, finding it in a wood, that this character is temporary, and will pass when the plant gets more light. Not a bit of it. *S. elongata* remains elongate in any state of life to which it may be called; a very lovely plant, rather shy-flowering perhaps, but then, with many of these Aeizoöns, their greatest beauty lies rather in their foliage. The third form is very handsome indeed, and I am quite satisfied with it. I discovered this below the Rosenlaui Glacier, a strong, stocky little plant, whose deep grey rosettes, flat, tight and small, are tinged, centrally, with red. The flower-stems are short and freely produced, bearing a moderate quantity of unusually large blossoms, whose ground-colour is white, but so thickly freckled with red that the whole surface looks pink. So far this delightful person has only received the undignified title of *Number Three*.

The colour-varieties of *S. aeizoön* are extremely rare and desirable. *Flavescens* I have found myself, as M. Correvon and I were exploring above Arolla. With what joy did M. Correvon discover it, and how generously did he allow me a half-share! Now, the prime colour in most of the Aeizoöns is a yellowish white, which at its best becomes pure, and at its worst turns to a dull greenish shade. *Flavescens*, however, produces sheaves of pale straw-coloured blossoms, quite distinct among a crowd of its kindred. *Lutea*, the other yellow form, is even more pronounced in tone, and both are quite as vigorous as the type. Then comes the rare and glorious *aeizoön rosea*, of whom I have a goodly host, with most lovely deep-pink blossoms, without spot or blemish. I think it was M. Correvon who invented this beautiful creature, but how, or when, or where I do not know. (My plants have taken an Award of Merit at the Temple this year.)

After sporting about from colour to colour, the name Aeizoön begins to indulge in vagaries as to size. *Altissima* is a stout, good form ; so is *rosularis*. *Sturmiana* is as near the imaginary type as anything conceivable, and is the most generally used of all, making thrifty great mats and flowering very abundantly. Its rosettes are flattish, while those of *rosularis*, besides being larger, are curved inwards. *Aeizoön thyrsiflora* is a fine stout plant from Servia, my stock of which has developed from two frail seedlings. The plant is solid in growth, with denser, larger spires of blossom than usual. And the finest of all these is *balkana*, rather like my *Number Three*, but with big flowers, even more densely spotted, and with more brilliant crimson. The growth is sturdy and dwarf, the panicle rather flat and few-flowered by comparison with the packed heads that prevail among many Aeizoöns.

Of minor forms of Aeizoön there are several. The first is *Portae*, which seems not quite to have made up its mind whether it means to be a type or a miniature. It is neither big enough for the one, nor small enough for the other, but a useful, bright-leaved little thing. Then comes a plant which was sent to me as *labradorica*. Whether the name has any real authority I cannot pronounce, but this form is a tiny, closely-packed little Aeizoön of the greatest charm. And even better, if possible, is another which came under the obviously false

name of *Zimmeteri*. In spite of thus usurping the title
and respect due to one of the rarest and most difficult
Saxifrages of the Umbrosa section, the impostor turns
out very valuable indeed—with serried, dense mats of wee
rosettes, and close heads of big, round, clean-coloured
flowers. (You can never be perfectly certain about an
Aeizoön's qualities until you have flowered him; for a
good many of the species have dull, dirty-coloured
blossoms.) Then there is an Aeizoön called *minima*, a
perfect miniature, very neat and tidy, like a close grey
moss almost. And after this again, a form I bought
under the decently unambitious description of 'Species
from Venetia.' This unclaimed little Tom Jones of a
plant is another of the tiny-growing Silver Saxifrages,
concise and wee as the others. And then, last of all, is
the one which I think I love best of all—a baby Silver
which bears the obscure title of *lagaveana*, or, as an
alternative, 'la Gave Dauphine.' Now, as a reverent
scholar I am going to propose an emendation to reconcile
these names. I believe they are both forms of one lost
original, and that that lost original is simply l'Agave
Dauphine. The corruption will be evident, and the
name is eminently fitting, for the plant is certainly like
a cluster of tiny, tiny Agaves (I've always called them
Aloes, and should like to call them Aloes still). Anyhow, l'Agave Dauphine is a most fascinating person, and
very distinct, even if he lacks a proper Latin name. All
these wee Silvers seem to like any amount of sunshine,
for on the hottest corner of the high rockwork, where the
bigger Silvers, some of them, blister and burn, l'Agave
and *labradorica* and *minima* thrive perpetually, without
ever seeming to suffer from anything—dense, tight clusters
of grey lichen from year to year. And I cannot leave
these pigmies without saying a last tender word for
them; they are the most fascinating and the most

satisfactory to me of all their great and fascinating group.

S. aeizoön paradoxa is a paradox indeed. I am fairly catholic, I hope, but I cannot see by what right this plant dares to call itself an Aeizoön at all. It has the loveliest foliage and the poorest flowers of the whole race. The rosettes are built of long, very narrow leaves, deep blue-grey, with a bright jagged edge of silver. And the flowers are stodgy, rather small, and greenish yellow, uninteresting and unappealing. However, the plant is so singularly beautiful, sprouting out of the rockwork, and so easy, too, that among the Silvers there is not one that stands higher as far as general desirableness goes.

There are a few others bewilderingly like it. In the first place, there is the true *crustata* as Correvon figures it—a brilliant plant, with better flowers perhaps than the so-called *paradoxa* (I think people are too fond of impos· ing names without due authority). *Crustata* is an obscure and ' diversivolent' creature. First of all, there is this plant, the true *crustata*. Then there is another, very near it, bearing the same name, but inferior. Then again there are at least two of the large intermediate Aeizoöns that are sold as *crustata*, fine handsome things, with big, neat rosettes of rather pointed leaves. For a few other neighbours of *aeizoön paradoxa* I must quote a very pretty, wee-leaved kind, with rounded tips to the leaves, which was sent me unnamed from the Engadine ; a remarkably bright thing called by the hopeless name of ' *circuenta*,' blue and silver, and hardly distinguishable from *paradoxa* ; and yet another, *circinata*, at whose title ' *circuenta* ' is probably a bold and unhappy dash. But these names are all dreadful together ; nor is it possible to get the question settled. The greatest authorities differ, and there is no one now able to deal with *Saxifraga* firmly, or to act as unquestioned court of appeal

among the many varieties. One learned man holds one
view, and one another; between them the race hangs
embroiled in confusion. To know how vain are any
efforts to get the matter straight, I will only mention
that some years ago, when I reintroduced *S. florulenta*, I
sent, for an experiment, a rooted specimen of it, with
another of *lantoscana*, to be named by an Authority so
high and infallible that charity forbids me to indicate it
even with an asterisk. Will it be believed that those
two plants—well known, easily recognised, absolutely
distinct—came back to me labelled, the one *Cotyledon*,
and the other *longifolia*! Now, when our horticultural
Popes can do this sort of thing, what can we expect of
those who are not Popes or even Cardinals ?

S. aeizoön leads on towards *S. Cotyledon* and *S.
longifolia* (with which it hybridises infinitely, to the
anguish of the classifier), through a group of large-growing intermediate plants, all (probably) of mixed blood,
all very thrifty and handsome, not many of them with
any very marked individuality of their own. *Engleri*
must be mentioned first as a warning. My *Engleri* is
very handsome in the leaf, making huge blue-and-silver
starry rosettes of narrow leaves. But, as the foliage is
like a magnified *paradoxa*, so also are the dull greenish-
yellow flowers that appear sparsely on the rare flower-
stems. *Hostii* was given me some years ago to name,
and this really is the genuine thing, I am told. (I
possess a spurious *Hostii* which is nearer to *aeizoön* in
appearance.) *Hostii* is a most amazing grower ; for I
was only given one small rooted shoot, which I rammed
two years ago into a crevice. That plant has now
absorbed not only that crevice, but another one beside,
and has altogether something like thirty good crowns.
The leaves are very dark greyish-green, like those of
paradoxa, but longer, less blue, and less brilliantly silver.

At the base of the stock they tend to turn crimson.
The flower-spikes are numerous, and, for this bluish
group, distinctly effective. To this section belongs
another plant to which I must propose and second a
hearty vote of thanks. Meekly, anonymously, it came
to me under the heading 'Species from Sicily,' and it
has earned my gratitude by thriving in a very dank,
shady spot, where nothing else but *Marchantia* prospers,
and where one would not have expected a Mossy, let
alone a sun-loving Silver from Sicily, to endure. However, this Sicilian of mine continues to make tall, sprayed
rosettes of long grey leaves, very distinct and light in
effect ; now I want anxiously to see what his flower will
be. Experience has made me fear that the Blue Silvers
imagine they have done enough for us in the beauty of
their foliage, and don't always think it worth while
putting themselves to the trouble of having pretty
flowers, on the principle of a very beautiful woman who
sometimes fancies that she may allow herself the licence
of being sulky and stupid. However, my nameless
Sicilian friend may prove a brilliant exception. Others
of a greyish persuasion are *cartilaginea*, *catalaunica*,
carinthiaca, and *carniolica*. These are all of goodly port,
sturdy and sound, if not precisely dazzling. Very possibly mine may have gone astray somehow ; I can only
say that these plants are thoroughly serviceable, but
without any great force or marked distinction of character. As for my Aeizoid *cristata*, whether it is really
'*crustata*' I cannot say. Why is it that gardeners
develop a peculiar illegibility of writing ? Horticultural
correspondence is something cruel ; Aztec or Tuscan
must be comparatively simple. The more learned and
high the authority, the more intense, says the rule
(apparently), must be the opaque obscurity of his hand-
writing. Consequently plants are perpetually arriving

with perfectly undecipherable names. Anyhow, my *cristata* is near *aeizoön paradoxa*; but where the name really belongs, or whether it actually exists, I leave to the brave soul who will venture into this labyrinth which yearly devours its toll of new Saxifrages, and adds them to the vast heap of unclaimed species. All I can do is to collect every one I can lay hold of, true or false, and simply hold them here in readiness at the service, for purposes of comparison, of any authority who really wants to work up *Saxifraga* once for all, and by collation make out definitely which is which.

Other of my hybrids or neighbouring forms of *S. aeizoön* are apparently the true *Malyi*—mark this, for *Malyi* is made to cover as many sins as Charity—*notata, australis, pectinata, cultrata,* and *brevifolia. Gaudini, elatior,* and *rhaetica* are handsome, distinct forms akin to *Hostii. Churchilli* is very effective, with pointed grey leaves in stiff rosettes. And all these countless varieties and species and mules are not only worth growing, but also easy to grow—two recommendations by no means synonymous in the rock-garden. But, good as they are, the best of the Silvers are yet to come—at least the best of this section, forgetting for a minute the Rosy, the Balkan, and the miniature varieties of *aeizoön* itself. For the royalties of this group are the three giant Saxifrages—*longifolia, Cotyledon, florulenta.*

Saxifraga florulenta takes precedence by right of age. In all probability it is a very ancient species, now dwindling rapidly towards extinction. There is only one district in the world where it dwells, and among the other Saxifrages there is none that stands near it. This strange, lonely plant, making its last stand against time and evolution, lingers high up under a few shady rocks in the Maritime Alps behind Nice. Even in this range it is rare, occurring only here and there, in colonies, on northern cliff-faces, on the Col de Fenestra, the Balloure, the Argentera, and above the Lakes of Vens. Here it makes huge star-fish rosettes, very slow - growing, and distinguished among all the rosetted Saxifrages by being quite green, dark and lustrous, spiny-looking, and without any trace of silver. And so, in the course of years, up comes a stout stocky flower-spike, carrying a dense viscid sheaf of rose-purple bells. This task accomplished, the plant dies without offsets, shedding its seeds at the cliff's foot, where they germinate among the rubble. Years ago I made a great pilgrimage to visit this wonderful, tragic personality, and was lucky enough to find a guide—may his name be ever blessed—who knew the plant and its stations. So he took me up and up the dark rocks, up to the level of the Primulas and the last pines, and there, in rifts of the unsunned precipice, shone the glossy rosettes of *florulenta*. I secured a goodly stock, and since then have experienced nothing but disaster. *Saxifraga florulenta* is not really a difficult plant to grow; it is far worse; it is one of those plants which are apparently quite simple, but which have a way of dying off abruptly after seasons of prosperity, without any ascertainable cause. I had it for three seasons prospering quite firmly in the Old Garden; then, in the fourth, it suddenly, inexplicably, began to rot at the centre of the crown, and so died. My frame-plants have had the same habit; each spring, each autumn, sees half a dozen established rosettes, or more, expiring without discoverable excuse or reason. As for flowers,—in all these years I have never seen that purplish spike. The Records of the R.H.S. show that *florulenta* was shown in the 'sixties; I hope it was the genuine thing. Perhaps it is heretical to entertain a doubt; yet carelessness among Saxifrages being what it is, and *florulenta* the notoriously slow-bloomer that every one finds it, I should like to see the blossoming plant before I can be quite happy as to the award of the R.H.S. Of *florulenta's* culture only one thing can be definitely said. It does certainly dislike sunshine, and, almost alone of its race, insists on a shady corner. There, in a well-drained crevice, in rich old soil protected from corroding damp in winter, nobody ought to have any difficulty in establishing *florulenta* for three or four seasons. As to what will happen after that I have more fears than hopes. It is comparatively easy to deal with a plant which has passionate dislikes, like *Eritrichium* ; real difficulty only begins with a plant that seems quite easy-going, if slow, and then develops a sudden, unaccountable pleasure in dying.

S. longifolia is the grandest of the great Saxifrages, making huge, sometimes enormous, rosettes of blue-grey, edged with silver, and then sending up a short, thick spike of pure white flowers, unspotted, and of clean colour. After this the plant dies without offsets, but matures seed so abundantly that one has no difficulty in raising as large a stock as heart can desire. The true *Saxifraga longifolia* may always be known by this inability to throw any secondary growths, which, I believe, is invariable. However, the plant hybridises so interminably with the lesser Silvers that out of a hundred seedlings hardly fifty per cent. will be pure *longifolia*, while among them you will find mules of every conceivable shape, size, and habit,—none worthless, and some of very high value indeed. These hybrids are generally Aeizoöns on one side, too, and make offsets in a pleasant and permanent manner ; but though they are almost invariably beautiful, I don't think any of them matches the genuine *longifolia* itself, with its stalwart, snowy pyramid of blossom. *Longifolia prolifera* is, I fancy, an Aeizoön almost pure and simple, and life would become quite impossible if one set oneself definitely to classify and name the intermediate forms and seedlings of *longi-folia*. Very probably all the Silvers of larger growth, such as *australis* and *splendida*, are sprung, on one side, of *longifolia* or *Cotyledon*. To have *longifolia* for their parent they must, of course, be Pyreneans, for the Fox-brush Saxifrage is, I think, restricted to the Pyrenees (with an occasional appearance in the French Alps), though, unlike many species of small range, it takes very kindly to cultivation in any good, deep, rich garden soil. I remember a plant at Edge, which, to my excited memory, seems to have been about a yard across!

S. Cotyledon, gracilis, nepalensis, pyramidalis, are all really one thing, practically—πολλῶν ὀνομάτων μορφὴ μία. *Cotyledon*, to take the type name, is the lovely Pyramid Saxifrage sold in pots during May and June in London. *Pyramidalis* is the title under which they hawk it; but I have never seen any solid difference between true *Cotyledon* and *pyramidalis*. The species is singularly beautiful, with tall, very loose, delicate spires of white crimson-dotted flowers, and one must not judge it by the habit of bought forced plants. For these are simply flowering crowns reft away from a clump and potted up, so that, after blooming, they die, and people are disappointed; whereas, normally, *S. Cotyledon* goes on forming larger and larger clumps that never want any attention, and flower gloriously from year to year. On one rock last season I had an old plant covering a yard of ground or so, who sent up sixteen most glorious great spikes; and this year, instead of taking a well-earned rest, it seems to intend giving me as many or more. There are various pretty forms of *Cotyledon*, though *nepalensis* seems inclined to be half-hardy—a grotesque thing to say of a plant identical in appearance with *Cotyledon*, and wearing all the robustious look of the group. *Gracilis* and *minor* are smaller varieties, as their

SAXIFRAGA AEIZOÖN PARADOXA

names denote. *Montavoniensis* is shorter and dwarfer than usual—a species of great brilliance and beauty. The finest of all rather dislikes me, unfortunately, and, I fancy, craves a soil devoid of lime. (They have, I hear, the same ill success with it at Kew.) I call the thing *Cotyledon icelandica*, because at St. John's, at Oxford, whence I had it, it had been originally collected, I believe, in Iceland. It is a most gorgeous plant as they grow it there—forming enormous, impressive flat rosettes of unusually bronzed, leathery, strap-shaped leaves, with great four-foot plumes of blossom almost incredibly splendid. Here, however, it only exists, and displays no such generosity. *S. Cotyledon* is the most widely distributed of all the great Saxifrages, and, of course, like *longifolia*, has hybridised lavishly with every *aeizoön* that it came across.

S. Macnabiana is a species frequently sold and frequently shown. But the name, I believe, is false, and the plant an impostor. *Macnabiana*, as sold, is obviously a hybrid of *Cotyledon* and a red-spotted *aeizoön*—possibly *balkana*. It is a very handsome thing, with shortish, few-flowered panicles of big white blossoms, heavily freckled with crimson. The true plant is quite different, very rare, and by no means less desirable. The true *macnabiana*, as I was given it on high authority, is an extraordinarily vigorous grower, making yard-wide mats, in no time, of big rounded rosettes of upstanding narrowish leaves; the flower-spikes are numerous and tall; the flowers creamy white or lightly spotted. I should guess the plant to be a secondary cross between *Cotyledon* and one of the larger Aeizoön intermediates. And all these big Saxifrages, except where I give them a bad character in so many words, are, in this garden at all events, of the easiest culture and the happiest possible temper.

After years of confusion and unhappiness I have been forced to the conclusion that there is no such thing as *S. lantoscana* or *lantoscana superba*. These are frequently offered in catalogues, and they are really forms —simply varietal forms—of *S. lingulata*. You will find them all passing from one to another in a batch of *lingulata* as you collect it, as you go up to St. Martin Vésubie, from damp shady rocks among the silver-grey cloudy tufts of the exquisite little yellow St. John's Wort, *Hypericum Coris*, that sweet-tempered treasure of golden beauty and golden value. *S. lingulata* is one of the very, very best of the great Saxifrages. A most variable plant, though ; some forms are quite poor in build, while others have earned such distinctive names as *lantoscana*. (St. Martin Vésubie used to be St. Martin Lantosque.) *Lingulata* makes rather tall, humped rosettes, with leaves of apparently unequal length, which at once distinguishes it from others—the old leaves being rather long, narrow, tongue-shaped, swelling at the points ; the young ones come up among them, and all, old and young, are of a lovely blue-grey, most brilliantly marked with silver. The flower-spikes are about a foot high, reddish, and very graceful ; the crowded flowers are the largest in this group, and of a brilliant, solid white. (I am talking now only of the best forms of *lingulata* ; worse forms are red-spotted, star-shaped, thin-petalled.) The whole thing is smaller, of course, in habit than *Cotyledon*, but, to my mind, even more beautiful and fascinating and bright. And, in spite of its shady habitat, I find *lingulata* quite pleasant and affable, in any corner of the rock-garden, exposed or not. It has a kindly way, too, of dropping seed about into rock-chinks, where they go on and thrive unnoticed, until you pass by one day and find a good clump of *lingulata* where you never sowed. I am now raising a batch of hybrids, between this and other species, especially the pink ones. (Every gardener's ambition is to get a good red Silver; there is the horticultural importance of *S. florulenta*, if any one could flower it.) There are about eight or ten babies, and every one is different from the others. So that, out of the lot, something distinct ought to emerge.

S. kolenatiana is a rare and valuable plant, which can hardly be overrated. It is very like a large *aeizoön*, with rather pale rosettes. Its special beauty lies, however, in its flowers, and these are of a soft coral-pink, very delicate and charming, rather paler than those of *aeizoön rosea*. (This is one of the sires I have used on *lingulata*.) It has a variety, *major*, otherwise *Sendtneri*, which I don't approve of. *Major* is certainly larger, but inclines to be one-rosetted and die after flowering, whereas *kolenatiana*-type goes on from year to year, making finer and finer masses of growth. Nicholson declares this species a close ally of *cartilaginea*. If this is so, then my *cartilaginea*, being a rather undistinguished Aeizoön, is absolutely false. Another obscure and very lovely species was given me at Glasnevin, where it was grown as *S. triternata*. When I saw it there, the whole thing was quite wee in growth, with tiny rosettes. Here, however, it has developed very handsome large globes of wedge-shaped leaves, like a big Aeizoön, and the flowers (which I hope it will now produce more freely than it seemed to do at Glasnevin) are of the same exquisite rose-pink that you rejoice over in *kolenatiana*. So fine are these colours that it is as well to give the plants they belong to a sheltered place, where the hot sunshine will not fade them. Otherwise the Pink Silvers are quite as easy and friendly as any other of the group.

S. cochlearis is a connecting link between the Silvers of this section and those of the next. *S. cochlearis* belongs to the Maritime Alps, though I never found him there, and seems a sun-lover in moderation, making round humps of small rosettes, with spoon-shaped leaves, light blue-grey, heavily edged and powdered with silver. The whole plant recalls a small edition of *lingulata*, though it is neater and more covered with whiteness. The flower-stems are the same reddish graceful spikes that you get in *lingulata*, but halved in size; the flowers have the same pure brilliancy of colour, and are quite as large. But *S. cochlearis* varies as much as *lingulata*, and it is not really safe to buy either of them except in flower, unless you get a guaranteed good strain. For there are many poor forms of both—forms as poor as the good forms are glorious, which is saying a great deal. Then there are the recognised varieties of *cochlearis*, a Major and a Minor form. The *major* is double the size of type *cochlearis*, with extremely beautiful spidery-looking rosettes. But even here there are divergences; for, among my imported Majors, I bloomed one year a plant so magnificent that I am now letting all my minor Majors go. The beauty has the same habit as the rest, but its flowers are half again as large, round, solid, and most dazzlingly white. *Cochlearis minor* is simply a minute and attractive version of *cochlearis*, almost as neat as *valdensis*.

S. valdensis is allowed specific rank under protest. It is really only a small variety of *cochlearis*. But such a precious little plant—no Saxifrage surpasses it. *Valdensis* differs from the lesser forms of *cochlearis* in a much closer, neater habit of growth, making tight, dense cushions of silvery pale blue, with little airy stems of white blossom. (All these Saxifrages, *lingulata*, *cochlearis*, and *valdensis*, have much looser, more delicate and graceful spikes than any of the Aeizoöns.) *Valdensis* is a precious treasure, and I believe it, like *cochlearis*, to be a sun-lover. But both, I fancy, dislike being parched. On hot, dry places they look unhappy, and their growths appear best on the sheltered side. And *valdensis* has astonished me by looking happy and sowing itself (almost the only Saxifrage that does) among the mosses and dankness of the Old Garden, where it appears in unexpected chinks, and soon makes fat round masses of blue.

S. aeizoeides is a great change from all these, though it belongs by courtesy to the Aeizoön section. It is a native, and generally a marsh plant of moderate elevations, extraordinarily abundant in the Alps. It forms mats of succulent-looking moss, glossy-green, with no trace of silver, and the numerous flowers are narrow-petalled and yellow. They have a golden centre boss, too, and their calyx-segments are yellowish, so that they contrive to look more effective than they have any right to do ; and they have also, in some forms, a tendency to bloom, or fade, of a ruddy copper crimson, which is lurid and imposing. Our native plant divides itself into two conspicuous varieties. The type dwells in sopping bogs, and blossoms in June. You will find it all over Upper Teesdale ; the variety *autumnalis* lives in high cliff-chinks, quite out of the reach of ground-moisture, and flowers in August and September. This is the form we have here. *Autumnalis* dwells on the western precipices of Ingleborough, and, as far as I know, the typical bog-plant is not found in this country at all. *Aeizoeides* is not a species, however, that captures much of my enthusiasm. In the bog it is a useful, easy-going ramper ; and in dryer corners it is really hardly worth a place.

But he is interesting because I suspect him of having a hand in the parentage of *S. mutata*. This sounds a fearful heterodoxy, as *S. mutata* seeds like any weed. However, I throw it out as a suggestion. *Mutata* is a curious species, from wet shaded rocks in the Eastern Alps, which makes rosettes exactly like those of a small, dull green *Cotyledon*, and then sends up spikes of very narrow-petalled, orange-copper flowers, after which the plant generally seeds and dies. *Mutata* is a rather rare species in gardens, and has no very great intrinsic attraction. Any cool moist corner will do for him. But certainly, considering many things, it does not look so very impossible that *mutata* is the result of an *aeizoön-aeizoeides* cross. *Mutata* certainly crosses back again, for the very rare *S. Hausmanni* (which I have only just succeeded in getting true), is a mule between *mutata* and *aeizoeides* itself. And all these Euaeizoön Saxifrages have no conscience about intermarriage ; *Burnati*, another novelty here, is a hybrid of *cochlearis* X *aeizoön*, which looks distinct, while I have raised a whole crew of little mules myself.

S. speciosa is a very fine stocky dwarf thing, clearly of mixed parentage, with *longifolia* on one side, certainly, and an Aeizoön on the other. *Speciosa* makes very compact tufts that never spread much. The rosettes are extremely handsome, dark green and silver ; the flowers, carried stiffly on short spikes, are big and solid and very pure white. *S. splendida* is yet another hybrid, between *longifolia* and another Aeizoön. The rosettes in this species are its chief beauty. They are lustrous and neat, hemmed with a neat silver margin. But the flowers are almost ugly, of that stodgy greenish yellow that occurs from time to time among the dark-leaved plants of the Aeizoön group. And of further *longifolia-aeizoön* crosses there is no end. I am now awaiting the first flower of a unique old seedling of *longifolia* which I marked for the beauty of its beaded grey-and-silver tuft ; and any one who grows *longifolia* and *aeizoön* in the same garden will have the same experiences.

S. aspera, *S. bryoeides*, and *S. bronchialis* have really no right here, as they belong to the Trachyphyllum section. Generally, they are all like rambling mosses, with rather large *hypnoeides*-like flowers, straw-coloured, butter-coloured, or dullish white, carried on tall frail stems. *Bronchialis* is abundant in the Rockies, and *aspera*, with its glabrous variety, *bryoeides*, is far too common on the Alps. They are associated with one of the bitterest days of my horticultural life, when I sallied forth innocently, from the Grimsel, to find *Androsace imbricata* on the Unteraar Glacier. I didn't know how far that hateful glacier was; I was alone, the day was very hot, and I was armed with my usual mountain-lunch of four Marie biscuits. All these things would have been pleasures—distance and heat and frugal fare (I hate the hollowed loaves, the dismembered cold hens, the cumbrous and unappetising paraphernalia that most people think it necessary to go and sit over on the edge of a glacier. In the mountains I only want and like the merest formal pretence at food)—if only the valley had been generous. But it wasn't. It was very long, and very stuffy and sterile. Then far ahead I saw what looked like a wall of cinders towering to heaven. This was the terminal cliff of the moraine. Up I scrambled with infinite pains, and wended on for toilful miles, knowing nothing except that *Androsace imbricata* was reported from the Unteraar Glacier. Well, I sweated miserably onwards and upwards till I very nearly reached the Dollfuss Hut—and, all that way, the only flowering plants I set eyes on were one mutilated *S. Cotyledon*, masses of little Mountain Sorrel, and acres upon acres of *S. aspera*. When at last I did sight a gleam of purple away on the right-hand precipice, and crawled timorously thither over fathomless crevasses, it turned out to be only a dreadful, common magenta *Epilobium*. Oh how hot the day was! How lonely and small was I amid mountains so horribly vast and depressing! And Oh those Marie biscuits, how arid and jejune! To make worse worst

H

I came upon two Germans drinking Asti from a bottle with loud gurglings of contentment. Though I ambled up and down and sought for plants all round them in a faint and moribund manner, they were not going to indulge any Samaritan weaknesses. So at last, when I heard the final glou-glou of the dregs go bubbling down those greedy throats, I stalked indignantly away with a sternly teetotal aspect, and, for the first time in my life, arrived at that hatred for the German which I am now given to understand is the hall-mark of the modern patriot. That, I think, was the first and last time in my life, too, when I returned absolutely empty from a quest. All that age-long day not a single thing did I see that I could even persuade myself to want. And I cherished a grudge against *Androsace imbricata* ever afterwards, until I collected it two years later above the Plan de Bertol. As for *S. aspera*, never, from that date, have I raised any feeling for him but a wearied and self-reproachful dislike. He is rather a dowdy little plant at the best of times, and has no brilliant loveliness or dainty charm to wipe off the slate of my memory the black mark which that day put against his name.

CHAPTER VIII

The Kabschia Saxifrages

WHY this last great group of Saxifrages should have such a repulsive sub-title is more than I can say. But in this section are to be found the rarest and noblest and choicest of their race—a clan of small-growing, clustered people from high open places all over the mountain-chains. And whereas there is much joy but no especial glory in cultivating the Silvers or the Mossies successfully, there is no less joy and far greater glory in growing the Kabschia Saxifrages prosperously. A fine clump of *S. Rhei* or *S. lingulata* is a lovely and commendable sight; but a fourteen-spiked clump of *S. media* or *S. Ferdinandi-Coburgi* is not only a lovely but also a remarkable and enviable sight. For in the Kabschia group are gathered the most exacting and the most difficult of the Saxifrages—brilliant, rare species that want special attention if they are to thrive permanently. Luckily the cultural directions that my experience teaches me are few and simple: light limy loam, an open but not too sun-burnt exposure, and very sharp drainage, with good top-dressing in spring, are the main requirements in this group as I grow it. And, in most cases, matters are very much helped by an abundant use of lime-chips, in the soil and on the surface. So far I have only one plant in this group that definitely objects to lime; all the others absorb it greedily, and render it again in the redoubled silveriness of the foliage. My *media* and my *Ferdinandi - Coburgi* are prodigies of vigour, sprouting among lime-rubble.

S. apiculata is an obscure plant which may well head the list, for it is at once the commonest and the least definite of the Kabschias. Nicholson's description of *S. apiculata* makes me perfectly certain that the ordinary plant is not genuine. What gardeners send out as *apiculata* is a dense, spiny-tufted species, that rapidly makes big mats of foliage, and rejoices early April with heads of soft primrose flowers. This Saxifrage is well-known, and of very easy growth. But its true place in the group is not certain. Nicholson makes *S. apiculata* —the real plant—a synonym of *S. Lapeyrousi*, a very rare Pyrenean miniature species, which I possess on very good authority, and which is absolutely distinct from *S. apiculata* of horticulture, so that if Nicholson is right, there is a big error somewhere. The other names worn by this common Saxifrage are *Alberti*, *Malyi*, and *Frederici-Augusti*—the two last being scandalous usurpations, the proper *Malyi* being an Aeizoön, and the proper *Frederici-Augusti* an exceedingly rare and august red-flowered Silver. But, to make confusion worse, *Malyi* and *Frederici-Augusti* and *luteo-viridis* are indifferently borne not only by *apiculata* but also by another dense green spiny species, whose proper name is *juniperina*. Between *juniperina*, again, and the so-called *sancta* of gardeners, I have never been able to make any real distinction. This plant, whatever its name, is the only uninteresting dowdy of the group—a glossy evergreen cushion, thriving anywhere, with spikes of dull, deep yellow flowers, whose chief merit is that they appear so very early in the year. Of the two, *apiculata* is far the better, and a really beautiful plant; the other is only notable in that it lies concealed under so many of the splendid, money-compelling names that flaunt in nurserymen's catalogues. Never buy *Malyi*, therefore, or *luteo - viridis*, *luteo - purpurea*, or *Frederici - Augusti*, unless you see the plant, or have it on sound authority, unless you are prepared to be fobbed off with the dingy *juniperina*. Yes, and *juniperina*, too, has yet another alias which rightly belongs to a fine rare species. For *juniperina* is often sent out as *scardica* (I have had it myself, from well-known gardens, under all these names at various times). However, with so much preface, and with this warning as to the depraved ass-in-lion's-clothing habits of *S. juniperina*, I can go boldly on with the Kabschias, for, with few exceptions, the race is not entangled in the polymorphous confusion that so bewilders one in dealing with all the countless developments of *S. aeizoön*.

S. burseriana is a variable and valuable North Italian, blooming in March, with tight thorny-looking little grey cushions, ruby-red buds, and snow-white flowers as big as a shilling. The type thrives in any cool climate, but is rather a shy flowerer. *Burseriana speciosa* is a more generous variety, with very short stems; *Burseriana major* is taller, larger, and freer than the ordinary form. But the glory of the species, if not of the whole group, is *S. burseriana Gloria*, a form that I bloomed some years ago out of an importation and named *Gloria* as a tribute to its inordinate beauty. *Gloria* is not only of quick easy growth and free habit, but the flowers come up from every shoot on five-inch stems, and are so large and brilliantly snowy that no foliage can be seen. Each blossom is as big as a florin, and the effect of a clump in full bloom is really quite sensational. The Royal Horticultural Society has just given *Gloria* an Award of Merit, and it is recognised, I think, as putting every other form of *Burseriana* com-

pletely in the shade—'knocking *Burseriana major* into a
cocked hat' is the usual expression, I find. Rumour says
that only one Alp produces this particular beauty, though
large-flowered forms occasionally turn up in general importations of *Burseriana*.   Another variety of great
size that bloomed here is called *Gloria Number Two*;
but *Number One*, beautiful as the other is, stands a
head and shoulders above all chance of rivalry, and is, I
fancy, unique among Burserianas in its distinguishing
tendency to produce sometimes (though rarely) two, or
even three, flowers on one stem. I am hoping now to
seed it this propitious season, and to use it as the parent
to good species of other colours.

S. aretioeides must come next, on account of the inti-
mate matrimonial alliances it has so profitably contracted
with *burseriana*.   *Aretioeides* is rather misnamed, for it
bears no very obvious resemblance to *Androsace vitaliana*;
it is a minute Pyrenean, with tiny ligulate leaves, grey
with silver markings in dense hard rosettlings, and few-
flowered short stems with yellowish flowers that vary
in brilliancy.   One particularly rare and lovely form is
the almost extinct *primulina*, with primrose - coloured
blossoms.   This and *aretioeides* are, I think, rather
troublesome delicate doers, and I am not sure if they
approve of lime. Here they go along happily for a few
years, then, rather inexplicably, turn pale and pass away.
It may be that they cannot do with a parching sun. My
Manager has a great theory that these dainty high
alpines would be thankful for the shade of rocks; I
myself, without going quite so far as that, have come
to the conclusion that they do sometimes resent being
scorched and sun-burnt on arid pinnacles of the rockwork. I had thought it likely that *aretioeides* and *primulina* might appreciate the Moraine Garden; but they
pitilessly expired there, although it appears to suit some

others of their close kindred perfectly. As to soil in general, I have only found, I think, two, of all the desirable Saxifrages, that genuinely dislike lime. Those two are *Cotyledon icelandica* and *Vandelli*. *Aretioeides* must have the benefit of the doubt; and all the others take to this garden as ducks to water.

Of the small Saxifrages *aretioeides* has given us most hybrids, so far—perhaps all the best hybrids. Of *aretioeides* and *burseriana* was born the famous *Boydi*—a spiny grey tuft, very slow-growing, with large yellow flowers, fairly intermediate in type. *Boydi* has a great repute, and fetches rather fancy prices; but I must say, pretty as it undoubtedly is, that I think its fame distinctly surpasses its merit. There are other yellow Kabschias far prettier, far more free-flowering, far more quick-growing. Even among the hybrids *S. Cherry-trees* is superior to *Boydi*. *Cherry-trees* is an extremely rare plant, of which a certain Scotch firm vainly imagines itself to have the monopoly, and is of the same or nearly the same parentage as *Boydi*. But its flowers are certainly more attractive, and its growth more willing and quite as beautiful. *S. Faldonside* is another hybrid raised by the same illustrious worker; but this, however delightful, looks rather grudging and dainty in habit, not much more vigorous than *Boydi* itself. There is a white *Boydi* too, absolutely different from the type—a ramping, rather untidy grower, with quantities of short-stemmed, snow-white blossoms that are very attractive. Then again there is a plant I bought years ago as *Boydi Number Two*, which turns out to be, in all probability, a *tombeanensis* cross, with several-flowered stems and fine white blossoms.

Not content with *burseriana* for a husband, *aretioeides* has sought a mate in *S. media*—a union almost as grotesque as that of Thomas Keyes and Lady Mary Grey. For while *aretioeides* is a wee dwarf like the poor Lady, *media* is comparatively as much a giant as the Queen's burly porter. And their offspring (not to talk here of obscurities like *luteo-viridis*) is the beautiful *ambigua*, with spikes of fluffy-cupped, flesh-coloured bells, a blend of *media's* crimson and the pale yellow of *aretioeides*. Years ago I saw *ambigua* represented in Bennett's painfully inadequately-figured, but otherwise useful book, and resolved that I must and would possess it. Well, many and many are the plants I have had as *ambigua*—a Mossy once, and then a pretty little Silver near *aeizoön paradoxa*, and then a big *rosularis*-form, but the genuine plant never till last year, although I fancy that we bloomed it one season, unknowing, in a batch of imported Medias.

S. media is the European type of a group that prevails in East Europe, and has hardly been brought at all into general cultivation. They want consideration, and are thoroughly deserving of it, these red Silver-Saxifrages. They make apparent rosettes like round-leaved Aeizoöns, bluish, and edged with white, but the spikes are in varying shades of crimson, and the rather minute flowers are enclosed in splendid great fluffy calyces of vivid red or purple. *Media* is a Pyrenean, and is one of my greatest joys and successes. Here it takes any amount of sunshine, and rejoices vigorously in abundance of lime-chips and rubble. Last season an old clump carried fourteen strong flower-spikes, and was so fine that I sent him up to be shown in London, after which ordeal he was reinstated in his place on the rockwork. Did he flag or faint? Not a bit. He at once set to work growing again, and is now as good a clump as ever, though only, I believe, throwing up three bloom-stems this year. However, the wonder is that he is still alive to throw up any. And besides all this, he has seeded himself freely over the bed.

S. Griesebachi is now becoming widely known, and is probably the most frequently cultivated of the group. Personally, I can't set him on a level with either *media* or *Frederici-Augusti*. Nevertheless he is doubly, remarkably valuable—first of all for the singular beauty of his blue, silver-hemmed rosettes, and then for the crimson flower-stems with their blood-red bracts, that come shooting up in the dark days of February. The spike, however, when fully unfolded, is hardly up to one's expectations, the flowers being so minute and the colour deepening to an opaque note. But there can be no doubt that this robust, kindly-natured plant is a newcomer of the first rank.

S. thessalica leads us towards a region of some uncertainty. For many years *thessalica* has been out of cultivation, and its name has been rather uncertain. Correvon once sent me a *Frederici-Augusti* that turned out to be the true *thessalica*, and the Kew plant called *porophylla* is, I believe, confessedly a synonym for *thessalica*. The species hails from East Europe, and is exceedingly rare and very distinct, with strange flat rosettes, very narrow-leaved, pale grey-blue, of an oddly attractive thorny appearance, with little thorny lateral growths, and red spikes of deep rich crimson flowers and bracts. I had long hankered after the plant and despaired of getting it true. What then was my joy when, one day, having imported a quantity of the almost equally rare true *Saxifraga scardica* from the Servian mountains, it arrived with several nice little spiny masses of *thessalica* wedged in tightly among its cushions. Now, though *scardica* is a good grower in all conscience, *thessalica* is showing such inordinate vivacity that it is strangling the parent clumps, and taking up the whole of each pot for itself. As for culture, I suspect that these red people from the East will endure and welcome a great deal more sunshine than would be acceptable to *caesia* or *aeizoön*. Otherwise, and with good drainage, they are not really in the least difficult, though deserving attention and showing gratitude. *S. Frederici-Augusti* is a name, as I said, which cloaks innumerable bastard species. I rather fancy I alone possess the rightful wearer of it (if there is such a person!), having imported it from Servia with trustworthy guarantees. Roughly speaking, the true *Frederici-Augusti* (what a fearful name! and whom does it belong to—Dante's great damned Emperor, or merely some gentleman called Frederic Augustus?) is a magnified *media* in appearance, with oval, not pointed foliage, in flattened rosettes. Its tuft may be (with difficulty) distinguished from that of *Griesebachi* by a rather greater roundness of leaf. The flower-spikes are freely sent up, most curious and fascinating. They are branched, densely covered with a kind of glandular rose-purple fur that glistens like pink crystal in the sun, and each branch, long and lax, has a curious tendency to weep like a trained cherry or Japanese dwarf. The flowers are rather small, pink, but enclosed in beautiful furry great purple calyces, and after flowering the sprays often turn stiff and straight upwards. Seed is abundantly borne, I am thankful to say, and germinates as freely as that of *mutata* (whose fertility is a byword here, so that if I see a thick pan of Saxifrage seedlings I always feel sure that it is only *mutata*). *Frederici-Augusti* was not a success at the very first; he took some acclimatising, and for a long time I felt doubtful about him, and many of my imported plants miffed away. Now, however, I have an old clump on the rockwork which, after ailing for a season or so, seems to have made itself at home in a rather sunny nook, and is throwing abundance of sound-looking laterals, with one stout spike. And with an army of seedlings coming on, I feel serene; for they will certainly prove even more amenable than old imported plants.

S. Stribnryi is the rarest and newest of this group. I have sent plants to Edinburgh and Kew, but the plant has not strayed into cultivation at all. I imported it from Servia as having similar flowers to those of *Frederici-Augusti*, but carried in a flat head, instead of a loose spike. So far, I must say, this character has not been very conspicuous, but the species must be believed to stand away from the other, if only in its greater vigour. It seems the most cheerful grower imaginable, and the way it comes from seed is nothing short of a marvel to any cynical mind which has learned that, as a rule, only tiresome things germinate profusely. The tuft inclines to be taller than that of *Frederici-Augusti*, making a four-sided mass, a rough square, with a big rosette on top, supported by four rosettes on each side. The flowers are very near indeed to those of *Frederici-Augusti*, though the spike is certainly not so tall as yet, and betrays already a tendency to be flatter, with branches of more equal length diverging more unanimously from nearer the summit. The leaves and rosettes have only the faintest possible divergence ; and frankly, when all is said and done, I dare not really maintain the two species as separate. Kew, I understand, makes *Frederici-Augusti* (like Correvon) a synonym of *porophylla* and *thessalica*, and would therefore lump my two last species under the one name of *Stribnryi*. And in this, so far as I can see, Kew is probably right. In fact, a stray bloomed here this season wearing a mistaken label of *media*, and it was only after much argument 'about it and about,' my Manager and I were able to agree definitely that it was probably *Frederici-Augusti*, not *Stribnryi*.

S. scardica heads an important group of these Saxifrages which form dense, very hard crusty cushions of rounded rosettes margined with silver. At least, one uses the word 'rosettes' as best expressing what one means; but these Kabschia-Saxifrages do not form rosettes in the strict sense, like the Aeizoöns, but a series of short branches so squashed and flattened down that in many forms they are almost indistinguishable from true rosettes, which, in the Kabschia section, are not genuinely produced at all, I think—though apparently by *Griesebachi, Frederici-Augusti, Stribnryi,* and *media,* with its children. *Scardica* has long been quite impossible to obtain true ; one was for ever deluded with *juniperina,* that many-aliased impostor. Then I got a nice little plant from a French gardener, which seemed nearer to the right thing—a neat cushion with pure white, rather thin-petalled flowers. This I hoped was genuine, until at last I had a chance of importing the true *scardica* from Servia. And the genuine *scardica* turns out to be really a valuable thing, sending up numerous flower-stems, which distinguish themselves among all their kin by carrying half a dozen snow-white flowers or more in a flattish head, vaguely recalling Cuckoo-pint. The foliage, too, is remarkably pretty, the mass being made up of rather pointed grey-and-silver leaves arranged in a collection of little hard rosettes. *Scardica* seems a very vigorous doer, and thrives with any decent kindness. I am trying to make him carry seed of different coloured Saxifrages, and especially of my beloved *lilacina.*

S. rochelliana is a very close ally of *scardica.* The leaves are much rounder, and the flowers larger but less numerous. *S. marginata* is a bigger, laxer plant, with very handsome blossoms. (All these white-flowered Kabschia-Saxifrages have a pure, solid tone, absolutely devoid of that creamy or red-speckled tendency that damages the colour so often among the Aeizoöns.) The greatest beauty of these scardica-cousins, though, is *corio-*

phylla—I think, a half-brother of *rochelliana*, but a little larger, a little more floriferous, a little more brilliant in every way. *S. Kotschyi* is a pretty little creature which I love more than my Manager does, although even I cannot muster any very warm passion for it. In growth *Kotschyi* is a smaller, pale-green version of *rochelliana*, but the numerous flowers are of a bright clear yellow. However, they are rather narrow in the petal and star-like in design, so that they cannot enter into any sort of competition with such glories as *Elizabethae* and *Ferdinandi Coburgi*. These *scardica* Saxifrages are easy-going rock-lovers from high hot elevations, of which *scardica* and *Kotschyi* are East Europeans, while the rest belong to the central ranges of Austria and the Tyrol.

S. Salomonii is a garden hybrid, I believe, having *burseriana* evidently for one of its parents, and possibly one of the *scardica* group for the other. The plant makes beautiful, rather lax tufts of spiny grey leaves (not so spiny as *burseriana's*), and sends up stems that carry each two or three large white blossoms, thus distinguishing it from the almost invariably one-flowered *burseriana*, which, for the rest, it much exceeds in height and size and habit generally. *Salomonii* is a very fine garden plant indeed, though of course it is completely killed, like every other of its kind, by the triumphant beauty of *burseriana Gloria*, which wipes all the other dwarf white Saxifrages out of existence as far as brilliancy goes. However, *Salomonii* suffers as little from the comparison as possible, only creeping into bloom when *Gloria* is passing over, and then, I think, it takes the lead of the rest in charm.

S. Elizabethae does for the common yellow Saxifrages of the group what *Gloria* does for the white ones. They all become inconspicuous and unnecessary. The plant is of comparatively recent introduction, and the Elizabeth to whom so many lovely things are ascribed is, I believe, Queen Carmen Sylva of Rumania. Some day, if I have brazenness enough and luck enough, I myself will raise a glorious thing and dedicate it under the name of another Elizabeth—' *Elizabethae Horti-Teutonici*.' But it must be a gay, fascinating creature, to deserve ascription to so gay and fascinating a lover of these delights. *S. Elizabethae* was a long time coming to its own here. For a season or two I was sceptical and incredulous as to my Manager's praises of the plant. It went on making dense deep mats of dark, glossy, spiny foliage—striking and ornamental, no doubt, but rather, it seemed to me, parsimonious and poor in the matter of flower. Now, however, that *Elizabethae* has matured and shown her true character, she stands revealed the sovereign, for gardening purposes, of the yellow Saxifrages, amazingly floriferous, with heads carrying three or four large round blossoms of a soft and bright canary-colour ; and so vigorous in growth that she makes great mats of emerald fur in no time in almost any position on the rockery. Her only requirement is a little low-feeding at times, for if too much fattened her branches get long and straggle about and fail to bloom. This is easily cured by poor soil and attention in spring top-dressing. And I must repeat here with emphasis that the other Yellows depart and hide their heads when *Elizabethae* begins to unfold. *Boydi* is to her as the moon to the sun ; and even the more lovely *Cherry-trees* can hardly enter into rivalry with the free-growing, free-flowering beauty of Queen Elizabeth.

S. luteo-viridis is a very rare strange person, hard to obtain true, though not, I find, very hard to grow. It is, I suppose, a hybrid between *media* and a yellow Saxifrage ; anyhow it makes largish grey-and-silver rosettes, and the ridiculous flowers, very small and pale yellow, in great fluffy greenery-yallery calyces, make the flower-spike

A LIMESTONE BOULDER IN THE OLD GARDEN

reminiscent of a Cowslip gone mad. *Luteo-purpurea* is another of this kind about whom some obscurity hangs. The true plant, now coming into flower, is quite unmistakable, with yellow-green flowers in purplish cups. But there are other plants sent out as *luteo-purpurea*. Of course, the wicked *juniperina* pops up here, never neglecting any chance of imposture. Then Nicholson makes *luteo-purpurea* a synonym of *apiculata*; and, again, I have a curious-looking creature sent me under this name which, so far, seems like a straggling *Elizabethae* run to seed, and in need of pulling to pieces. These two plants, *luteo-viridis* and *luteo-purpurea*, are evidently crosses belonging to the *ambigua*-class, children of *media*, *aretioeides*, and so on, among whom there is such diversity that confusion is pardonable. *Luteo-purpurea* must be the reverse cross to *luteo-viridis*, for the whole growth of the plant is very much smaller, in tufts, not rosettes, making growth altogether like a slightly enlarged form of *aretioeides*; and the same must be said of *Lapeyrousi*. Nicholson makes this a synonym of his *apiculata*, which shows conclusively that there is a mistake; for anything more unlike the *apiculata* of gardens it would be hard to imagine. *Lapeyrousi*, of good authority, is a neat little plant like *luteo-purpurea* (these, and Sundermann's *ambigua*, seem only to differ in foliage, the greenish flowers being almost indistinguishable; but, indeed, there is no certainty about any of these plants). All are prospering delightfully in the Moraine Garden, where *Boydi* languishes and *Vandelli* expires, and even *aretioeides primulina* has become sickly. *S. patens* is also thriving there—a new plant of this section, which I have only just bought. Its flowers seem smallish and creamy.

S. Vandelli is not a common nor an easy species. You will find it in the North Italian lakes, in the hills above Garda, and so forth. I saw it years since figured in a book of Alpine plants, and coveted it eagerly. After much difficulty I acquired it, and then saw it figured by Correvon with nasty little black lines running about all over the petals, which, in the first picture, had been snow-white. My plants, however, have the proper pure white blossoms and are pretty. *S. Vandelli* makes the hardest, densest growths of all, a serried close crust of spines, which hurts you sharply if you rest your hand on it unadvisedly. Then come up the short, three- or four-inch flower-stems, each carrying several blossoms in a head. As to culture, my pot-plants are a perpetual pleasure in their vigour and floriferousness, but I have only just succeeded well with it in the open, and I am coming to the conviction that this Saxifrage is a positive lime-hater—perhaps even a lime-hating development of *bur-seriana*—though not nearly so attractive (in fact, it ranks low among the Kabschias). One significant symptom is the absolute greenness of the leaves, without touch or sign of silver. This, of course, should mean a contempt for chalk and lime. I am trying it now, therefore, in soil as free as possible from lime, with peat and leaves and grit and wedges of sandstone.

S. diapensioeides is another difficult species, but very, very much prettier than *Vandelli* at its best; in fact, *diapensioeides* stands among the most fascinating of the smaller Kabschia-Saxifrages. The plant, unlike *Vandelli*, is a fanatical lime-lover, and occurs rarely along the line of the Southern Alps—as, for instance, in sunny chinks, quite ungetatable, of the great square Pierre à Voir, which you see from the Gemmi, far away, looming high over the Val de Bagne. (This, I am told, is the western limit.) The plant forms very small, very hard, very dense tufts of very hard, very dense little rosettes exactly like those of *Diapensia lapponica*, but tighter, tinier, and of a lovely blue-grey, picked out with silver. Then, on sturdy, short stems, come up large, round, snow-white flowers. In cultivation, this most worshipful species—I love it almost more than any other, though one never dares really to make a preference, because it is sure to be unsettled again the next minute—is rather dainty and capricious. It must have a bright, open place, and abundance of lime, in the soil and on the surface. Here I have it thriving, thank goodness, very happily on the moraines, where it has had a spring covering of lime-rubble, and is already showing signs of appreciation. I have always found in this garden that it dies promptly if you attempt to put sand with its compost. Now I give it nothing but loam and lime.

S. Ferdinandi-Coburgi is close to *diapensioeides*, a very rare newcomer, and the peer of *Elizabethae* among the small crusted Saxifrages. It makes firm cushions of blue-grey spiny-looking wee tufts, and sends up a very generous display of bright golden-yellow flowers (almost too sharp and shrill in tone), carried four or five to a head. To my surprise and joy, this little Easterner is among the best and easiest growers of the group; one established clump of mine, high up on a blazing hot piece of the rockwork, is at this moment a glory of fourteen brilliant flower-spikes. This plant, too, as far as I can see, demands and delights in abundance of lime. Here it perks up among the lime-chips, and seems to be the happier the more lime you scatter on top of it. In has two august neighbours, in *S. media* and *Edraianthus pumilio*, both of whom are thriving notably in the same conditions. But you can generally make a guess, from the appearance of a Kabschia-Saxifrage, as to whether it likes lime or no. Any greyness, any silver punctuations, are almost certain proof that lime, as the doctors say, is indicated.

S. squarrosa is an even tinier form, very close to *diapensioeides*—halfway, indeed, one may say, between *diapensioeides* and *caesia*, but almost devoid of silveriness. The plant makes such minute growth as to look like a small green splash of lichen. The flowers are large, pure white, carried on frail stems. I have never had any difficulty with *squarrosa*, although it looks at first sight as if it might be a lime-hater. But, if you study closely, you will see a miniature chalk-pit in each leaf, though so small as not to produce the usual grey effect; and *squarrosa*, then, comes among the general crowd of lime-lovers. Anyhow, it is certainly a success here—really, I think, more permanently satisfactory than *caesia*, though it must be remembered that so very tiny and choice a plant requires looking after, for fear that bigger things may shade it or worry it. *S. tombeanensis* is midway between *squarrosa* and *diapensioeides*; in fact, is looked upon by some as the North Italian form of *diapensioeides* itself. I find it quite distinct, and much less beautiful, making very hard, tight little masses entirely devoid of silver, and much more spiny in their minute way than the lovely splayed clusters of *diapensioeides*. The flowers of *tombeanensis* are pretty, though, and the plant quite easy to grow, and generous in the production of its snowy cups. In fact, it is, I find, easier than *diapensioeides*, though lacking that rare plant's extraordinary charm.

S. caesia is the commonest and one of the most beautiful in the group, an essentially limestone plant, quite blue in colour, with heavy punctuations of silver. In growth it is like a laxer *diapensioeides*, not so tight in growth or serried in leaf, and you may find it abundantly here and there all along the Alpine chains, growing, as far as my experience tells, in shady rather than in hot places, and occurring, as a rule, between the Alpine and sub-alpine zones, near or just above the last limit of the woods. It never, I believe, goes very high (*squarrosa* takes its place

at great elevations), and sometimes comes down accidentally with the torrents, to germinate in the river-beds
far below. It is a beautiful plant to see, so neat and
blue, with lovely great white blossoms, on wiry, very frail-
looking stems. And it is also a delightful plant to
collect, for it loves to grow wedged in among rocks, or
among the *débris* at the foot of a limestone cliff; so that,
in the precipice, it is a joy to prise away the rotten stone
with care, and reverently extract the whole black fibrous
mat of roots; or, among the *débris*, to lift away block by
block, until out comes the whole flattened shape of the
plant. When you do find *S. caesia*, too, you find it in
abundance. On the Vorder Wellhorn, below the Rosenlaui Glacier, you will see it on your direct way; and yet
again, coming down from the Gemmi towards Kandersteg,
just as you turn the corner beyond that desolate inn
sitting above its pool, where Guy de Maupassant's dreadful
little story of the Alpine winter has its scene—there,
growing about freely in the fallen rocks, you will find it.
The plant is very 'thankful,' as the Germans say, in
cultivation; but, at the same time, it wants a certain
amount of top-dressing and general attention. In any
case it is extremely fascinating and beautiful; one year I
showed it at the Temple, in clumps amid a great violet
mass of *Edraianthus serpyllifolius major*, and the contrast
of the big purple bells and the brilliant snow-white stars
was quite as beautiful as I had ever hoped.

As *S. caesia* they grew at St. John's, Oxford, an
Aeizoön which has absolutely nothing to do with the
noble plant whose name it bears, but which, like many
of these impostors, is a charming thing in its own right,
with no need of such adventitious aids as an unjusti-
fiable alias. This Saxifrage is very easy, and makes
quick-growing, dense mats of rosettes, rather narrow in
the leaf, and flattened in form, with vividly jagged edges

of clear bright silver. The whole tone of the plant is blue, and the effect of a fine sheet of it very remarkable indeed. The flower, too, is fine and telling—showy compact heads of creamy-white. I wish some one of authority would give it a good name. It is quite possibly the genuine *S. crustata.*

The true *caesia* is joint-parent with *mutata* of the true *Fosteri*, a very rare plant that I have only just succeeded in getting after many failures. First of all, I was sent one false *Fosteri*, which turned out a large Aeizoön intermediate, rather stout and stodgy; then I was sent a false, false *Fosteri*, which proved to be a neat, dear little plant of delicate appearance, belonging to the Geum group, to which belongs also the true *Zimmeteri*. Now I must bend my energies towards growing the genuine plant—very small and delicate, and ominous in appearance. *S. Boryi* is a rarity from Greece that I have not yet got.

And now, last of all this glorious race, but first in novelty, in rarity, in delicate, unexpected charm of unusual colour, comes *S. lilacina*, the only large-flowered purple of the group. This is a very rare, newly-introduced Himâlyan, whom I mention with the utmost contrition. When first he bloomed I turned up my nose at him, and snarked, and said bad words; this year he has bloomed in character, and I have never in all my life seen a more exquisite creature. He is a quick, easy grower in any shady place, making mats of dense, dense wee rosettes, like an even more minute *squarrosa*, without any silver markings. Then, from this lichen-like carpet, spring innumerable (I never saw such floriferousness) stems about an inch high, each carrying one big flower, of a rich blue-lilac with dark eye—a perfectly lovely colour, soft and delicate and appealing. A very little more, one way or the other, and it would be a bad washy magenta; as it is, the colour just strikes the right note, and is a blushing lavender.   *S. lilacina*, too, gives every sign of being a really good, willing little plant, and has already made large beds of itself at Kew.   Its principal requirement seems to be the rather uncommon one of shade, for excessive sun-heat withers the growth and burns the colour of the flowers.   *Lilacina* ought to cross with the other Kabschias, and bring its unusual lilac into a race with larger growth and flowers.   I am trying it this year with *scardica*, carefully picking off all *scardica*'s anthers, and then secluding the fertilised blooms in a frame by themselves.   So as, at all events, to do what I can towards securing purity.

CHAPTER IX

From Sedum to Edelweiss

OVER the Sedums I will not linger, for I don't like them ; over the delightful Sempervivums I dare not linger, for I like them so much. Other things are calling me onward. *Epilobium Hectori* and *Epilobium glabellum* I only mention as warnings. They look so meek and deceptively modest in habit, but in reality no two more awful little ramping weeds were ever invented ; and, if you once admit them, your life will be one of alarms and excursions ever afterwards.

Epilobium obcordatum is a good plant in a family filled with iniquity. He is a prostrate Rocky Mountain species, who hangs in fine sheets from a crevice and bears abundant large flowers of a bright cherry-pink. I am not quite certain how hardy he is, though, for my plants look very sickly, so far, after this terrible, incalculable winter, which has killed a few hardy things, and made so many tender ones blossom like the bay-tree or the wicked man. *Anemone vitifolia* is as lively as a grig already, on an exposed corner, too, and quite unprotected ; for the first time in my experience the South European Antirrhinums, *sempervirens* and *glutinosum*, have triumphantly survived ; and yet the *Aethionemas* look sorry for themselves, and *Pyrethrum densum* seems dead, while even *Epilobium obcordatum* has a rather unpromising appearance. However, one can never dare to prophesy what an apparently defunct plant may do a little later, in the way of breaking from the base.

E. Dodonaei is the red-flowered, shrubby species that one sees in the Alpine torrent-beds. He is my favourite of the whole race, and I think him a particularly charming, useful little plant, who is certain never to make a nuisance of himself, or die off, or do anything tiresome. He is, unfortunately, hard to get hold of; seed does not seem to come very freely—at least mine never did; and the plant has such an awful woody root that it is sheer madness to try and dig him up from the river gravel; for it is a hundred to one against your getting it intact, and if you don't the plant is almost certain to die, being very parsimonious about making secondary fibres. Luckily, after much search, I found one season a batch of babies, and dug them up with such success that now *E. Dodonaei* glorifies my garden yearly, in the rather dull months of July and August, when so many of the alpines are over. Of course, if you wish to carp, you can say that *Dodonaei* has rather more than a shade of magenta in him. Well, so have all the red-flowered Epilobiums; and they are so brilliant, and, in the case of *Dodonaei*, have so brown a scarlet in their alternating calyx-segments, that the magenta is quite condoned and carried off. So much cannot be said of *Geranium sanguineum* and *Erodium Manescavi*. But *Geranium argenteum*, the little Pyrenean, with silver leaves and rosy blooms, is a jewel of jewels, though hard to increase, while all the other Erodiums— *chrysanthum, cheilanthifolium, macradenium, supracanum, guttatum, Sibthorbi,* and the wee *Reichardi*, are among the most fascinating of plants, with aromatic ferny grey foliage, and delicate white or rosy or yellow flowers, most exquisitely feathered and streaked with purple. And all, though Easterners, are quite easy on any open bank.

The great Natural Order of the Umbrella Bearers offers quite astonishingly little of horticultural value, its children being, for the most part, large splendid weeds all very much of a muchness. The clan, too, is distinguished as producing the two most fearful pests that the gardener ever has to wage war upon—Goutweed and Pignut. However, in *Eryngium*, *Bupleurum*, and *Astrantia*, the Umbelliferae lead off with some good things. *Astrantia major* is a very well-known sub-alpine—a big herbaceous plant, with leafy, petal-like bracts enclosing a tight umbel of small, stamen-like flowers. The apparent petals are of a chaffy substance, and of a dullish rose in colour. The plant thrives anywhere, but is beaten out of the field by its cousins, *A. carniolica*, *A. Biebersteinii*, and *A. helleborifolia* (of which *helleborifolia* is, I fancy, a synonym only of *Biebersteinii*). This is a stout plant, growing two or three feet high, with greener, shinier leaves than those of *major*, and abundant flowers of a really delightful brilliant rose-colour, produced all through the season. *A. carniolica* is similar, though smaller, I find, and much slighter in growth.

A. minor is, to me, one of the most precious of alpines, and I cannot understand why so supremely lovely and dainty a little plant is not more worshipped or cultivated. I first saw it years ago in mossy woods on the way up to Rosenlaui, and nothing could now persuade me to live without it. *A. minor* has small, very deeply divided leaves, narrow, lobed, dark and glossy, and then a few frail delicate stems, perhaps eight inches high (in a strong plant), each carrying, on long peduncles, two or three pure white flower-heads that have an airy, sprayed effect (there is a pink form, too, of which I have seed). I find that this delightful treasure of mine thrives quite happily with any ordinary care, so it cannot be its difficulty that has obscured it in cultivation. Every time I see my clumps I am as proud of the plant as if I had invented it—such is the joy of discovering a little-known or neglected beauty.

For the rock-garden, the Natural Order Caprifoli-aceae means *Linnaea borealis*, and nothing but *Linnaea borealis*. Here and there in the North of England, here and there in the Western Alps, abundantly in the Eastern Alps and the far North of Europe, will you find the name-flower of the great botanist trailing long frail branches over the moss of the forests, and sending up, above each pair of tiny round leaves, a dainty stem from which hang swaying two fragrant pendulous little trum-pets of pale pink. My only European sight of him was over boulders at a half-shady turning on my way up the Meiden valley, where I collected a few plants that, with care, have thriven. For *Linnaea borealis* requires care, I believe—light soil and humidity around, and a lack of parching sun. But *L. borealis* is utterly put in the back-ground in every way by its American twin, *L. canadensis*, no doubt only a local form of the same plant, but Oh how different, how superior,—in beauty even, in vigour, in general desirableness! I collected it abundantly in the woods round Laggan in the Rockies, and even then was struck by the great robustness, the tolerance of sun, the brilliancy of blossom displayed so generously by this *L. borealis*, as I thought it. All over the light soil under the pines it grew, not apparently requiring moss or shade, but covering warm, dry, sun-hot banks in fine vegetable earth. Thence I collected a quantity of plants, and, in the course of years, I do not think that a single one of them has flagged or failed in any way. *L. canadensis* is undoubtedly a perfect pearl of merit, and if one adds to this that it is even more beautiful than *borealis*, one makes a bold statement indeed, but not, I think, an exaggerated one—for the bells of *canadensis* are richer in colour than the other's, and marked inside with two blotches of a brilliant carmine-rose, rich and velvety in texture. *Canadensis* thrives anywhere in the rockwork with me, in sun or shade making vigorous great trailing shoots.

I should want pages of rhapsody to deal with two sweet-tempered treasures in *Hypericum reptans* and *Oxalis enneaphylla*—the one a prostrate autumn-blooming St. John's Wort, with great luminous blossoms of a sunny pale gold with pink reverse; the other a garland of pearl-white Convolvulus flowers nestling among crinkly glaucous-grey leaves. The first loves sun, the second any cool shady nook, and both are splendidly amiable and hardy. And so with such scant notice I hurry on to the vast horticultural desert of Compositae, so full of names, but so barren of good things—though to Asters, of course, and their hybrids, we owe a great debt.

However, lovely as are *acris* and *amellus* and the water-loving *pyrenaeus*, when one mentions Aster in connection with the rock-garden, one has but one thing in one's mind—*Aster alpinus*. *Alpinus* is essentially a plant of the highest Alpine meadows, and you begin to find him just above the last limit of the woods, and continue in his company until you are very close on the moraines. In his upper reaches he shares whole lawns with the Edelweiss, and the contrast of white flannel and violet silk is perpetually brilliant against the grey rocks. The Aster varies indefinitely—the type bearing very large single flowers, each on one stem, of a lovely clear colour, with a bright golden eye; but I have collected, at different times, forms of the most ardent red-violet, pure white, or imperial purple. There is also a *roseus* form; and the plant varies a good deal in development too: *baldensis* is a long-stemmed variety, *longipetiolatus* is taller, *superbus* is almost as fine as the magnificent new *diplostephioeides*, while *himalaicus* is, I think, on the whole, the bluest and most vigorous of the lot. But they are all such lovable, dear little plants, that one must possess every one of them, and yet never have enough. *A. alpinus* is perfectly easy and comfortable in cultivation; he deserves a choice place, though, for his loveliness, and glorifies it too. As for me, I declare that, my garden, though it swarms with *A. alpinus*, is the last place in the world where his charms can be studied. For, if ever a stout bushy clump begins to shoot up, along comes a beauty-loving slug or an æsthetic-minded mouse, and in the morning there is absolutely nothing left but a dozen raw stumps, where each rosette has been gnawed off with perfect neatness close to the ground. Mice and slugs have for this Aster, in fact, a passion which I can but describe as morbid; only at the cost of disfiguring your garden with horrible little ring-fences of zinc round each plant can you hope to preserve *A. alpinus* in his pristine glory. I know few things so utterly disheartening as either this peril or this remedy; slugs seem impossible to cope with, for all so-called slugicide mixtures seem to be planticide as well. I suffer daily woe, and feel like a hardy perennial Prometheus as I wander round each morning and find my Asters, my *Campanula Zoysi*, my Primulas of the dainty Minima group, eaten flat down to the soil. A flourishing plant was there overnight; now, nothing but a dreadful mutilated, bleeding trunk. True, the plants will certainly break again later on, but nothing can ever quite recover that first fine careless rapture. And the more slugs you hunt down by night with lettuces and a lantern, the more there seem to be left to wreak wickedness unchecked.

Very close to *Aster* comes *Erigeron*, of which there are many large handsome herbaceous species, and two or three miniatures of the utmost daintiness. The big plants are *Erigeron glabellus*, *salsuginosus*, *grandiflorus* and *speciosus*, with *speciosus maximus*, this last best known as *Stenactis*. It makes a great bush, ultimately, of crowded stems, each carrying through the summer a quantity of flowers like small purple China Asters, with a greenish-yellow eye. Cut it down early and it will bloom again for the autumn. *Glabellus* I collected abundantly in the Rockies; it is very handsome, but not nearly so rampant, with large blue-lilac blossoms. *Salsuginosus* (the true plant) comes between these two in general appearance—a very useful vigorous late-summer and autumn bloomer, perfectly hardy and robust and thrifty, with abundance of medium-sized flowers, that vary from dirty white, through the typical lilacs, to rose and deep violet. All these large Erigerons are fine on the rockery, high up, or in the border or wild garden. These are the best species that I grow. *Aurantiacus* is a common kind, with countless gold or orange daisies; *Neo-mexicanus* I have rather slipped from my memory; I fancy it is a little pinnate-leaved trailer, that rambles about quite happily in a neglected corner; its Bellis-like flowers are pinkish. *Roylei* is a Himâlyan, and, to my mind, rather like a smaller and slightly inferior version of *salsuginosus*. Near these Erigerons, too, is the useful little *Vittadenia triloba* (sometimes called *Erigeron mucronatus*), light and graceful in growth, with a profusion of little flowers like pink daisies, carried on airy stems all through the late summer.

The choicer species are *compositus*, *trifidus* and *pulchellus*, minute things, if my plants be true, very neat and charming indeed for a choice corner, with mauve daisies for flowers. The gem of the race, however, is the exquisite *Erigeron leiomerus*. Where this rare newcomer hails from I cannot tell; I first saw him at Kew, and never rested until with great difficulty I had secured him. Now he is well established here and there in the rockery, and I can already see minute flower-buds forming, if only the mice and slugs will be reverent! *Erigeron leiomerus* is quite a tiny plant, making a small tuft of a few wandering twigs. The leaves are narrow and grey-green; the large flowers are of a peculiarly exquisite, very pale violet, almost verging towards a bluish white. This sounds washy and undecided, perhaps? Very unlike the flowers, then; a more delicate, serene tone was never imagined. Though this dear little *Erigeron*, I fancy, wants no special care, yet I would not trust such a jewel in any common place. It has select nooks in different quarters, and is thriving very happily indeed, having taken no hurt by the winter, which I was rather afraid of, not being certain as to his native country. Our own very rare native *Erigeron alpinus* is but a poor thing, like an inferior, shabby-flowered *Aster alpinus*, with flowers curiously stodgy and frowsy, by the side of that glorious purple Margaret.

Townsendia wilcoxiana and *Aster Pattersoni* must come together, as rare, very choice dwarfs. The *Aster* I have only just got, with huge expectations—'reizend, hell-blau, im April blühend,' is enough to excite even my Anglo-Saxon mind. This species has a dear wee rosette of narrow leaves, and shall take up his residence in the moraine, where *Townsendia wilcoxiana* is already established with every symptom of perfect contentment. (These Asters, Erigerons, and Townsendias are all very much the same thing, speaking from a gardener's rather than a botanist's standpoint.) *Wilcoxiana* also makes dense rosettes in a tuft, and is very dwarf indeed, with large, golden-eyed flowers of a soft lilac-blue. If there is any difficulty about these alpines, as I rather suspect there may be, they will probably thrive best in the moraine, as *wilcoxiana* is certainly doing already. And I only say this because the little things are obvious alpines, and because I am absolutely ignorant of where they come from, or in what sort of condition they grow normally. I should suspect them, instinctively and perhaps quite unjustly, of being American species; and all Americans, as far as I have found, thank you for much lighter soil and quicker drainage and warmer position than are demanded by most of our European mountaineers.

And now we come to the arch-impostor of the garden —the Flannel-flower of the Alps, so ridiculously sought after and marvelled at. The man who first called it 'Edelweiss' was a master of humour; the plant is neither noble nor white. I am far from denying the strange, wonderful beauty of the thing—the hoary leaves and hoary star-flowers are marvellously fascinating. It is the monstrous claims of the plant that I protest against. Many people regard it as a typical alpine plant—as *the* typical plant of high, perilous peaks; many people yearly topple off precipices in their attempts to find it; and the first question that all strangers put on entering a rock-garden is the reverent whisper, 'Do you grow the Edelweiss?' Now, so far from being *the* typical alpine plant, the Edelweiss is not even an alpine plant at all. It is a desert plant (from the great Siberian wastes), whose fluffy seeds allow it to spread far and wide. In the second place, far from being a peak-plant, what Edelweiss really enjoys is a scrubby, stony, flat lawn, where it grows like any daisy among chips and sparse herbage (I know great level stretches of it in the high Alps, where as you walk along a gentle valley you are trampling Edelweiss at every step). Only by an accident does the *Leontopodium* ever appear on cliffs and pinnacles. His chosen dwelling is always the very highest reach of the alpine meadows, where they begin to verge upon the moraines. But he seeds himself almost anywhere, and you are never secure against finding him, either in the moraine itself, or even in the torrent bed four or five

A LEDGE OF SAXIFRAGES AND EDELWEISS (S. LONGIFOLIA, S. MACNABIANA [TRUE] AND ANEMONE DICHOTOMA)

thousand feet below in the valley. For, in the third
place, there is no sort of horticultural merit or glory
about growing the Edelweiss.   A more robust weed
doesn't exist.   Any dryish treatment suits it, and the
only way in which you can ever hope to lose a clump, if
you want to, is to plant it so low that it gets too much
wet in winter.   Plant it high, give it poor soil, and a
dressing of lime to whiten it; then there isn't anything
of stouter health in the garden.   (As for a typical peak-
plant, a sight of whom *does* necessarily involve either
danger, or fatigue, or both, you need go no further than
Eritrichium nanum.)   But this lovely Siberian interloper
has no shadow of a right to any of the claims that are so
absurdly made for him.   Every mountain-chain possesses
him, and I grow a very fine Himâlyan form, as well as a
giant variety from seed off the Engelhoerner.   But the
thing is a pretender all round; even his flowers are not
really flowers, but only a bundle of leaves gone mad.   So
that one cannot, as one would like, acquit the plant of
all share in the legend that has been built up round him.
If only Edelweiss would stand on his own merits, and be
content with recognition as a very beautiful, interesting
Siberian, that would be all right; it is when this alien
immigrant presumes to pose as the type-plant of the
mountains, that we are forced to unveil his imposture,
and declare him the easiest of border-species; when he
falsely absorbs the homage that is really due to *Eritrichium* and *Androsace*, that we find ourselves bound to
denounce him as a flannelette fraud, composed entirely
of deception, without and within, a bunch of whitened
leaves masquerading as a blossom, and an easy-going,
sand-loving parvenu from the deserts masquerading as a
peer to the real, proud-tempered aristocracy of the
mountains.

CHAPTER X

The Smaller Campanulas

THERE is something at once brilliant and useful about
the Campanulas that takes the gardener's fancy almost
more than the manifold admirable qualities of the
gorgeous, incalculable Gentians, the easy-going but not
dazzling little Saxifrages, or the striking, slug-beloved,
rather capricious Primulas.   Not that the Campanulas
are slug-proof, sadly far from it.   *Elatines, Raineri,* and
Zoysi are perpetually used, at least in this garden, as the
staple of very successful slug dinner-parties.   But, on the
whole, I think no great alpine race quite approaches the
Campanulas in general, well-deserved popularity.   For
the most part they are so delightfully easy to grow,
combining good temper with extreme prettiness; and,
even when you come upon the difficulties of the race,
they are at once so very difficult and so very beautiful
that there is an enormous amount of both pride and
pleasure to be got out of their prosperous cultivation.
Very few Campanulas, and none of the alpine groups, are
anything but lovely; only in the biennials and rarer
Levantines do you sometimes meet with comparatively
uninteresting species.   But of those generally grown the
fascinations are innumerable; although they generally
keep varying round different shades of blue and white,
yet their contribution of beauty to rock-garden and
border is simply incalculable, while they redouble their

services by offering them when the other alpines are gone back to rest.

The family falls into two main groups, of which the one, containing comparatively few species of first-rate importance, is tall-growing, robust, woodland in taste, and suited to ordinary borders; while the other, by far the larger and more typical, is essentially a rock-loving, open-air race from high slopes or rock-faces or moraines, finding the centre of its distribution, not, like Primula, in the Himâlya, not, like Saxifraga, in the Alps, but in the Caucasus and the Levant and the islands of the Aegean. However, no race has suffered so awfully as Campanula at the hands of the nursery-gardener, who in dealing with it has displayed a redoubled wickedness in the matter of false, needless, or unauthorised names. Is there any one who has not bought some high-sounding Campanula from a catalogue, and then, having paid his long price, discovers at last that his purchase—*Raineri*, say—is only *G. F. Wilson* after all? And lives there a man with soul so dead, as, suffering these things, not to make up his mind to seek clearer knowledge on the subject? Then let him go to my friend M. Correvon's admirable articles in *The Garden* of 1901 on the smaller Campanulas. As for me, I will deal with the matter as best I can, claiming no authority, but retailing for the help of others my own disasters, and pointing out such mistakes or frauds or synonymities as I have come across myself. As for arrangement of the species, of course the alphabetic has its obvious conveniences. But then it means so much jumping about in the matter of description that perhaps it will be best for me, as usual, to take the great species as they fall together.

Campanula Allioni heads the list, alphabetically as well as by any other rule of propriety. For it is the type of the most difficult Campanulas of the most beautiful alpine group, of the *débris*-loving section. Every race of plant has its particular vice—the Saxifrages go in for appropriating each other's names in a most shameless manner, the Primulas vary indefinitely, the Columbines intermarry with shameless promiscuity. The especial vice of Campanula is a vanity that leads to a perfectly appalling plurality of epithets. Every species has about half a dozen different titles, and it is thus that such confusion reigns in gardens and catalogues—each grower choosing the name he likes best, until no one knows what his plant really, definitely, finally is, but wallows in a hopeless muddle from which the only escape is to buy every mortal Campanula you see advertised, until you get some hang of what each garden means. Even *C. Allioni* sins in this matter. It is catalogued as *alpestris*, *nana*, and *trilocularis*. However, the genuine plant is so very distinct that most nurserymen cannot help sending out the true thing if they possess it. I once had *C. nana* from a French garden, though, and my experience of it was altogether happy. For, though a real *Allioni*, it is certainly a more vigorous, even if a slightly smaller variety, and continues to grow here with a vigour not usual in the typical form. For *Allioni* is a well-known gardener's problem—difficult to collect, because of that long fleshy carrot which so resents disturbance, with all the fleshy little stolons round it, that each has roots, and looks as if it would grow separately, but, as a matter of fact, horrifies the unwary by refusing to do any such thing. *C. Allioni* haunts the slides of *débris* in the Western Alps—a limited, dying species, weak in reproduction, and incapable of any great spread. It forms, ultimately, what look like colonies on the bare bank (for the plant is never strong enough to compete with grass on more inhabited slopes), but these are, in reality, only so many offshoots of the main parent stem, each sending up its tiny rosette of long, narrow leaves, silver with stiff hairs, and, in the middle, one great blossom like a violet bell. There are certainly different forms, however, for my *Allioni* has much broader foliage than my *nana*—glossy, and brownish at the ciliated edge; while Backhouse's original plant, which is still flourishing here, is very similar, but rather larger in growth. In flower they are all the same, though Backhouse's, perhaps, is a little bigger and bluer. The great difficulty with *C. Allioni*, I believe, is rather treatment than compost. The plant is always thought of as a lime-hater, nor do I dissent from this. It is usually, and probably rightly, taken as a type of the irreconcileable lime-haters. But in this garden I have established this and the other difficult alpine species of its kind by putting them in the moraine, and saving myself and them any bother about soil by the simple expedient of not giving them any, or just the merest dash. For my pet heresy is this—what these stoloniferous high alpines hate and dread is not so much lime or peat, as a clogging weight of earth round their rootlets in the winter. In garden-soil, however carefully prepared with grit, peat, sand, chips, every sort of fuss, I could never persuade *cenisia* or *Allioni* to survive the winter. But, ever since I put them in the moraine, I have given them no more attention and had no further difficulty. *Cenisia*, by now, fills a yard-wide bank of moraine all to itself, where it appears each season brisker than ever among the chips, and from July onwards is such a miracle of blossom that the number of its flowers almost spoils their beauty. *Allioni* is more recent in a similar place, but is showing quite as much increase of strength, so that I have real hopes that the plant is established.

C. cenisia is of the same blood as *Allioni*—an underground, creeping species, from the very high moraines,

where you find him among the last vegetation of all,
making mats of blossom between the grey stones. Personally, I consider *cenisia* a very much underrated plant;
he is an old friend of mine, and all my specimens have
been collected by my own trowel. *Cenisia* has far
smaller flowers than *Allioni*, quite different—little wide
open cups, rather flat, and of a curious clear hard electric
blue. Mr. Robinson did not 'find this species very
attractive in its native haunts'; but I must confess there
are few high alpines that I find more so. The plant is
of a far finer constitution than *Allioni*, too—a vigorous
spreading species, that pervades the whole mountain-
chain, though considered a limestone plant as a rule.

C. excisa is curiously beautiful—a rare kind occurring
here and there in the high screes of the Binnthal and the
Saasthal, but not, like *Allioni*, rare on account of old age
and debility. For *excisa* is a very ramping little plant,
who takes every opportunity of thriving and spreading.
In growth he is thin and wiry, with erect, airy stems, and
nodding bells of pale violet, which, at the base of every
lobe, have the trait that gives the plant its name—a
small, round, regular hole, as neat as if cut out with a
punch. *Excisa* I have in the open ground in peat, where
I believe him to be doing well, though he has not appeared as yet this season. I have also planted him just
lately in the moraine, where he will probably wage war
with everything else. The plant, I truly believe, is a
real lime-hater, though; and, at all events, is better
treated as such. To this high, difficult section belong
also the genuine *uniflora*, which I have never got
(*Barbata uniflora* or *rotundifolia uniflora* or *Cenisia* too
often serving for it in catalogues), and *morettiana*, a
lovely wee fissure-plant, Arctic and Alpine, which I by
no means despair of yet; for though my first and, so far,
my only experience of him was a failure, yet the plants I

had were so small and mutilated and poor, that I cannot
consider my experiment any fair test. Some day soon I
hope to have him thriving with *Allioni* and *Allioni nana*
in the moraine.

C. alpina is a very rare species in cultivation, but extremely beautiful. In too many nurseries the name
covers inferior commoner things (I know of one first-rate
garden where *C. alpina* stands for a *valdensis*-form of
rotundifolia). The true plant is quite distinct among
Campanulas, standing nearest, in many ways, to *C. barbata*, which it replaces in the high pastures of the limestone Alps. *C. alpina* makes a small, dense tuft of
narrow, hairy, greyish leaves, and then, at the side, sends
up a six-inch flower-spike, very densely set with pendulous bells of a rather dark, steely blue. After this the
plant too often dies, following that dreadful monocarpous
tendency which is so frequent among spiked Campanulas,
and which I will always, in fairness, bring up as a charge
whenever a species deserves it. *C. alpina* is otherwise a
very good little doer—a lime-lover of quite easy cultivation here, though small and rare enough to claim a choice
corner.

C. barbata, its big brother, is one of the loveliest of
alpine plants. No one who has ever seen a meadow hung
with those exquisite great pale porcelain-blue bells, all
fringy with hairs, can ever reconcile himself to a garden
without *C. barbata*. Few plants are better to grow,
either, on any fair sunny slope. The plant is not a limestone species, but with us is obliging enough to have no
fads at all in the matter of soil. The one danger with
him here is that of rot from excessive damp in winter,
unless he is planted high and dry. The white form is
even more beautiful, if possible, and the one-flowered
form is delightful in the high Alps, though so far I have
not proved it constant in cultivation. Though *barbata*

makes fine tufts and grows more than a foot high, he can
be trusted never to presume on his space, and, despite his
size, is certainly to be reckoned among the aristocracy of
the mountain-race.

C. caespitosa I can never distinguish from *pusilla* and
pumila and *modesta*, and all the other synonyms that
are academically held to cover two species. I wonder if
any one else can? Anyhow I will speak, as far as my
own garden goes, of *C. pusilla* only—the shorter and the
prettier name. The differences, if any, are so minute
and variable as to have no importance in horticulture.
The type plant is the commonest of all little Campanulas
on the Alps in shady or sunny places, on rock or moraine,
as well as in our cottage-gardens, where the dainty white
form—the Religieuse des prés—is abundant everywhere.
But the ordinary blue form is lovely enough, ramping about
everywhere among the rocks, with its glossy rounded leaves,
and its clouds of little swaying bells. This plant is, of all
weeds, the most beautiful. It must never be admitted to
any select corner of the garden—but for carpets, or for
neglected plots among the rocks, nothing is so valuable.
The varieties that I have collected include a very dwarf,
large-blossomed form, from a high moraine, which, much
to my surprise, seems inclined to be more or less constant
in cultivation, and a most lovely silver-pale variety from
rough rocks on the way up to Arolla. Then *tyrolensis*
is not, I think, anything more than a fine, robust *pusilla*
under a more sonorous name—a splendid thing enough,
a little larger than the type, perhaps, but not conspicuously worthy of differentiation. *Bocconi* is sometimes
sold by tradesmen, but generally turns out to be *pusilla*,
of which the real *Bocconi* is apparently only a variety, as
also is *Vensloi*, not easily distinguishable from the ordinary *caespitosa*.

C. Zoysi is a minute high alpine from Styrian *débris-*

slopes, with tidy wee tufts of small ovate leaves, and abundance of the quaintest bright blue flowers, shaped like minute soda-water bottles. One would expect this species to be rather a miff—but no ; there are few high alpines that I find more grateful and happy than this exquisite and peculiarly charming little oddity. He has never given me the slightest trouble in any soil, and in any aspect—except by reason of the inordinate concupiscence with which he inspires every slug within a six-mile radius. In the Old Garden I had a glorious clump of him for five years and more, until at last the gods were jealous, and sent a snail to eat him flat—every bud and shoot. With all a plant's pathetic bravery he broke again heroically at every stump, and soon was budding all over with green. Then the jealous gods took care to send another snail, and not even *C. Zoysi* could stand two murders in one summer.

C. Raineri is a rare dwarf species from Northern Italy, which is always very highly praised in catalogues. He loves a sunny chink, and is quite easy to grow, though, like *Zoysi*, is very much affected by slugs. However, I must confess that I have never set *Raineri* high on my list of Campanulas. The plant is inclined to be leafy, and the large flowers are not quite large enough to carry off the leafiness. I myself should describe it, very irreverently, as a hairy little Esau-version of *turbinata*, lacking the big-flowered decisive loveliness of the commoner species. Perhaps I am a little embittered against the true *Raineri* by my love for the false *Raineri*. A few years ago every nursery of any pretensions was selling, as *C. Raineri*, an extraordinarily lovely dwarf thing which I now believe to have been the genuine *turbinata*, or a form of it—a very small plant, with very large cups of pale blue or white sitting close to the leaves. And I far preferred the false to the true *Raineri*. However, lest one good custom should corrupt the world, the nurseries have now changed their ascription, and if· you order *Raineri* to-morrow you will most likely receive, not the genuine plant, nor even my dear little false form, but simply *G. F. Wilson*—either the type or the ugly yellow-leaved variety.

The true *turbinata* is not, as a matter of fact, quite the same thing as my pet false *Raineri*, but it is, nevertheless, a rarish plant of the highest possible value—the thriftiest of growers almost anywhere, with immense purple flowers on quite short stems. I now have a *compacta* form which is even more dwarf, a lovely *alba*, and a *pallida compacta nana*, which must indeed be lovely to make it worth one's while to learn such a name. Sundermann produces all these marvels, and now chronicles a *turbinata* X *Raineri* hybrid, which might be extremely beautiful, and might be rather plain. From *turbinata* on through the common garden forms of *turbinata* to the genuine *carpatica*, is a succession of steps so small as to become almost a slide. The genuine Turbinatas are, I believe, dwarf and one-flowered ; the genuine Carpaticas are taller and several-flowered, but the two species vary and cross so infinitely that there are a whole crowd of excellent plants which can scarcely be ascribed to either with any certainty, but which are all excellent for any ordinary place in border or rock-garden, flowering throughout the season. I myself have raised a very pretty pale-flowered dwarf of *carpatica* ; others have produced the wide-flowered, deep-blue Isabel, and its albino counterpart White Star, and the vigorous, brilliant Riverslea. And now I am awaiting blossoms from a whole flourishing batch of crosses.

C. Elatines and *C. elatinoeides* are two rare plants, standing fairly close together. They are both from Southern France and Northern Italy, sun-loving, wet-hating species that require a good deal of attention, I find. *Elatines* has a glabrous and a hairy form, of which the smooth is, as one would have expected, the hardier and the better in every way. I have had both species; now only *Elatines* dwells here, in a hot crevice, where the slugs eat him flat as soon as they get a chance. I saw him two days perking up in a neat tuft of greenery. The next day I pass by—*nothing*, only a bare brown stump, with trails of slime all over it. And I do so hate zinc rings, to say nothing of the impossibility of fitting them round plants in a crevice! However, when all is said and done, I do not think either *Elatines* or *elatinoeides* really has any conspicuous merit among Campanulas, or ever could have, even if they were not tender and wet-hating. They send up branching stems, and the flowers are small, shaped like flat stars, and of a bright or dark blue, not very brilliant in tone.

C. fragilis is a species one must be very firm about. Here are a few of the names that stand for *C. fragilis* itself, or for varieties of it, or for Campanulas so very close to it in appearance and requirements as to deserve no separate mention: *fragilis, garganica, garganica hirsuta, versicolor (Tenorii), isophylla, Barrelieri, rupestris, balchiniana, Mayi, muralis*, with variegated-leaved forms. Not that all these are synonyms of *garganica* or *fragilis*, but they all belong to the same group, are endlessly confused, and require similar treatment. *Rupestris* and *versicolor* are novelties, on whose names I cannot pass judgment. They are both, I believe, bad, biennial, or monocarpous species from hot rocks in the Aegean, and have no especial beauty to set them above *garganica*. This is really a first-rate garden plant for any warm, well-drained place, forming sheets of smooth or downy foliage, with abundant big, open-eyed flowers, blue or white. *Isophylla* and its variety *alba* are glorious sights

as grown in cottage windows, making perfect curtains of
blossom; but none of this heat-loving, drought-loving
section can ever be expected to be happy here in the
open, and I have some time ago renounced the hope of
making them so. Nor do I mean to make any longer
effort with another Southerner, the pretty, biennial
Campanula laciniata. Where soil or situation permits of
adjustment, one may fairly continue to cope with difficult
plants; but where it is a matter of commanding the sun,
all who do not emulate Joshua will do well to take refuge
with more amenable plants from more northerly quarters.

That *C. isophylla* or *C. garganica* should ever pass as
muralis is a wicked shame. For the true *muralis* is a
perfectly distinct and admirable species, making great
mats of smooth, shining leaves, covered with lovely
purple flowers which, unlike those of the *garganica*
group, are not starry but bell-shaped. *Muralis* has a
splendid constitution, too, and is one of the most trustworthy plants of his race. The variety *bavarica* is only
a rather larger form of *muralis*, and *triflora* a very close
cousin, while *portenschlagiana* is yet another synonym of
this poor Campanula, except when, by those who should
know better, it is used to cover a singularly fine little
Campanula which no one yet it seems has named with
authority.

This jewel is sometimes called *C. Erinus*—a name
patently false, as the real *Erinus* is a worthless annual
species. At other times it is talked of as *muralis minor.*
This name is nearly as bad as the other, for the plant
bears little or no resemblance to *muralis*, while it obviously comes very near the *garganica* group. Taking all
things into consideration, I feel certain that M. Correvon
is right, and that it is best to be described as *garganica
compacta.* However, this *garganica compacta* is so distinct as to deserve a place to himself. The plant is quite

small in growth, making dense flat cushions of serried bright green, glossy leaves, reniform, crenulate, with a leaf-hiding profusion of bright china-blue flowers with a clear white eye. But these flowers, instead of being bell-like, after the model of *muralis*, are flat, star-shaped, exactly like those of a small *garganica*. Where the plant originated I have no notion, nor what its history may be; all I can say is that *C. garganica compacta* of my garden is an absolutely first-rate alpine, hardy, easy, immortal, and of an amazing floriferousness, unquestion-ably a head and shoulders above all others of the *garganica* group for outdoor culture in this damp Northern climate of mine.

The star-flowered section contains one more delightful and very distinct rock-plant in *C. waldsteiniana*, one of whose synonyms is *rupestris* (nowadays labelled on to a miffy monocarpous Greek Islander). *C. waldsteiniana* hails from Dalmatian regions, and makes a neat little bush about six inches high, of stiff, wiry stems, clothed with narrow leaves, and crowned with lovely bright blue stars with a white eye. This is one of the easiest and best of the minuter Campanulas to deal with, and has none of that ominous downiness which foreshadows delicacy and dislike of damp in too many of the Southern species. It is smooth and sturdy, deciduous, and quite impervious to autumnal wet, so different from the other star-flowerers, who fear so much less the summer sun than the furious winter's rages.

C. tommasiniana must find a place here, if only that he and *waldsteiniana* are sometimes made synonymous or forced to exchange names. In reality *tommasiniana* is quite as distinct, and, in his own way, quite as pretty, as *waldsteiniana*. This species also makes little bushes, but the erect stems are clothed with long pendulous narrow bells or tubes of pale purple, exceedingly quaint and attractive. M. Correvon, as far as I can understand, describes this species under the name *waldsteiniana*, and says nothing as to the other plant of that name. However, my *tommasiniana* and my *waldsteiniana* are as different as any two things could be, except in ease of growth. Both are perfectly good-natured, though perhaps *waldsteiniana* is the more indestructible of the two. *Tommasiniana*, too, is hard to get hold of nowadays. Last year a whole consignment of him came in, and proved to be the even rarer *Stansfieldi*, of which I guess *tommasiniana* to be one of the parents. Both *tommasiniana* and *waldsteiniana* are prettier, I think (because more frail and graceful), as young plants than as old-established clumps. And both are quite tolerant of rather rich soil in a more or less shady position on the rockwork, a treatment that in my gardens would be fatal to so many Campanulas of the Garganica persuasion.

Of the little Alpine Bell-flowers the sovereign is *C. pulla*. When you have faced the fact that *pulla* really *does* dislike lime, you have said, I think, the only thing that can possibly be said against him. The plant is a dainty ramper of the most irresistible nature, filling up a peaty or cool sandy corner, whether shaded or sunny, in no time, and sending up his bright pale green leaves every season further and further away from the old plant. And then the flowers; I dare not admit that any other of his little kindred can surpass the beauty of his flowers, though he has a very formidable rival in the newer, larger *C. collina*. *Pulla*, as all the favoured know, produces on each threadlike stem a single pendulous bell of the most splendid deep imperial violet—a lustrous, glorious colour, with a silky sheen about the texture of the flower that makes the glory of it complete. He blooms late in the season, too, after that most precious habit of the Campanulas which so doubles their value;

and altogether *Pulla* ranks unquestionably among the dozen indispensables. Don't ask me to name the dozen; if I attempted to, the number of indispensables would certainly swell to a hundred, and then probably to a thousand.

A very, very seldom seen species—what my Japanese servant would call 'a very sometime person'—is *C. macrorhiza*, from the French Riviera. Why does no one seem to grow this plant, one of the most valuable of all the race? He is perfectly hardy, perfectly easy to establish, and has the supreme merit of blossoming, even in my Yorkshire garden, right away from October through the winter, unless violent frosts cut off his flowers. (No frost can affect the plant, it seems.) I give *macrorhiza* the very highest character in every way, and a special mark of commendation, because one would not expect him to be so pleasant. For *macrorhiza* inhabits rock crevices along the range of the Maritime Alps, and one might expect him to have some of the hygrophobia—I cannot go on saying 'dislike of damp'—that painfully distinguishes his fellow-countrymen, *Elatines* and *elatinoeides*. *Macrorhiza*, as his name implies, makes a vast fleshy rootstock, and then tufts of leaves, with innumerable light branching stems loaded with blossom. The flowers, far more in number, are like those of the Harebell, but a trifle less in size, a trifle more open in shape, and of a distinct vinous-lilac. A shower of this little Campanula, pouring from a rock-face in November, as I collected it years ago on my way down over the hills from St. Martin Vésubie, is one of the most inspiriting paradoxes that that Lenten period ever produces. And *C. macrorhiza* is not a scrap less late or lavish in my own garden. Was ever an alien so tractable?

C. rotundifolia shall have his fair meed of worship, though in less exalted phrase his name is the common

Harebell. But I love the common Harebell, and can never weed the sprightly beauty of him up without an apology and a feeling of ingratitude. The white form is beautiful, too, and so are all the other forms—even M. Correvon's double one, with blossoms like little blue roses. The *major* form of the white variety is excellent, too; in fact, the only Harebell at which my heart does not open and shut, like Mrs. Caudle's at a rose, is *rotundifolia soldanellaeflora*, a Ragged-Robinish thing, with untidy, tatterdemalion flowers that seem to me to have lost their regularity without acquiring any counterbalancing charm. No plant varies more than the Harebell, and with *rotundifolia*, too, we get back into the painful land of minute differences and unnecessary distinctions. A very conspicuous plant, however, is the true *C. Hosti*—a fine sturdy, stocky thing, with more flowers and larger flowers than *rotundifolia*, carried on stiffer stems and more simultaneously. Some people deny, perhaps with reason, the existence of a genuine *Hosti*, claiming the plant as a mere variety of the Harebell. But I must say I have always thought it very distinct, and, in some ways, more valuable; it is much neater and less untidy in growth (for *rotundifolia* first of all grows tall and then flops in a most annoying way). I once found what I believe to be *Hosti*, and still grow as *Hosti*—one single plant in a river-bed below Rosenlaui; and, whatever his family history, the plant seemed then and seems still to have a very distinct personality of his own, and to be very desirable —a foot-high bush, covered with big purple bells. Both *Hosti* and its pretty albino are almost border-plants, so easy are they to grow. *C. Scheuchzeri* one first sees in the Alpine meadows, and goes quite mad over. At least I did. *C. Scheuchzeri* is simply a Harebell with enormous blossoms, deep satiny-violet in colour, and most gorgeous to behold. *Scheuchzeri* loves very wet places, and in England proves nevertheless to be absolutely good-tempered. But—ah, what a change! With me the flowers have always dwindled and shrunk, until they lost all their pristine glory, and became indistinguishable, except by their sparseness, from a good Harebell. I wonder if many people in England maintain *Scheuchzeri* at his splendid alpine level of brilliancy and size? There is a white form, too, as of nearly all Campanulas, which I collected below Meiden one year. *Linifolia, valdensis,* and *subpyrenaica* are all varietal forms of *Scheuchzeri* or *rotundifolia,* as far as I have ever been able to make out. So is *Baumgarteni,* and so is the false *carnica,* I believe. *Valdensis* is attractive, having a grey down all over him which enhances the violet blossoms; otherwise these Campanulas, though interesting enough for a full collection, are unnecessary for ordinary purposes, I find, and many of them revert in a season or so, notably *Scheuchzeri,* to *rotundifolia,* of which they are all probably local or generic developments, like the indistinguishable *alaskana.*

Very distinct, though, is the rare and attractive *C. stenocodon,* which I had and lost, and have now replaced. It seems to hover between *rotundifolia* and *pusilla* as far as its habit goes. In growth it is slight and stoloniferous as *pusilla*; but the flowers are curiously narrow, not comfortably bell-shaped like the others—long, close, little dark-blue trumpets, very unusual and pretty. I forget how my plant originally departed, perhaps it was sold; anyhow, there is nothing about *stenocodon's* appearance that would lead one to anticipate any sort of difficulty in its cultivation. It is hardly conceivable that a plant so free and brisk in growth should not be as robust as *pusilla* itself under ordinary reasonable conditions of cool moist soil and plenty of rock.

C. tridentata and *C. saxifraga* are generally spoken of as if they were synonymous—at least in catalogues. I cannot pronounce on this, but from what I gather I should suppose that they are very likely two different forms of the same species—*saxifraga* hailing from the Caucasus, and *tridentata* from further south, in the Lebanon ranges. (Although the two plants seem to be found together in the Caucasus.) However, the differences between them are of a minute nature, and they may be treated as one in the garden, where they are very happy in any decent, well-trained corner, with good drainage, light, and air. Their habit is close and tufted, their flowers large, short-stemmed, and of fine blues and purples. I think them superior in every way to the true *Raineri*. As for the slugs, they refrain from any such invidious comparisons, and devour all three species with impartial zeal whenever they get a chance. (As a rough rule, smooth-leaved Campanulas are fairly safe; down spells danger.) I have just reared to flowering size a splendid batch of young Tridentatas, out of which I hope for some fine things, if I am ever allowed to see them in bloom.

As far as my garden goes, this closes the list of the small true-born Campanulas. There are, however, some very beautiful Campanulas by marriage, belonging to the small as well as to the larger-growing groups. The first in beauty, as in all-round merit, is *C. pulloeides*, whose history I cannot be quite sure of, though *pulla* is obviously one parent, and I should suspect *turbinata* of being the other. Any way, the plant is a most magnificent creation, a glorified *pulla*, twice the size of the original, forming a stout clump, and with flowers of the same marvellous violet silk (not *always*, I fear, trustworthy in winter, wild as the accusation seems for a plant of such parentage). Not only is *pulloeides* a first-rate grower, but it astonished me last season by setting a quantity of apparently sound seed. Now what, if anything, is likely to result? I used to think I had two forms of *pulloeides*, one from Kew, and one from a friend's garden. Of these the Kew plant appeared the better at first; but as soon as the other developed its character the two forms merged into one, and there was no longer either difference or superiority between them.

C. Hendersoni is a *carpatica* cross, throwing up great pyramids of shallow purple bells. I used to have the worst possible opinion of this plant as a miff, and its constitution had always appeared to me profoundly untrustworthy! (It evidently has biennial blood in it,— *Medium*, very likely.) However, this year I must make apology to it, at least as far as resisting power goes, for the plants are coming up as sturdily as ever from open, unprotected ground. But still, of course, remains the question whether *Hendersoni* will manage to survive, for once, its blooming stage, and prove that a plant which flowers and grows away may live to flower another day. And of this, I confess, I am still rather sceptical.

C. haylodgensis has *pusilla* and *carpatica* for parents, and has turned out a very easy, useful plant, with yellowish-green leaves, and innumerable pale blue bells in summer and autumn. Of similar race, I think, is *C. Profusion*, another late-blooming, beautiful hybrid, which, like *haylodgensis*, only comes on when *pusilla* has gone to rest, yet betrays the influence of *pusilla* in the bright blue colouring and the bell-shape of its flowers. For shady corners and ledges these two plants are simply invaluable, thriving anywhere, and looking after themselves,—*haylodgensis* being, of two excellent growers, perhaps the better, as far as pervasiveness and vigour goes, though the flowers of *Profusion* are, I fancy, just a trifle more graceful.

Pulla and *carpatica* give us another of the great hybrids in *Campanula G. F. Wilson*. This plant has quite as much merit as either of its parents, and I say this with a full sense of my candour and the plant's compelling beauty, for I have often felt harshly towards it, so frequently of late years has it been sent me instead of the true *Raineri*, or instead of my far more beloved little *turbinata*-form of *Raineri*. But *G. F. Wilson* is worthy of its name,—a lovely, vigorous little thing, running about all over the place like an even more vigorous *pulla*, and with shallow, semi-pendulous bells of soft violet with a paler centre, exactly intermediate between its parents, and only a little smaller and paler than those of the unrivalled *pulloeides*. There is, though, another form of *G. F. Wilson*, which ought to have lapsed from cultivation,—a feeble, golden-leaved affair, which is altogether unworthy of comparison with the better seedling,—the robust, little, greyish-leaved ramper that one means when one mentions *Campanula G. F. Wilson*.

Whether that potent gardener whose name it bears is the creator of *C. Stansfieldi* I cannot say; but the plant, anyhow, is a very notable thing. It makes no sort of effort to compete with the other hybrids in vigour, but contents itself with growing into a solid little, deciduous bush, of perfect health and perfect hardiness, and perfect good temper, in any cool, well-drained corner (preferably, I think, in shade of rock, where it comes stronger year by year). The parentage of the plant lies between *carpatica* and *tommasiniana*,—the growth is in all ways that of *tommasiniana*, but the stem-leaves are much broader, and the numerous flowers much larger, of a tapering bell-shape, shallowish and widely open,— suggesting a compromise between the roundness of *carpatica* and the narrow trumpet design of *tommasiniana*, while in colour they are of a soft vinous lilac not unlike those of *macrorhiza*. The plant, I believe, is still extremely rare, and little known. What, then, was the mixture of my feelings one day, when, as I have said, a very precious and long-looked for consignment of *C tommasiniana* turned out, one and all, to be nothing else than the even less common *Stansfieldi* !

In leaving the dwarf Campanulas for the larger-growing plants one reflection crosses my mind. We are passing from the section that (with the exception of the Southerners) will tolerate and even enjoy the shade, to a group which, for the most part, insists on exposure to sunheat on open banks. In the dwarf kinship only those that follow *barbata*, *garganica*, and *Raineri* insist on sunshine and heat. The rest are all happy among unsunned rocks. In the next group, with the exception of the *latifolia* cousinhood, all the species are plants of arid, sun-baked slopes, and may be treated accordingly, though they are seldom very exacting in the matter.

CHAPTER XI

The Greater Campanulas and their Relations

My collection of the larger Campanulas has recently been enriched by a friend's kindness with some very interesting things of which I must speak, though I cannot yet describe them, as they will only flower this season. These are the very rare true *Steveni* (the *Steveni dasycarpa* that I have had from St. Petersburg looks a *macrantha* seedling, whereas the true *Steveni* has long, narrowish, glossy leaves), a thrifty, beautiful alpine to be cultivated like *barbata*. Then comes *C. incurva*, which gives *Leutweini* as its synonym (Correvon's *Leutweini* being a biennial), *longistyla*, a species I can nowhere trace, though quite distinct, of course, from the annual *macrostyla*, and *raddeana*, a peculiarly attractive-looking thing so far, if its Harebell flowers rival its charming rosette of long-stalked heart-shaped crenulate leaves. *Laciniata* also is only a seedling with me, and, I am afraid, is biennial. *Sarmatica* is a fine species of the *barbata* kind, which I now have (the true plant, too, after many spurious ones), a goodly batch that promises to flower well this year. The same may be said of *americana*; as for *amabilis*, my one plant of this has made a great clump since last season in the open, and is already sending up six or seven good spikes. I was once promised, too, seed of a plant most barbarously named *C. chrysoflora*, but the promiser unfortunately died, and his executors or heirs had other views as to the disposal of this golden Campanula.

C. abietina makes mats of small, close, green foliage, and then throws up a multitude of rather tall, very slender, but stiff stems, with a few large, wide - open flowers, almost starry in shape, of a fine red-purple. The plant is perfectly easy, but requires attention, I think, in the way of dividing and top-dressing, and so forth. *Bononiensis* is another starry-flowered species, and so is our own rare native, *patula*. Neither of these appeals to me very strongly, though they are undoubtedly very useful and beautiful, producing flowers till far into the autumn, and seeding so abundantly that their tendency to be biennial is not really to be counted against them.

C. cristallocalyx I bought seed of, simply on account of its fascinating name. But, alas, though the calyx is certainly studded with curious little crystal bristles, the whole plant is very ineffective here,—a gawky, great *persicifolia*-form, with poor, small flowers huddled on the stems. *Persicifolia* itself, of course, is one of the best known, and probably the best, all-round garden Campanula, quite irresistible with its huge, yet graceful, blue bells, and its cheerful habit of seeding itself, as well as of growing on into fine clumps. The plant has even established itself here and there in England, so as to gain admittance to our Floras. There are innumerable varieties,—double, semi-double, Picotee-edged, white, *grandiflora, hermosa, Moerheimi,* and so forth. *Grandiflora* is the best, I think, gaining in size, and losing nothing in grace. For the doubles and semi-doubles I can feel no affection.

C. collina is a comparatively new comer from the Caucasus, and a plant in whose praise it would be very difficult to say enough, so perfectly hardy and thrifty and perennial it is, besides having a rare and brilliant loveliness even among Campanulas. It is of medium growth,

and finely downy all over, which makes one yet more
surprised at its indomitable good temper. The leaves
are greyish, stalked, and oval-pointed, while the flower-
stems rise to about a foot high, carrying each six to
ten pendulous blossoms, large, long, bell-shaped, and of
so glorious a silky violet that they rival those of *pulla*.
On a hot, rubbly, rubbishy bank, abandoned to colonies
of Campanula, *collina* is now sending up stronger clumps
than ever, nor do slugs seem to persecute him as they do
the downy-leaved dwarfs. In fact, the only fault I can
possibly find with *collina* is that his flowering season is
rather shorter than one could wish. Perhaps, though,
if one could dispense with his seed, and cut away his
flower-stems in mid-July, he might be persuaded to push
more in September or early October. Of the middle-
sized Harebells I would almost be bold enough to proclaim
that *collina* is out and away the best of all; *barbata* himself, for general purposes, would have to yield, were not
his own particular beauty, of those great pale bearded
bells, so distinct from the purple sheen of *collina*. And
yet, between Campanulas, who will dare to make preferences?

C. divergens, as I had it, was an obscure and rare plant
of biennial nature, which has since died out. *Sibirica* is
either another name or a variety of this; and, while I
have seen very inferior, worthless developments of *divergens*, which may, or may not, have been typical, my own
batch of seedlings all turned out extremely handsome,—
middle-sized, much-branched things, with innumerable
fine big purple flowers. Never since that first season,
though, have I had the same display, though last year a
self-sown mule of *divergens* flowered from between a chink
in the brickwork of the frames,—such a beautiful dwarf
thing, with *collina*, perhaps, for its other parent, a small
loose pyramid, with abundance of large violet blossoms.

SAXIFRAGA COTYLEDON, CAMPANULA PERSICIFOLIA ALBA AND
SILENE ALPESTRIS IN THE OLD GARDEN

But, alas, it was obviously biennial from the root, and entirely failed to set seed.   Other Campanulas that I am now growing on from seed are: *cervicaria, Argaei, tomentosa, cymbalaria, lingulata, reuteriana, caudata,* and *caucasica* (this last germinating with such prodigal generosity that surely it cannot be anything but a biennial?)   Yet Nicholson says nothing of any such fault, and, from his description, I most heartily hope my plants will go on well and faithfully, for his *caucasica* is starred as a beautiful thing.

Of *C. michauxioeides* I expect to have news again this season, after a blank year or two.   It is a very handsome species, but monocarpous, with rounded leaves, on long, thin stalks, and very tall spikes of tiny, airy flowers. However, with these exotic Campanulas, it is never perfectly certain to my mind whether death after flowering is so absolutely inevitable as is generally thought.   At least I have had one startling exception to all accepted rules, which has very much shaken my convictions on the point.

C. elegans and *C. pulcherrima* are two rather obscure species.   Correvon makes *pulcherrima* a synonym of *peregrina,* whose description in Nicholson my plants answer closely.   *Elegans* is almost indistinguishably near it, and is sometimes very wickedly known as *speciosa,* — like half a dozen other Campanulas, including *glomerata,* that have no shadow of right to the name.   And both *elegans* and *pulcherrima* only differ horticulturally from our own beautiful weed *rapunculoeides,* in being a trifle less rampant and invasive.   They form dense clumps, sending up tall spikes of many graceful, bright purple bells, like those of *rapunculoeides;* but the roots travel less underground, and are more bent on concentrating into a mass than on occupying as much territory as possible.   However, they are both terrors for seeding, which *rapunculoeides* is not ; and, altogether, beautiful as they are, all three, they are far too vigorous and greedy for admittance anywhere near choice beds. Magnificent, indeed, for wild shrubby places, I have had, at last, to banish them from the near neighbourhood of the New Garden, though, in the Old, I take advantage of their capacity for growing outrageously where other things will not even survive. Needless to say I had *elegans* and *pulcherrima* from seed, lured on by their seductive names, of which, to speak the hard, chill truth, I do not think that they are conspicuously worthy. Such splendid epithets must be very well justified, if they are not to annoy, and I feel that *elegans* and *pulcherrima* do not deserve superlatives of admiration, while far finer species are fobbed off with a mere personal remark, abrupt, inadequate, and cold,—*barbata, pulla, collina.*

C. grandiflora (*Platycodon*) is the great Japanese Balloon Flower, a splendid thing, with glaucous leaves, and immense bloated-looking balls of bluish violet. *Mariesi,* a dwarfer, neater form, is the one most prevalent in cultivation, I think, with a charming white variety. And this year I am expecting flowers from my seedling of *Platycodon minimus,* an even smaller form, quite minute, so far, in development. All these Platycodons are easy plants for the rock-garden ; but slugs or mice, or some abomination of the sort, take undue pleasure in them ; and they must also be put where they will run no risk of excessive damp in winter, for their fleshy masses rot off rather easily at the neck, if any stagnant moisture or fat wet soil hangs heavy round them in the resting season. They are gorgeous in blossom, and endure till very late in the season, unless the weather spoils them. They make the Meibuts', or special autumn spectacle, on certain Japanese moors, and are as common in classical legend and poem as rose or violet in ours.

C. glomerata is a native, not uncommon in the Southern Counties, but valuable for the garden, especially in some of its varietal developments. Notably quaint is *glomerata acaulis*, a dwarf freak, with a huddle of violet clusters, sitting close on the tuft of robust-looking downy leaves. In the type-form the flowers are carried in a head at the top of stems about a foot high or more; and in the variety very wrongfully called *speciosa* or, better, *dahurica*, the clusters are larger, more frequent on the stem, and of a most gorgeous brilliant violet, which is the more valuable that it appears in autumn when all the other Campanulas, except *macrorhiza*, are gone.

C. lanata is also known as *velutina* and *althaeoeides*, an extremely rare and precious plant, so wonderfully attractive that it breaks down all my wise rules of abstention from Southerners or heat-loving monocarpous kinds. And *C. lanata*, I think, understands my affection, and, in part reciprocates it, for I have had a good deal of very unexpected success with this difficult species; at least, to flower it well in the open in West Yorkshire, and then to get good seed, is surely something to be pleased at? *C. lanata* is a rock-plant of rock-plants, inhabiting rock-fissures in the blazing gneiss cliffs of Rhilo and Rhodope, whence it is almost impossible to pluck its great fleshy root-stocks. You have only to look at the plant to see what a sun-lover it is. For the big rounded leaves are hairy and flannel-like, to absorb every scrap of moisture that the air may hold, in the plant's certainty that no surface moisture will ever afflict it or damp it off or rot it at the neck. Both these dreadful things occur to it in an English rock-garden, unless you are very careful indeed, and put it where every ray of sun can be focussed on it, with no danger of rain mouldering the downy foliage, or damp in the soil clogging round the neck or root. It is hard to import, too, as any life-preserving humidity is liable to rot the leaves to such an extent that the plant finds it difficult to recover. However, many plants from my importations survived, and I can proclaim *C. lanata* as well worth all the trouble she requires. The flower-spikes are short and sturdy-branched, and gracefully bowed; the blossoms, which M. Correvon describes as greenish, are far more lovely than such an epithet seems to foretell; for my plants were never greenish at all, but the large hairy bells were of a most delicate primrose-saffron, tinged, in one lovely specimen, with a gentle pink. And then, having flowered, the plant is supposed to die. It has an entirely monocarpous reputation and appearance. No one would ever doubt that it must die after blooming and seeding, nor should I dare to entertain or insinuate a hesitation on the point, had not my pot-plants, after flowering and producing sound seed last year, astonished everybody beyond measure by quite refusing to expire; now they are sending up sturdy green growths, which look perfectly trustworthy, at the side of the old withered ones. As for the seed, it is now so busy germinating that I ought to have a goodly batch before long of *C. lanata* in a hardier, home-bred strain.

Of the only other difficult yellow Campanula I have no such pleasant tale to tell. *C. petraea* is the very rare western counterpart of *C. lanata*, a woolly-leaved saxatile creature, occurring only, I fancy, in the Vallée de l'Esteron in the Maritime Alps. The plant is a very stout, vigorous grower in cultivation, far too rampageous-rooting to be happy in a pot, with heart-shaped, downy grey leaves. and stocky spikes, which differ from those of *lanata* in being unbranched and much less graceful than the bending lines of the Rhilo Campanula; while the flowers of *petraea*, small, and of a dullish yellow-green, are carried at the top of the stem in a dense crowded head, like those of *glomerata*. *Petraea* dies after flowering, and is no very appalling loss, whether it seeds or not. My only plant is rooting about on the rockwork now, and looking quite happy, but I am resolved not to bother any more about cosseting it up in pots.

A far more valuable biennial Campanula with yellow flowers is the far commoner *C. thyrsoidea*, with big rosettes of long, narrow, hairy leaves, and sturdy, very dense spikes of crowded straw-coloured flowers, which have the very uncommon advantage among the Campanulas, of a sweet, delicate fragrance. *C. thyrsoidea* is a limestone plant entirely, but is quite easy to grow anywhere, I believe, on any sunny slope, though seed should always be looked for after flowering, if the plant is to be perpetuated. *C. spicata* is very close indeed to *C. thyrsoidea*, so close, indeed, that at Kew they intermarried of their own accord. Possibly *spicata* is only a granite or gritstone variant of *thyrsoidea*, the growth being almost indistinguishable, and the spike only differing in being, perhaps, a little narrower and more cat's-tailish in shape. The serried flowers, however, are of a bright purple, and the plant is as perfectly biennial as *thyrsoidea*, and as easy to grow.

To conclude the yellow-flowering species, as far as they are known to me, I will take *C. punctata*. Whether or no this is simply a varietal form of *nobilis*, I cannot say; but anyhow it is a valuable and very free-growing Japanese plant, with long, heart-shaped hairy leaves, and few-flowered spikes of big pendulous cream-coloured bells, hairy and spotted inside. I collected it from the track-side over the pass from Shoji down to Yoka-Ichiba on the Fujikawa, and now it roots about quite happily underground in sunny light soil, sending up its slight rosettes at will. There is also a *rosea* form which I grow and think very pretty, almost as delightful as the pink-tinged *lanata*. The one thing to be careful about in

establishing *punctata* is to get sound, well-rooted plants.
It is not always easy to start the plant; though, once
started, it makes haste to show itself quite at home. The
best place for these pendent flowered Campanulas is high
up on the rockwork where one can see the full beauty of
their blossoms without grovelling. The true *nobilis*, if
there be a distinct *nobilis*, I have never had, though now
a purple *punctata* has just arrived from Japan, and is
probably Nicholson's *nobilis*.

C. Medium is our common and garden Canterbury Bell
in its primitive form. And to this, I am convinced,
belongs a certain lovely purple-belled spire that I collected seed of years ago in the Maritime Alps. The plant
turns out quite biennial, but very free and self-helpful
about seeding, as well as remarkably pretty. I have
tried to hybridise it, and now seedlings are fast coming
towards the flowering state. What they will turn out,
' quien sabe ? ' as poor Queen Mary said ; so far they look
painfully like true-born *Medium* babies. Another very
fine big Bell-flower here is *C. lactiflora*, whose identity
with *celtidifolia* I see that M. Correvon denies. Whatever
my plant may be, *lactiflora* is a singularly inadequate
name; for the great flattish flower-heads are of a soft
electric blue, varying towards white. My *lactiflora* is an
immense stout plant, often biennial (but by no means
invariably), and when one sees its five-foot leafy stems,
with their crowns of blossom, it is almost impossible to
believe that the whole thing has developed in a few
months. Yet so it is ; *lactiflora* gives me no trouble at
all ; he flowers profusely, and then, by October, when the
heads are dry and sere, I smash them about with a stick,
and take no more thought for the morrow, knowing that
all will be well. And surely, as soon as April is in, up come
the seedlings all over the place, and, by August are five feet
high or so, with great heads of blue or greyish flowers.

C. latifolia is our own native giant Bell-flower, the best of all big Campanulas for a damp shady place where no choice things can suffer from his invasions. *Eriocarpa*, which I am raising from seed, is only a synonym, or, at best, a variety of *latifolia,* and *macrantha* is a very fine improvement on the type, less obstreperous in growth, but rather taller, with larger, darker bells. *Burghaltii* and *Van Houttei* owe, I am persuaded, a share in their existence to *latifolia.* They are both extremely valuable plants, very close together, and mainly differing in the flowers, which in *Burghaltii* are pale purple, and in *Van Houttei* are of a richer shade. They are small-growing, neat hybrids, with rather slender but stiff stems, about a foot or eighteen inches high, each bearing a few enormous pendulous bells, rather narrower and longer than those of *latifolia*; though this distinction may be merely apparent, owing to their frailer growth and more modest leafage. All these Bell-flowers are delightful for any rockwork or border, perfectly hardy and thrifty. *C. versicolor* is a recent introduction from the Levant. I have not got it, and shan't get it. It is biennial, and, to my taste, rather coarse and ugly, with a good deal of hispid leaf and stem, and undistinguished, smallish, starry flowers in two tones of blue.

C. nitida takes us back almost to the alpine section. This species rarely grows more than a foot high at the most, with rosettes of shining leaves, and stiff loose little spikes of very large flattish flowers of a clear blue or a rich pure white. *Planiflora* is a synonym, and the plant is charming for a cool corner of the rockwork, perfectly hardy and easy to grow, though very slow to spread. To my mind, it is like a minute and infinitely prettier form of *C. pyramidalis,* the vast Chimney Bell-flower that so many people so greatly admire; a fine, huge, showy thing, yes, with its big glossy rosettes and its six or seven-foot spires of flattened flowers. But to me it says nothing. The gawkiness of the stems annoys me, and the mean, spasmodic manner in which the flowers sit tight upon them and open one by one, here and there, in a disorderly, anarchistic sort of way, a few at the bottom and a few at the top, and a few scattered about among the rest for no obvious reason. So the plant has no place either in my garden or my affections, though I dutifully confess that it is very useful for a corner of the rockwork, where, it is true, I still have one old plant, which blooms every year, and makes me feel that I ought to like it much better than I do. *Grandis* seems between this and *persicifolia*.

Take a silverless rosette of *Saxifraga Cotyledon*; stick into it a rather small-flowered pale-blue Canterbury Bell spike, and you will then have *C. mirabilis*, that most ancient of all Campanulas, a plant almost geologic in its antiquity, of which only one specimen has ever been discovered, and that with only one sound capsule of seed. But *C. mirabilis* has now taken a new lease of life, and, for so hoary a patriarch, is now showing himself almost skittishly robust in gardens. When M. Correvon first introduced the plant to cultivation from the solitary capsule found on the solitary specimen that Alboff collected in the Caucasus, the plant was ushered in with a mighty blowing of trumpets, and an escort of highly-wrought advertisements. Consequently, since that day, there has been a reaction, and we are a little disposed to underrate *C. mirabilis*, in apology to ourselves for the extravagant way in which we overrated it on the first appearance. Say that the plant is frankly monocarpous, and you have said the one bad thing that can be said against *C. mirabilis*; otherwise it has no shortcoming, even if it be not the unsurpassable miracle and *ne plus ultra* of excellence that its introducers made us take it for. But their rhapsodies have damaged the plant's reputation; and now the really remarkable loveliness of these pyramids of great pale blue bells hanging above the glossy rosette is not nearly as generously appreciated as it ought to have been, and would have been, if our expectations had not been so artificially inflated. Such are the evils of advertisement that even now I can never worship *C. mirabilis* in a spirit of unreserved enthusiasm; I am always haunted by the dream - *mirabilis* of our first raptures — a beauty that never was on land or sea, but which nevertheless makes one's inmost heart still say, ' Oh yes, *Campanula mirabilis*, very pretty and charming, of course, but not *quite* as wonderful as one had expected. A charming, rather overrated thing.' Poor *mirabilis*, this is so unjust; and the plant is so good too; it does its best, grows quite happily in any well-drained chink, and flowers profusely and makes us abundance of sound seed, does everything in its power to mollify us and make us forget our first wild predispositions, and take a beautiful plant on its own naked, unadorned, but pre-eminent merits.

C. speciosa has been made to lend its name to innumerable impostors, but the real plant is a marvel of splendour. I used to think it a little alpine; now I know better. Imagine a great hirsute rosette a yard across or more, with a foot or more of stiff solid spike, heavily hung with large pale-purple Canterbury Bells. There you have *C. speciosa*, that rare and difficult rock-plant, as it can be grown in a hot heavy loam on an ordinary bank. M. Correvon approximates this species to *Allioni*, but I have found it very different in every way, not only in size and height, but also in the far greater robustness of its temperament. It is the limestone substitute, in the Cevennes and Pyrenees, for *C. barbata*, which, though not at all irreconcileable, is not by original choice a limestone plant. *Speciosa* infallibly dies after flowering, but sets abundance of excellent seed, which germinates with the

laudable profusion shown by so many of these rare monocarpous people. I have grown him and flowered him
superbly, too, in an American peat corner, as well as in
loam, so that, for general amiability he stands as high as
for beauty.   My list of genuine Campanulas closes here
with the common, easy-going meadow-plant, *C. rhom-
boidalis*, and its white form—like big, leafy, stiff Harebells from Swiss pastures, thriving anywhere, anyhow, in
any soil, and remarkably gorgeous in their display.

With *Wahlenbergia* and *Edraianthus* we go back
into the region of dwarf alpines.   To *Wahlenbergia*
are assigned, nowadays, our native *C. hederacea*, and my
own particular delight, *E. serpyllifolius*. However, one
may still continue to call the one *Campanula* and the
other *Edraianthus* without fear of any but an extreme
purist's correction.   The Campanula runs about among
the long grass in marshes of Wales and the West—a
most dainty wee trailer, with pale, ivy-like little leaves,
and very frail, airy flower - stems, each carrying one
brilliant blue bell, bright but tiny.   This delightful
plant I have always found impossible hitherto to establish. I rather fancy, though, it resented being planted
in naked ground, with no coarse growths to ramp among.
So now, having nursed up a fine specimen, I am going,
with good hopes of success, to put him out in a wild wet
place where he will have to look out for himself and
make his own way about through the weeds.   He is
found on the southern side of this valley, but I myself
have only seen him among the bogs of North Wales,
round Capel Curig.

Edraianthus serpyllifolius stands very high on the list
of the six most indispensable indispensables.   Nicholson
calls him *Campanula serpyllifolia*, and the R.H.S. gave
my notable *major* form an award as *Wahlenbergia serpyllifolia*. However I will stick, if I may, to *Edraianthus*,

and, in what I say must be understood to be speaking, not of the ordinary plant, but of the very extra special variety that strayed into my hands seven years ago, and is now to be numbered by many thousands. *E. serpyllifolius major* came to me as typical *serpyllifolius* from a famous nursery, and it was not for some time that I was persuaded that the thing really deserved a rank of its own. Then at last I realised that my plant's unusual brilliancy could not be accounted for either by culture or climate, and that it must be, in fact, an extra-fine variety of the type. The plant is a Dalmatian, and, as far as I have seen the type exhibited, is smaller and paler in the bloom than my own treasure. This, in any comfortable chink of the rock-work, with depth of good, light, rather rich soil, and plenty of sun and air, makes a loose mat of little thyme - leaved purple - stemmed branches, which all lie about on the ground, or drop in a fringe over the edges of the rock. Then, in June, every branchlet produces one enormous bell - shaped flower, upturned cheerfully to look you in the face, and, in colour, of a most gorgeous brilliant violet, as silky as, but even more luminous and vivid than, those of *Campanula pulla* or *Campanula collina*. No other plant —I think I can say this in cold blood—is quite so wildly floriferous, and, quite certainly, no plant in the garden is more beautiful, more fascinating, or more perfectly robust in health. In any decent treatment the plant goes on and thrives imperturbably without fuss or protection, looking after itself serenely from year to year, and for ever growing stronger. The flowering period, worse luck, is not very long, but while it lasts, every one who has seen the imperial purple splendour of my Temple exhibits can bear me witness that the spectacle is one of quite unsurpassed magnificence. This praise is fair; 'magnificence' is the essential quality of this

E. serpyllifolius major; the claim can be made for very few other alpines;—brilliance, purity, exquisiteness, vividness, yes, but just that solemn opulence of the Edraianthus is almost impossible to match, though we may allow a good share of it to *Rosa alpina, Viola pedata bicolor, Primula decora* and the Campanulas *pulla* and *collina.*

E. pumilio has come at last to rank near *Eritrichium* as the test of wise and fortunate cultivation. The plant is very dwarf and neat; a Dalmatian, loving rocks in the sun, and forming small, close mats of spiny-looking, bright silver little shoots, each one of which ends in a big upturned bell of pale purple. But why the plant is generally found so difficult I cannot say. Probably my climate is particularly favourable to these small alpine Campanulas, for they all show a wonderful alacrity here, which makes me believe my cultivation to be lucky, seeing that I dare not claim that it has any special wisdom. In any case *E. pumilio* has never given me any difficulty at all. I have it in ordinary soil in a very hot place high on a choice ledge, where, between the Saxifrages *media* and *Ferdinandi-Coburgi*, it has grown into a goodly solid little clump; and again in the moraine, where it is quite as vigorous, though rather closer and smaller in growth. In both places the plant is heavily top-dressed each season with lime-rubble, through which covering its silver-green shoots pierce bravely and rejoicingly, turning to their lovely silver as they get ripe. *E. pumiliorum* is, to me, a rather larger, looser, less silvery, less beautiful *pumilio*, untidy in growth, and in no way to be compared with *pumilio*, though I am told that it is more amenable in general cultivation. But as I (and, I am sure, many others, fortunate in soil and climate) have found nothing in the world more amenable than the lovely *pumilio* itself, why bother about its inferior relations? Of the other

species of Edraianthus (I shrink from saying 'Edraian-
thuses') none captivate my fancy. As far as I know
dalmaticus, *graminifolius* and *tenuifolius*, they are not
particularly beautiful or, at least, not particularly choice
or brilliant plants, making rosettes of leaves (large and
slug-beloved in *dalmaticus*), with drooping stems that
each carry a close dense head of purple bells. This is
a great change from the neat single-flowered loveliness
of *serpyllifolius* and *pumilio* ; and, to these demerits is
added a rather presumptuous objection to winter-wet,
with a tendency to rot away at the neck on any excuse.
It is all very well for a rare and haughty seven-and-
sixpenceworth, fresh from Thibet, to affect these airs
and graces, but they are intolerable presumption in
common little plants of no especial beauty or charm.

Phyteuma comosum is a most weird thing from North
Italian cliff-faces in the limestone, a fleshy-rooted species,
with clumps of crenulated, round, greenish-black leaves,
and then, sitting among them, great solid heads of what
can only be described as small purple soda-water bottles
with their nozzles all turned outwards and a long feeler
protruding ; the plant has a rather bad reputation as a
grower, I fancy, though I cannot understand why. It
is quite successful here, even in the Old Garden, where
it has taken possession of a chink all to itself, and,
whatever the winter may have been, perks up again
quite happily in the spring without any care. Slugs,
however, look on this plant as we look on oysters, and
would, I believe, crawl a mile to destroy a leaf of it ;
so that in this direction, at least, the plant does need
special care. The only other preferences that *Phyteuma
comosum* seems to have is for good drainage, lime, and
such a position that it will have plenty of root-room,
but no clogging weight of moisture at the neck.

Phyteuma pauciflorum, *Ph. hemisphericum* and **Ph.**

humile are dwarf high alpines from the upper and uppermost pastures, *pauciflorum*, I think, being the earliest found. In growth they make a wiry little tuft of narrow leaves with a few three- or four-inch stems, each carrying a head of bottle-shaped deep-blue flowers. I once found a white form of *pauciflorum* above Meiden, and collected him with the great difficulty attendant on the removal of these little alpines, with their immense straggle of roots. Last year he throve in a high hot place on the rock-work. But he has not yet appeared this season, and I cannot tell whether he still lives, though I have no reason, except a gardener's habitual diffidence, to think he is doing otherwise. And, of these little Phyteumas, *pauciflorum* is immeasurably the prettiest, with far larger flowers, more bloated and more brilliant in every way than anything attempted by the others. But I do not think he is common in cultivation, and I certainly have had more trouble about establishing him—even if I have succeeded—than anything ever cost me by the far worse-reputed *comosum*.

CHAPTER XII

Primula

For the most part, Alpine Primulas are not such climbers as other rock-plants. They begin lower down, and rarely go up to the glaciers. They are fully alpine, indeed, but prefer the lowest limit of the alpine region, hanging in curtains and cushions among mossy rocks where the sun is rare or not too violent. One's first glimpse of *Primula viscosa* edging a shady boulder is one's first blessed sign that one is getting up out of the shrubby sub-alpine level to the realm of wide open spaces and stony lands of botanical promise. *Viscosa*, too, is a good little companion; it bears one company for a long way up the mountain-side, grows stunted and wizened as it goes, and finally deserts one with the last traces of grass. But the Primulas, though never, or rarely, plants of the open stony deserts, are true rock plants. They clamour for cliffs to root into, and deep rich crevices into which to dig their enormously long roots. As for the question of sun or shade in cultivation, it is impossible, of course, to speak dogmatically, but I have a notion that the species with smooth, coriaceous, leathery leaves, like *P. clusiana* and *P. calycina*, will bear a great deal more sun than the less glossy-leaved almost viscid sorts such as *Allioni* and the rare true *spectabilis*. I know, though I have never collected it, that *P. clusiana*, takes basting heat in its rocks above Como; on that fact, among others, I base my guess, and in cultivation have found it answer. But I must at once confess that I have not seen many of the species *in situ*. Primula is a very scattered race; each mountain district may have, perhaps, two or three ruling species; then, to find the others you have to wander over vast alpine chains, and search all the other districts. Certain kinds, *viscosa*, *farinosa*, *Auricula*, are, of course, almost universal; but the rarer kinds have each a limited range. Besides the common ones, I have only collected *marginata* and *graveolens* (*latifolia*),—in the Maritime Alps. But, wherever I have found Primulas, it has always been on more or less shady cliffs that they have been most luxuriant (I am not talking now of *farinosa* and the marsh - loving section, only of the typically rock species). But it must be borne in mind that shade in the rarefied pure atmosphere of the high mountain region is very different from the same amount of shade in the damp-clogged air of a lowland garden. In cultivation, all Primulas will take a little more sun than they choose in nature, though they always retain a disapproval of torrid heat. Another thing too I find they hate, is the rain that washes away the soil from their chinks. Add to that, they are the worst of all alpines for lifting out of the ground in winter. When spring at last arrives, you will probably find all your cherished plants lying about on their heads, with silly great white roots flaunting in the air. They all, it follows, want stern, squashy planting and a good-top-dressing as soon as 'the season of snows and sins' is over. Beyond this, and with a few exceptions, I cannot say I have found the Alpine Primulas cross-grained in nature. For one thing, this climate, damp and fresh, with its cool, pure mountain air, is exactly what the mountain species love; besides which, the fat soil they are in suits most of them. This reminds me—as to soil—every one

JANKAEA HELDREICHI

must buy his own experience. Some Primulas are lime-lovers, others peat-lovers; but with me, neither section seems to have any very violent views on the point; good loam, with or without peat, and plenty of stone about them, and perfect drainage seem to give them all satisfaction. It must never be forgotten that they detest being splashed about and messed and upset by torrential rains in winter, and that the downy-leaved species, like all the woolly-leaved alpines, get exceedingly annoyed if their foliage remains long in contact with cold, sodden earth; so that, though I never glaze them over here, some such treatment might help them elsewhere. A rock-crevice with deep, deep rooting-room, and the least possible amount of soil-surface, will always be the most pleasant treatment for the rocky Primulas.

Of course there are many kinds and many sections, all of which I must treat of, so that the foregoing comments are only meant to apply to the cliff-haunting species such as *viscosa* and *graveolens*. And now, before I go on to deal with the race individually, I must stop to pour out my wail for the deficiencies of our experience. There are many very worshipful Primulas in cultivation already. The family dwells right across the world in all the great mountain-ranges of Europe and temperate Asia, and our gardens are stocked with delightful kinds from all the European ranges and the Caucasus. But what, Ah what, of the very focus of the race? For Primula seems to have its central radiating point on the northern and the southern face of the Himâlya; and, great as the beauty may be of our Lombard or Austrian Primulas, they fade and pale before the countless gorgeous little species that dwell all over the great slopes which lead the Himâlya gently down through Yunnan to Ichang. Here is the very Paradise of Primula. Here they are indeed high alpines, going right up to the last limit of vegetation,

where *concinna* makes patches of rubies on the ultimate moraines, and *rosea* bursts through the very ice.
Their very names cast a spell of longing :—*pulchra, bella,
concinna, sapphirina*, Lady Pretty, Lady Lovely, Lady
Dainty, Lady Sapphire ; to say nothing of all the others
that we hear of, and, apparently, so vainly yearn for;
soldanelloeides, glacialis, calliantha, yunnanensis,—it seems
as if their discoverers had wickedly named them for our
especial torment.   Who, *who* will procure us these jewels ?
Let us promise him a statue at Wisley, and a new
Primrose Day.

Some of these outlandish people we already have, indeed,
though their loveliness only makes us long the more for
their unknown kindred ; and year by year, new ones are
slowly introduced.   Veitch has some rather uninteresting species, *Veitchi, vittata, reflexa*, poorish Capitatas and
Sieboldis, and a hideous black-brown one, called I think,
tangutica.   Then there was the gorgeous orange-coloured
cockburniana, which I am only just trying, and the very
beautiful *pulverulenta*, which is practically only a mealy
form of *japonica*.   In telling of the Primulas we grow,
it is so difficult to arrange them in sections, that I think
I may as well treat them alphabetically.

P. Allioni very properly heads the list (Allion, whoever he may have been, seems to have a monopoly of
extra difficult plants).   If you can keep *Allioni* happy,
you need be in no anxiety about its many cousins.   *Allioni*
is a rare and dying species, found inside rocky hollows
and unsunned caverns in the valleys above Mentone.   It
is very small-growing, making wee little cushions of its
downy rosettes, flat upon which lie, in their season, the
abundant big rosy flowers, large as a shilling, with a white
eye.   It is a wonderfully beautiful little plant, and bears the
reputation, not unjustly as far as my experience goes, of
being a perfect little devil to cultivate.   Absence of sun

and absence of surface moisture are its two first demands,
and then if you satisfy those, it very soon finds some other
fault with you and expires. In pots, on the other hand,
I have always found it quite amenable and good-tempered.
It is worth any amount of trouble, but luckily, it has a
twin brother, so like as to be indistinguishable, called
tyrolensis, which is as cheerful to deal with as *Allioni* is
captious. The two plants are but geographical forms of
the one species, probably, but a world of difference lies
between their temperaments.

P. Auricula is too well known to need description.
But why is it not more grown? Has the existence of
the many beautiful hybrid Auriculas driven out of
people's minds that radiant loveliness of the type, with
its whitened leaves and its flowers of that true pure
yellow which is so very rarely seen. It is precisely that
rich clear colour which is the Imperial yellow of the
Chinese Court, and which I last saw in the palanquin
that was conveying the Empress Dowager to the railway
station in Peking. *Auricula* is as easy as a cabbage,
almost; and so is a very beautiful hybrid of it which
I have grown for years as *decora*, bearing big flower-
heads of a lovely deep blue-violet. *Balbisi, similis,
Obristi,* and *bellunensis* are, most likely, local forms or
seedlings of *Auricula*, differing mainly in their slightly
different shades of yellow, for *Auricula* varies freely, and
even *decora* has given me some splendid forms from seed
—a few very pale and poor, but others of an even richer
violet than the type, and some of a lovely art-nouveau
paleness specially beloved of M. Correvon.

P. calycina. This is one of the easiest and the loveliest of the rock-haunting Primulas, and it is the type of
so many others that I will only name them as I go—
*carniolica, glaucescens, clusiana, integrifolia, intermedia,
murettiana, serrata* (this is not the true plant), *wulfeni-*

ana. All these make tufts of more or less shining, leathery, pointed foliage, and bear loose flower-heads of the most brilliant big pink and purple blooms. They are among the most attractive of alpines when once you have surmounted any objection you may have to that faint suspicion of magenta or excessive blue that mars the pure colour in so many of them. Very few of them escape it, and none that I know of the rocky section. But a bank of *P. clusiana*, as I once saw it at Kew, with its huge bright rosy-lilac blossoms, is a very great joy. *Clusiana*, while, to my mind, the loveliest of this group, is not (with me, at least) quite the easiest. In the open I have only just begun to suit it. I suspect it will tolerate more sun than I can bring to bear. *Murettiana* is the smallest of these Primulas, belonging, together with its other little brilliant cousins, *flörkeana*, *juribella*, *daonensis*, *dinyana*, and *portenschlagiana*, to that great group of hybrids which ranges between *viscosa* and the Calycinas, or *viscosa* and *minima*.

These little people are not at all less beautiful or less amiable than their parents, and their colours are, as a rule, lighter than the rich crimson purples of *calycina* and *carniolica*. *P. spectabilis*, with its variety *Kitaibelii*, stands rather out of the group, but must be treated here, as *wulfeniana* is described as a form of it, only differing in the more pointed leaves. *Spectabilis*, as its tempting name tells you, is an extremely beautiful species. It is also extremely rare, and rather hard to grow. Hitherto *calycina* or *intermedia* has always been sent me for *spectabilis*. I have only had the genuine thing for a couple of seasons, and so cannot tell much about its ways, except that it seems to be thriving in a very rich leaf-mouldy soil, with plenty of broken crock, sharp sand, and elaborate drainage underneath. It makes large rosettes of rounded leaves, with the usual brilliant pink blossoms. *Glutinosa* is another rare difficult species which properly comes here, being the parent of *P. flörkeana.* It is a strange species, frequenting marshy places above Gastein, and bearing narrow leaves with rather small, almost blue flowers. It stands alone among European Primulas in this merit, which would be greater if it could ever be induced to produce these flowers in cultivation. I have grown it now for many years, and I have never seen a blossom yet. Taken as a whole, this group of rocky Primulas, together with the secondary group of hybrids between *minima* or *viscosa,* make up about as brilliant and easy-going a family as you will easily find.

That well-known plant, *P. cashmeriana,* brings us into another section, of which *denticulata* is the recognised type. These species produce rosettes of large, primrose-like crinkled leaves, and then send up stout stalks carrying round heads of lilac flowers. These species are all robust, and, to my mind, rather coarse, and lacking in appeal. They are very showy and fine early in the year, and imposing in their luxuriance. *Denticulata* is the most grown; its flowers are, generally, more numerous, smaller, and duller in tone than those of *cashmeriana,* whose attractions are further enhanced by a lovely golden meal that covers the underside of the leaves. Both *denticulata* and *cashmeriana* vary endlessly in tone and brilliancy, and, of course, there are some truly beautiful forms to be found amongst them, especially among the seedlings of what is called *cashmeriana grandiflora hybrida.* But the section contains one unexpected jewel (to say nothing of the wee, wee bright blue *sapphirina* of the Himâlya) in *P. capitata.* This, like *sapphirina* and *denticulata,* is a Himâlyan. Its foliage is grey with meal, and resembles, afar off, an enlarged rosette of *farinosa.* Then, in autumn, or late summer, if you please—not spring—up comes a powder-white stem, carrying a globular head of bloom. But such bloom! A pure deep violet-blue, contrasting with the grey and whiteness of the plant in a most satisfying way. *P. capitata*, unfortunately, has a bad reputation. That deadly word, 'biennial,' is whispered against it. Perhaps our cool mountain air may have something to do with it, but, all I can say is, not only do I find *P. capitata* one of the easiest of all my Primulas, but I also find it a most trustworthy and hearty perennial. How well I remember astonishing Mr. Wolley-Dod with the news that I then had a four-year-old clump of *capitata* that went on improving from year to year. That same specimen lived to be seven. Now, on the rock-work in the New Garden, I have a great slope of old plants that are a glory in September. It can be well raised from seed, too, though it does not vary like the others. However, out of one batch I did rear a plant of far greater vigour than the others, two seasons ago. That individual proved no less superior in flower than in growth. His babies are now growing on, so that I hope I may in time perpetuate this large, vigorous form of the species. All the *denticulata* group love rich, cool, moist corners, except *capitata*, which, I believe, prefers a well-drained slope in some sound light soil. There is a white form of *denticulata* now, and a ruby form, not to mention a dwarf and a bluish variety. Then there is a big-flowered pale one called *J. Boyd*, which beats all the others into fits. Its history I do not know; it seems rare, and I only possess one plant—planted on a choice bank where its round heads and big, pale lavender flowers appear very early in the season.

P. cortusoeides is the typical wild Japanese species, the parent of the many fancy varieties known as *P. Sieboldi*, which take endless varieties of size and colour.

To this section belongs also *P. Veitchi*, and, probably, for
gardening purposes, those two tiny gems, *P. Reidi* and *P.
Reini*. *Reidi* is from the Himâlya, whence also in time
we may perhaps hope for its other kin, *uniflora*, *soldanelloeides*, and the rest; *Reini* is from the Japanese Alps.
All of this group have stalked, crinkled, downy, deciduous foliage, in texture resembling those of a primrose, and in shape, very roughly, an ivy leaf; the flowers
are not very numerous, but of truly enormous size and
exquisite brilliancy. *Reini* is, I believe, unknown, and I
dared not at first believe it to be distinct from the white-
starred *Reidi*, but, after all, *Reidi* I knew existed, and
there seemed no reason why Rein should not have had a
Primula named after him just as well as Reid. *Reidi* I
have cautiously cultivated in pots, but of *Reini* I have
just had such a delightfully promising importation that
I am now planting it out freely in rich, well-drained soil,
carefully made for this and a few other treasures. It turns
out a real jewel, too, this tiny Japanese, only a couple
of inches high or so, with a tuft of wee, crinkly, stalked
leaves, and then one or two very large pink flowers. As
for *cortusoeides*, *amoena*, *Veitchi*, *Sieboldi*, and the larger
varieties generally, any well-nourished soil, not wind-
swept, will please them, and they'll grow happily even in
a border. Only it must be remembered that they die
clean down in late summer, so that one has to be careful
about noting where they are. In Japan you see *Sieboldi*
with its—yes, magenta-crimson—flowers hanging over
every alpine rock as the train carries you northwards
towards Aomori on your way to the Hokkaido.

P. cottia is a very rare little treasure belonging to the
group of *viscosa*, which accordingly I will now take in
hand. The Viscosas are the easiest, for the most part,
of all the rocky Primulas, and among the most lovely.
Their one drawback is that mice and slugs share my

views as to their attractiveness. *Viscosa*, I have said,
makes curtains over all the big mossy boulders as you
pass up towards the Alps above. It forms perfect sheets
of downy rosettes (the leaves oval, light-green, toothed),
and then, on short stems, carries one to five big rose-lilac
flowers with a white eye, sometimes clear and sometimes
blurred. *Cottia, pedemontana, ciliata, helvetica, Portae,
balfouriana, pubescens*, are hardly distinguishable, from
the gardener's point of view. They are all much alike,
and each as charming and desirable as the other,
differing mainly in shades of colours and botanical
particularities, *cottia* being frilled, and *pedemontana*
having pretty little round flowers. Of *viscosa* itself,
too, there are colour-variations, while *ciliata* has—(some
of these names, of course, are even synonymous with
others, so much need is there of a firm hand to straighten
out nurserymen's complicated dealings with Primula)—
ciliata has a purple and a scarlet variety, *purpurea* and
coccinea, which are as lovely as they are rare. Crowning
the whole section stands the plant which gardeners
(again!) have, with a superfluity of naughtiness, called
P. nivalis. The true *nivalis* is a not very desirable
Caucasian, not in cultivation, with purplish blooms, and
called *nivalis*, presumably, because it lives near the snow.
P. nivalis, of gardeners, is nearly the most lovely of all
cultivated Alpines, and is called *nivalis* because its colour
happens to be snow-white, which ought, of course, to be
rendered *nivea*, if the thing is to have a specific name at
all. As a matter of fact it is an albino form of either
pubescens or *helvetica*. Albinos occur all through the
Primulas—the pink Primulas, at least,—Albinos occurring as commonly among pink- and blue-flowered races,
as they do rarely among yellow ones. *Cottia* gives a
lovely albino; so does *farinosa*. But none can beat the
gardener's *nivalis*. It grows as robustly as a cabbage,

and, indeed, rather resembles a very tiny cabbage in its buxom little shape. And then comes in spring a great swelling cluster of snowy-white flowers, not very large, but extraordinarily crowded and abundant. Add to this that *nivalis* is perhaps the most happy-natured and vigorous of even the *viscosa* section. All it asks is good soil and a few stones, and to be let alone. They none of them ask more than that, in fact, though I rather fancy *viscosa* itself has a lingering love of peat. And they all, of course, like every other Primula, resent being parched and scorched by excessive sun and an arid air.

P. Deorum, the Primula of the Gods—and why it should be the Primula of the Gods no one seems able to declare —is a recent introduction from the stony edges of mountain-rills high up in the Balkans, and, though such a new-comer, has already acquired a bad name as a shy-flowerer. It is a handsome plant, stout and sturdy, which should carry big heads of rich purple blossoms (rather small in proportion). Mr. Hindmarsh of Newcastle has flowered it grandly, as figured in the *R. H. S. Journal*, and I myself have a large stock of it that I imported long ago from the Balkans. Last year nearly all the pot-plants flowered—not with any very great enthusiasm indeed, but still they did flower. The plants in the open contented themselves with growing, and that they did so happily and persistently, that I felt it would be unjust to ask more of such a new-comer. This season, however, I see the flower spikes are pushing bravely. I have it in every kind of position ; dry, damp, and sopping, and in all it seems to thrive with equal pertinacity. *P. Deorum* belongs to a scantily-represented section, of which *P. Parryi* is also an ornament. *P. Parryi* hails from the Rockies, likes the same wet treatment that nature indicates for *Deorum*, has a similar but rather larger habit, and larger, less numerous, and more brilliant purple flowers. Both species have my warm affection, and every one should grow them.

P. farinosa. I won't give rein here to my feelings about this dazzling little jewel of the Craven Highlands; it bulks naturally large in any talk of British alpines, and it is sufficient to say that both *farinosa* and its very rare albino form, are among the most precious plants that the heart of the gardener can yearn over. *Farinosa* is perhaps the cheeriest of all Primulas, and has the further merit of being the widest distributed. In every temperate mountain-range of the world, whatever Primulas may or may not be found, you are always certain of finding *farinosa*. From the North Pole to the South, from the Arctic Circle to the Straits of Magellan, across the Stony Girdle of the World, from the Himâlya through the Rockies, over the Alps and the fells of Northern England, *P. farinosa* is everywhere to be found in the mountain marshes—a hearty energetic little species, not like *Allioni*, dwindling and dying, but always (at least with us) spreading from meadow to meadow and hill to hill. Of its kindred to be treated here are its variety, *scotica*, from Sutherland, a delightful stocky dwarf form with bigger purple blooms; *longiflora*, a very much magnified, drawn out edition of *farinosa* from the Alps, and *frondosa*, another enlarged likeness, a very robust vigorous plant from Thrace, in some ways attractive, thrifty and good to deal with, though really inferior to *farinosa*, except in so far as it is much leafier and larger in growth, and blooms much earlier, though with rather second-rate flowers. Nicholson says its blossoms are of a 'pleasing blue.' With me, *frondosa* is of nearly the same lilac pink as a poor *farinosa*. But descriptions of colour are painfully apt to be vague; I know an estimable botany book that describes *Saxifraga florulenta* and *Androsace glacialis* as blue. Neither

longiflora, frondosa, nor *scotica* wants the wet treatment
here which *farinosa* will take. In fact, *frondosa* dislikes
excessive moisture, and rots away promptly if annoyed
by it. On a well-drained corner of the rock-work, however, I have great fat perennial tufts of it; and lower, in
a damper, peatier bed, great old clumps of *longiflora.*
As for seed, *farinosa* and *scotica* have an agreeable emin-
ence among Primulas from the brisk and ungrudging
way in which they germinate. At this moment I have a
seed pan where uninvited self-sown plants of *farinosa*[1]
are busily engaged in squeezing out of existence some
very choice baby Gentians. But at such a mercy of the
gods who will be so ungrateful as to carp? As for
P. algida it seems to me like a large poor *farinosa.*

P. involucrata or *Munroi* (the two plants—if they
really are two—are horticulturally one). Enthusiasm is
apt to pall, and I hope before long I may come to a
Primula that I can be cold about. But I cannot be cold
about *involucrata,* not even to avoid monotony. I sometimes think that this plant pleases me more perfectly
than any of the others. There is something about it so
remotely, coldly pure; and, besides, the fragrance of it is
celestial. *P. involucrata* is Himâlyan, a representative
of a little-known section. It is essentially a 'wet-bob,'
and must have a good sopping marsh to be happy in. At
least they say so But I have one self-sown clump of
involucrata that sat itself high up in a shady corner of
the rockery, far away from any bog, and there flourishes
happily from year to year. In the autumn its little,
round, smooth, dark-green leaves die quite away, and nothing is left but a fat bud and yellow, thready roots that
soon begin to kick about in the air. The flower stems rise
in early summer. There are not many of them, and they
bear few blooms. But those are very large, and of a

---

[1] They have turned out albinos; no one knows why.

white so icily pure, that it sometimes passes into a gentle, thin, bluish tone, and from this again to a soft, pale purple. And the scent of them is beyond description— so clean and sweet and dainty—like all the Primula scents in clean daintiness, but sweeter than any of the others. In drier south-country gardens I am certain it will always be safest to treat *involucrata* as a plant of the wet marsh. Even here I should never, of my own choice, put it far away from water.

Now, at last, I think I have come to a Primula that I need not praise. *P. japonica* is large and stout and coarse and splendid, and its colour is of a violent crimson-magenta. Like a cabbage it grows, and sends up tall spikes, carrying whorl upon whorl of those fiery blooms. It is a fine thing for the big bog-garden, or for naturalising in a mass in a cool, woodland dell. It loves moisture and rich soil, nor does it object to shade. When suited it seeds itself generously about, and some of the seedlings, to do them justice, bear blossoms of purer colour. (My own prevailing form is almost a true crimson.) As for the white and other varieties advertised and sold, I have always thought them downright ugly—mean and dirty in tone, and without the gorgeous vigour of the type, which, at its best, and in a fine colony, and a good strain, certainly makes a very memorable show. But neither *Primula japonica* nor *Primula pulverulenta* is a plant for the small or the choice rock-garden.[1]

P. latifolia or *graveolens* (but why the poor thing should be thus called 'Stinker' when, in my experience, it is almost as fragrant as *involucrata*, is more than I can

[1] Here I must note Veitch's glorious hybrid Unique (*Pulverulenta* x *cockburniana*) with the build and vigour of *pulverulenta*, and a lovely salmon-scarlet flower, softened from the fierce orange of *cockburniana*. This appeared triumphantly at the Temple Show of 1907—a splendid instance of prompt and prudent hybridisation.

say). I collected this species, far too uncommon in cultivation, from shady rocks high up in the Maritime Alps, close under the habitat of *Saxifraga florulenta*. Nicholson calls it a variety of *viscosa*—well, anyhow, it is absolutely distinct from a grower's point of view. It is much larger and laxer in growth, the broad, oblong leaves are soft, greyish, and velvety ; the scented blossoms are abundantly borne, and are of the loveliest pure gentle purple. The plant is altogether kindly and pleasant, lovable too, and grows without any difficulty whatever in a rocky crevice.

P. luteola stands rather by itself. It is a Himâlyan species, very sturdy and stout, with rosettes that, while unfolding, look not unlike a *denticulata*. But the flowers are not borne till about August, and then come up great heads of rich golden yellow on stalwart stems. *Luteola* thrives very easily in any cool, good loam, not parched or wind-worried. It is a plant for any garden, and a most delightful species.

P. marginata. Now go we back to the Maritime Alps, to the same crevice whence I plucked *latifolia*. Thence pluck we also *marginata*. *P. marginata*, of all the rock species, is, I think, the easiest, and the most fascinating, and the most beautiful. The large, pointed leaves are of a hoary grey-green, and their deep-toothed edges are most delicately scalloped with white meal. Mealy too are the stems, and then the flowers are very large and of a soft, clear lavender blue. (There are better and worse forms of course.) *Marginata* does not so strongly insist on rock as others of its cliff-haunting kindred. With me, indeed, it certainly prefers rock, but elsewhere I have seen it growing rampantly in the open border, like an Auricula. Its most annoying trick is that of coming out of the ground in winter, and, ultimately, of becoming lanky and leggy in growth. When this happens it must be taken up, cut to pieces, and replanted. Every bit will grow and shoot again and bud.

P. megaseaefolia is a new-comer from Rhazistan, in many ways resembling *obconica*, especially in foliage. The flowers are much larger, and of a strong magenta-lilac. They appear in mid-winter, and so are frequently spoiled, and this detracts from the merits of the plant, though it is absolutely hardy and extremely easy to grow in any comfortable, shady nook. The colour of the flowers displeases me, and their unseasonableness is a nuisance, so that I cannot do generous justice to this trustworthy, interesting species.

P. minima is a parent who, with *intermedia* or *calycina*, has given so many of the brilliant babies I have talked of earlier. *P. minima* is tiny, tiny in growth, and runs about, I believe, among short, delicate Alpine herbage. Its flowers are virtually stemless, and enormous for the plant—the size of a shilling or more, bright pink or white. *Minima* is not very satisfactory in growth with me. I rather fancy that, like several other alpines, it misses the fine vegetation among which it normally grows. It is one thing for a tender alpine to make, as it were, a thread in a whole big carpet of dwarf growths, and quite another for it to be sat in splendid isolation all by itself in the cold, dank soil of an English rock-garden pocket. I am sure a great many difficult things would be easier if we gave them the protection they are accustomed to by planting tiny Poas and things among them; but then what grass can one trust not to eat one out of house and home in the fattening conditions of a rock-garden? *Minima* is a conspicuous treasure, and yet, like Letizia Bonaparte, she is famous by virtue of her brilliant child. For *minima* is the mother of *P. Fosteri*, the most audaciously splendid of all the small Primulas. *Viscosa* is the father, *minima* the mother, and

the child is a dwarf plant, very robust, very healthy and
easy to grow, and very floriferous, with bright carmine
flowers that, on well-grown tufts, are literally as large as
five-shilling pieces. *P. Fosteri* is indeed a sight to be
remembered. Nature was the nurse too of this Napoleon
among the alpines; he hails from the Gschnitz (Heavens!)
valley in the Tyrol.

Now sliding briefly over *P. Rusbyi*, a queer, deciduous
Mexican with dark brownish-purple flowers, we come to
the glory of the bog-Primulas. I do not think in the
world there is such another colour as that of *P. rosea*—
a dazzling, virulent pink that takes you between the eyes,
—absolutely clean of any magenta taint, of any blue, of
any purple—simply pure, almost appalling, carmine-rose,
with a golden eye. *Rosea* is a Himâlyan, and climbs, as I
said, up on to the very edge of the everlasting ice. Think
what it must be to find it there glowing with that
jewel-like intensity, that ardent pink which seems to be
actually luminous! *P. rosea*, given its requirements, too,
is a joyous inmate of any English garden, making enormous masses, and throwing up, before the leaves, dozens
upon dozens of its glowing flower-heads with their
great round blossoms in a loose ball of glory. But
water it must have, water it must and will have, its
feet in running water (if you can manage it), all
through the summer. And then it will give you news of
its happiness, yes, and seed itself about too in the most
heartening unexpected way. And if ever its forces wear
out, all that the clump requires is dividing and replant-
ing. There is a *grandiflora* form of *rosea*, and a late-
blooming form; but I love the type so much that I
cannot love its varieties any better. *P. Poissoni*, with
its whorls of lilac-purple flowers, and its flaccid, rather
unpleasant leaves, with their pale midrib—that always
remind me of a cold, froggy hand—is a rather beautiful

Asiatic from Yunnan (Yunnan is *par excellence* the place where the Primulas come from it seems, or at least would if they were brought—Oh, *bullata, calliantha, serratifolia, glacialis, secundiflora, spicata, yunnanensis,* make haste and come from Yunnan!) which may be put between *rosea* and *Sikkimensis*—though not from any botanical affinity, for the whorled habit approaches it in appearance to *japonica.* *P. Poissoni* is supposed to love wet places and to be rather particular in its habits. All I can say of it is that it comes from seed like any annual, and that it seems very robust, and that I cannot muster up any great passion for it, especially as it is distinctly tender, all my hundreds of plants having died off last winter, while *Anemone vitifolia* and the southern Antirrhinums took no hurt.

P. Sikkimensis brings us to the last great group, of the deciduous marsh Primulas, very largely represented in the Himâlya, and very poorly in our gardens. *Sikkimensis* is a singularly splendid and yet graceful person who dies quite down in the winter and then sends up stout, wrinkly crinkly, dark-green leaves, obovate and narrowing to a footstalk, and then, on tall, waving, powdery stems, great heads of pendulous, soft-yellow bells, deliciously sweet-scented. *Sikkimensis* is reported to cover miles of bog in the Himâlya; and, with us, it demands deep, cool soil and abundant moisture, if it is to do well. Given those requirements, there is not a robuster, more long-lived plant in cultivation. Belonging to this group again are many other glories, most of them known to us only by hearsay. *P. Stuarti* is a splendid, golden rarity whom I have never succeeded in getting hold of. His purple variety must be no less splendid, and there are many others of whom it is a vain grief to tell: while *pannonica* and *anisiaca* are simply forms of Primrose.

SILVER SAXIFRAGES SPROUTING FROM A ROCK IN THE OLD GARDEN

CHAPTER XIII

Androsace

NEARLY all Androsaces are beautiful; but, while some are of the easiest culture, others take rank among the famous difficulties which it is a gardener's expensive pride to overcome. Among the children of the rocks none are so typical, so brilliant as the Saxatile Androsaces; they are far more 'high alpine' than most of the Saxifrages, and far, far more intractable in disposition. The zebra is supposed to be difficult of domestication, but the man who drives a well-broken four-in-hand of zebras is but a tiro compared with him,—if such a fortunate person there be,—who possesses large tame tufts of *Androsace imbricata*, or *A. glacialis*. In fact these perverse plants only yield the palm to *Eritrichium* for incalculable crossness. And, unluckily, like *Eritrichium*, they are so irresistibly fascinating that one must needs go on pleading with them, and coaxing them to survive.

First and foremost, there is the difficult mountain section of Androsace, comprising *glacialis, helvetica, imbricata, cylindrica, pubescens, pyrenaica, wulfeniana, ciliata, Haussmanni, Charpentieri,—alpina* being, Nicholson says, the proper name of *glacialis*, and *argentea* that of *imbricata*. There is not one of these that is not beautiful, and there is hardly one of them that is not more or less short-lived and querulous under cultivation. For the most part they dwell at great elevations, in dry clefts of

sunny precipices, increasing in frequency towards the
Southern and Eastern Alps. In their close crevices they
sit tight, year by year, and form fat little grey or silver
cushions of minute, rosetted foliage, like so many velvet
pincushions. Then, in spring, they break out into
brilliant flowers, white or pink, starry, with white or
yellow throat. They grow, like so many of the very high
alpines, as much as possible out of the way of direct
moisture, where only the air is damp, and that only in
the warm, bright days of melting snow, when the glittering streams are pouring down incessantly over the rock-
faces from the snow fields above. Then follows their
brief and glorious flowering time, still without surface
moisture, and then, in a little, the Alpine winter is on
them and their spirits go back to bed again, dry and
comfortable in the crevice, or, perhaps, no less cosy and
dry under a good thick felt of frozen snow. Never do
they suffer surface damps; their main liquid refreshment
being, as a rule, imbibed from the atmosphere of the
evaporating wet rocks in their neighbourhood. Therefore,
after the prudent method of their kind, they have all
armed themselves, more or less thickly, with a fine, close
down of soft fur, that sucks up every scrap of humidity
that may be floating near. They become little animated
sponges, agog to soak up all available moisture. No
fear, up in those blazing or frozen heights, that their
hairy coats will become overloaded. And, in the worst
droughts of the mountain summer, their down saves them
from parching, while, in those clear, rarefied altitudes,
the sun's beams have no such devastating power as on the
lower slopes.

But, when brought into English cultivation, what a
change! Their growing season too often parching, their
sleeping time almost invariably soaking and sopping.
Alternations of sleet, rain, snow, and thaw diversify our

British winter, and the little sponge-cushions of Androsace become unbearably loaded with wet,—and at the wrong time of the year too. So the burdened hairs clog and grow rotten, and in the spring nothing is left but a melancholy brown mess. Androsace has gone to its long home. No one who has seen *imbricata*,—(I can't help it,— Nicholson or no Nicholson, I must call the plant by the name I have always known it under,—there are already enough changes in this transitory life without adding to them by altering every plant-name that we have ever laboriously learnt),—nobody who has ever seen *imbricata*, nestling close into the granite precipices above the Plan de Bertol, over Arolla, will wonder at the ill-health from which the poor thing suffers in England. Those precipices reflect and refract the sun until the heat of them is something unbearable. And there, in every bone-dry crack, far from any moisture, huddle the ash-white cushions of the *Androsace*, shrinking, fiercely, tightly, into the blazing cleft, and rooting far, far back into the heart of the cliff. He clings like a limpet to its arid home, and vain indeed are all efforts to dislodge him. He seems to guess what fate threatens, and resists the utmost blandishments of trowel, finger, or tie-pin. Indeed the trowel becomes nothing but a derision and a mock where the rock-haunting Androsaces are in question. It was not until I had quested along all the frontage of that great amphitheatre, jigging and crawling across a slide of fallen rocks the size of pianos, that I came at last to a little granite cliff, disintegrated by time and weather, whence I was able to wheedle a few specimens of *Androsace imbricata*, with roots intact. *A. imbricata* is rather a rare plant, the most beautiful of all the high alpine Androsaces. Almost pure silver-white are its tiny, round tufts, and the flowers white also. It occurs sporadically in the Alps southward of the Rhone valley, and abhors

the limestone formations. *Charpentieri* and *Haussmanni*
are rose-red, and dwell, the one in the Lombard Alps,
the other in the Eastern. *Wulfeniana* and *ciliata* are
also pink, and inhabit Tyrol. All these, however, lovely
as they are, have not quite the densely tight minuteness
of the three essentially high Alpine species,—*imbricata*,
pyrenaica, and *helvetica*. *Pyrenaica* I have never collected,—in fact the only ones of this section that I have
collected are *imbricata*, *helvetica*, and *glacialis*.

Helvetica is much less uncommon than *imbricata*, and
is, all things considered, a remarkably good-tempered
little plant. He closely resembles his cousin, *imbricata*,
but his down is not silvery. He grows quickly and
robustly into fat little masses, and, even in England,
lasts over several seasons with any reasonable amount of
attention. I first saw him years ago in the Bernese
Oberland, and for a long time (he was out of flower)
could not imagine what he might be. Though easy-
going enough to put up with most kinds of rock, *helvetica*
has the, to me, great recommendation of being essentially
a limestone plant. *Imbricata*, on the other hand, is
sternly granitic in its inclinations. *Helvetica*, given a
good chink, makes a fine round lump of greyish rosettes,
and then erupts into the loveliest abundance of pearl-
white flowers.

As for *A. glacialis*, the first sight of it is an epoch in one's
life. You have got high, high up towards the glacier, far
above the stretches of *Arnica* and *Gentiana acaulis* and
Viola calcarata. You have trampled lawns of *Aster alpinus*
and grey-flannelette Edelweiss, and now the last vestiges
of grass are disappearing. Beyond you now, and around,
is a gigantic desolation of tumbled wet rock and shingle
leading upwards to the shelving screes of the mountain.
In a little while you know that *Ranunculus glacialis*
will be at your feet, already the high Alpine forms of

R. alpestris are snowy here and there, besides the sodden-looking rills, and in dank hollows from which the snow has only just fled, the Soldanellas are timorously blooming. Farther above, on the stony barrens, shine little jewels or pure sky-clumps of *Gentiana brachyphylla*, replacing *G. bavarica*, which in turn had outclimbed *G. verna*. Among them here and there you will find *Viola cenisia*, *Campanula cenisia*, perhaps *Saxifraga biflora*. As you wander on in expectation, suddenly, under your very boot, lies a mass of pink. No leaves are visible, nothing but a mat of pure, soft rose-pink,—a yard across perhaps. It is *Androsace glacialis*. Nothing so beautiful could the unaided mind imagine. Its colour is so pure, its profuseness of blossom so amazingly generous, not to say prodigal. Unlike the other high alpines of its kindred, too, it is growing loosely, rooting compactly in mere wet *débris*,—the easiest thing in the world to dig up adequately, all in a lump. So, think you, here is a glory for my garden,—this wonderful cheerful little person that is evidently as good-tempered as a daisy. You get it home. You plant it, you cosset it, you ultimately weep salt tears over it. Does it flower as it did, does it ramp as it should, as it promised to do? No such thing. It dwindles, and pines, and languishes; if your culture is very fortunate you may have half a dozen pale sickly blossoms. No more. *A. glacialis* soon sulks itself into a better world. And, Oh, it is indeed a heavenly beauty. Distrust appearances, however; the difficult-looking little cushioned *Androsace helvetica* is really far more trustworthy and rewarding than the easy-seeming *glacialis*.

Though I grow all the other species in this section I cannot speak of their native places from any personal acquaintance: they all require, it seems, much the same rocky treatment. *Pyrenaica* is, roughly speaking, midway in appearance and in temper between *helvetica* and *imbricata. Pubescens* connects the cushion Androsaces with the larger *cylindrica*, that beautiful rare little plant only found, I believe, on the rocks of St. Bertrand on the Pyrenees (*magellanica* is the same thing, I believe), and *cylindrica* leads on towards *brigantiaca* and *hedraeantha. Pyrenaica* has the most fascinating rosettes and golden-throated, white stars, but all the others run its beauty neck to neck. Until we get to the Himâlyan and the biennial Androsaces, there is not an ugly one among them. Now, then, to speak of their culture.

I have been successful, as far as success can be called, with *A. glacialis*, by growing it on a steep, sunny bank in a mixture of coarse, gritty peat with sand and plenty of sandstone chips. Here it grew audaciously all the summer and I was overjoyed, until I saw that about ten pallid little flowers were to be all the wool succeeding so great a cry of prosperity. *Helvetica, pyrenaica, imbricata,* require, and get, with me, a cleft in a rock. And here they all do well,—but never for very long. The life of a good collected plant of *imbricata* I should put at about two seasons—*pyrenaica* you may keep for four, and *helvetica* perhaps for five. As for *A. glacialis,*—well, my vigorous clumps of last year are now looking but poorly,—what an Oxford friend of mine once described as 'pale and emancipated.' Possibly spring weather, if it ever comes, may still awaken their dormant possibilities,—though, I fear, their sleep is too profound. The great worry about dealing with the crevice-loving Androsaces is not the Androsace but the crevice. A normal crevice in a normal boulder probably has not got enough soil, or cannot be properly packed, or, if it can, then follows the awful question of poking in the yard-long silken roots of an Androsace two inches high. One weaves oneself into a wild cocoon in the process, which almost invariably ends in disaster. Remains the other

alternative. You must build an artificial precipice, and
make an artificial crevice. And this requires better
craftsmanship than I hitherto have proved myself capable
of. The making is all right, and the planting is all right,
and the summer is all right, and you think that there *A.
imbricata* is going to sit tight for a quarter of a century.
Then winter comes, and the winds blow, and the rains
descend, and the frost works like a hateful mole, and so
the rocks shift and start, the soil washes this way and
that, the crevice gapes, until at last Androsace, not
recognising its pleasant chink any longer, suffers from
Heimweh, and departs to that bourne whence no traveller
returns. I dream, however, one of these days, of building
a really cyclopean cliff, capable of standing any weather,
and there, I verily believe, the cushion Androsaces will
flourish. But it will always, I fancy, be vain to expect
of them any great longevity. In fact, my idea is that we
ask too much of all our alpines in that way. Mr. Wolley-
Dod once said to me that he believed the average life of
an Alpine plant, such as the high mountain Androsaces,
would hardly exceed five, seven, or perhaps ten years.
Now, when the collector sallies forth to work, if he be
very inexperienced, the plants he brings home are middle-
aged, if he is wiser they are younger, but few collectors
are fortunate enough to be able to get seedlings. (In
my rotten rock I had the luck to find seedlings of *A.
imbricata*. Result, my pot-plants are growing and thriving still.) So that, by the time a plant is well established
in a rock-garden, it is certainly more than three years
old, possibly more than five. And thus, though individual
plant-vitality varies, even from the same seed pod, as
much as human vitality, the established specimen has
seen its youth, and, after a season or so of advancement,
under careful culture, will naturally and quietly expire of
old age. The gardener, however, not recognising this

factor in the great plant-problem, is apt to scold the memory of so capricious and ungrateful a species. Whatever one may think about robust creatures like the Alpine buttercups, I am strongly inclined to believe in the short life of the typical rock-plant,—as distinguished from the bog- or the moraine-plant. I have certainly seen on the Alps many stark-dead masses of both the cushion Androsaces, which looked as if ten years or so had been their natural term of life. As for the culture of the other species in this section, I need not say much. They are not really of any great difficulty as compared with *glacialis* and *imbricata*, whose needs are theirs also. Here they all appreciate being wedged tightly between stone, in stony peat. And it goes without saying that in a wet winter climate like ours of the West Riding, every single Androsace, easy or hard, must have ample glass protection from the rain. Of cold, of course, they will stand any amount, but winter wet is absolutely fatal. The only species not requiring such shelter are *vitaliana*, *carnea*, *Laggeri*, and *brigantiaca*, all plants whose leaves have none of that fine down so characteristic of the high-mountain species, and so intensely resentful of any excessive moisture. Every one of the others, even *sarmentosa* and *lanuginosa*, are protected, in my garden, through the winter.

Leaving now the European mountain section, and omitting easy beauties like *carnea*, *Laggeri*, the golden *vitaliana*, and the lovely rare new *hedraeantha*, from the Balkans, there are the delightful Asiatics that have already blessed us; no doubt there are more to follow. Two of them, *A. foliosa* and (or 'or') *strigillosa*, are a little large and coarse. They are leafy and big, with heads of dullish lilac flowers. But *A. sarmentosa*, *Chumbyi*, *lanuginosa*, and its variety *oculata*, are among the most cherished of plants. *Sarmentosa* is very stoloniferous, and has great, round, silver-green, fluffy cushions, ramifying from each other, that often cover yards of ground. Then up start the red stems, carrying verbena-like clusters of rosy flowers. *Chumbyi* is smaller, neater, still more silvery in tone and more brilliant in flower; *lanuginosa*, with its opposite, ovate leaves, pure hoary grey, goes trailing down over the rocks in a cascade of silver, throwing up, all the summer through, lovely heads of pink. *A. sempervivoeides* is another treasure of this Asiatic section, not so silvery as the others, rather small and neat, with bright rosy flowers. All these species are grateful and refreshing as Epps's Cocoa. There is about them no nonsense of airs and graces. Give them a sunny corner, a clean, well-drained, warm loam to run about in, and they go on happily for years without much attention. Indeed, I only glaze them over in winter to make surety surer; and I notice that even after this late appalling winter of 1906-7 a plant of *A. lanuginosa* (confessedly the tenderest of the group, and a species which has frequently departed from me in the winter), that had been overlooked, is now pushing up fat, silver buds, though ill-planted in heavy, sourish soil, in a dank and shady corner.

The silver-rosette Androsaces now bring us back to Europe, to the consideration of three charming and cheery little people—*A. Chamaejasme, A. villosa, A. arachnoidea.* They have a small habit, and (with all due respect to Nicholson's description of *villosa*) white flowers, large, round, borne in heads, changing from pearl-purity to pink, and yellow-eyed. *Chamaejasme* is common in the Alps. I have always found it blooming in the Oberland in August on the higher Alpine meadows. It runs about among the grass, and is indeed like a little ground-jasmine. In cultivation I have had perhaps less pleasure out of it than out of the others, and this

although it appears to be a lime-lover. It does not scuttle
about as it should. It sits quiet and grows only moderately. Perhaps it misses the grasses of the Oberland.
Arachnoidea is a very charming, silvery, fluffy-rosetted
thing, better than *Chamaejasme*, and not quite so
good as *villosa*, which in general habit it exactly
resembles. This last, of all the easier Androsaces, is
perhaps the loveliest, its flowers are so big, and so
profuse, and so pure; its disposition is so serene and
cheerful. It is essentially a limestone plant, but I
cannot believe that it could be really peevish anywhere.
Last year I had a quantity of pot-plants of it, in full
flower, to show among similar masses of *Eritrichium
nanum*, and the beauty of the comparison was a thing to
remember for ever. To this section also belongs *A. obtusifolia*, a very near relation of *Chamaejasme*, and, like
many near relations, on the worst possible terms with
its kinsman. On one side of the Arolla valley lives
Chamaejasme, on the limestone, on the other side of the
valley lives *obtusifolia*, on the granite. They are not
to be reconciled. *Obtusifolia* is not quite as pretty as
Chamaejasme. The growth is a little larger, the flower a
little smaller and not of so brilliant a white. It is, however, very easy to cultivate, though I cannot say I think
it really deserves such worship as its kindred. But shall
I ever forget the moment when I found on the Torrent
Alp above Leuk a ruby-rose-flowered form of it! That
had been a grim day. The Torrent Alp was painted to
me a miracle of floral generosity; I climbed and sweated
up its abominable great slopes, and found nothing whatever. The season, it is true, was growing late, but still
one can always tell a plant from its foliage, and not even
a leaf did I see to stir my pulses. Then the friend I was
with careered away up a mountain and got lost, and the
hotel fed me on stale marmot, and altogether life was very

gloomy. Then, after the marmot, I strolled out on to the Alp again, where the hotel wash was hanging to dry. And there, in the flapping shadow of a shirt, shone two plants of *A. obtusifolia*, bearing the loveliest brilliant pink flowers—deep, glorious carmine—that any one could imagine. I dug one up with huge reverence, sent it home, and ultimately divided it into eight. Every one of them grew ahead like so many seedling groundsel. What a rosy prospect for next year. Next year comes. All the eight push up strong flower-heads. And they all flower a dingy white!

CHAPTER XIV

Gentiana

No flowers of the rock-garden give more pleasure and more pain than the Gentians; pleasure when they do well, pain when they, so much more frequently, do ill. So far as I know, *Gentiana* might be called a water-loving race. Not by any means that they are bog-plants, but moisture in some form is essential. They are not as a rule very high climbers, and as found in Europe may be roughly called plants of the lower alpine limits. Of the Himâlyan species, I have not yet got hold of *G. ornata*, and only just succeeded in acquiring *G. Kurroo* (and I don't believe it is true), so that neither of these nor of many among their Asiatic kin can I speak with experience and authority. But indeed there is no family of plants among whom authority moves with so timid and cautious a step. About Gentians it is impossible to dogmatise. No race is so incalculable, no race so disconcerting.

All one can say is, if a Gentian will thrive with you you cannot go wrong with it; if it does not thrive, not all the king's horses nor all the king's men will induce it to do so. And this, as a cultural direction, is vague and unsatisfactory. However, this has been my experience. My country and climate fortunately enable me to grow *G. verna* and *G. acaulis* anywhere, anyhow, splendidly; but, like Morleena Kenwigs, I am not in the least proud, not only because pride is sinful, but because I know my success is mere luck. Which brings me to the broad rule which governs the cultivation of the Gentians. Give them pure, cool air. They are as much dependent on good, bracing air as Mrs. John Knightley and her babies. They might almost be called comparatively careless about soil if only the atmosphere be moist and clean. They demand, in fact, hill air. This is not to say that they are indifferent to soil as a race. Very far from it. But I would insist that it is in the quality and temperature of the atmosphere that their health or ill-health mainly lies. There are gardens—I know one within a mile— where *G. acaulis* is left quite to itself, makes yard-wide edgings to half a mile of border, and flowers till the whole place is like a fallen Heaven. And yet, again, over so much of England, this, the easiest of the Alpine section, is either a shy-flowerer or a bad doer, or both. Even with me it will blossom abundantly in one place and sulk in another, though both clumps have the same soil and aspect. As for *G. verna*—well, an English wild plant surely ought to have patriotic feeling enough to thrive in an English garden, you would think. But *verna* is notoriously ill-tempered over a great part of the island; and what is worse, as I hinted before, it is not with the Gentians as with any other difficult alpine. There are no definite difficulties whose overthrow will enable the plant to thrive. No, if a Gentian is cross, cross it will stay. The very utmost a gardener in the hot, dry South can do is to give *verna* moisture, and even then she may still prove flowerless and peevish. I will say again, and will say it ' if I was to be led a Martha to the stakes for it,' the Gentians are like the Swiss and Himâlyan nationalities: take them away from mountains, and they pine and peak and die of Heimweh. They feel as Jeanie Deans felt when she passed out of sight of Ingleborough. (And how she ever managed to come

into sight of Ingleborough at all, on the direct way from
Edinburgh to London by the Great North Road through
Berwick, Newcastle, and Grantham, is one of Nature's
most stupendous problems.   I commend it to Scott
commentators.)   As for *G. verna*, here you put it anywhere in the open garden, and away it romps.   But even
Mr. Wolley-Dod at Edge could only keep it barely alive,
with barrels, and granite, and all manner of contraptions.

Of course one great obstacle to the cultivation of
Gentians is that they are so very irritable about root-
disturbance.   Collected plants rarely turn out to be of
any use.   I have often collected *G. verna*, but never with
any great success.   The plant makes comparatively few
thready yellow roots that run far and wide underground,
in a lax and disorderly manner.   But if you mutilate one of
them the plant becomes annoyed, and takes several seasons
to get over it, and this can only be achieved by a year or
two of careful pot-culture, which, however medicinal, the
Gentian hates.   On the whole, I think *G. verna* is the
most difficult plant to collect properly that I have ever
come across.   As for the Gentians of the *asclepiadea*
section, with their vast root stocks, they are almost
impossible to dig up entire.   Luckily, however, this group
is better tempered than the Alpine section, and is so
far from objecting to root mutilation, that almost any
shoot with the merest stump of a root will grow on, if
carefully treated.   Buyers, too, must remember that it is
not safe to purchase unknown Gentians with handsome
names.   For there are—low and reverently be it spoken
—a number of Gentians that are not only plain, but
even ugly.   Such of them as I know, I will signalise as I
go along, and my curiosity has brought me many dark
experiences in the matter.   The race may be roughly
divided into the alpine, the herbaceous, and the annual
sections; *G. acaulis* stands for the first, *asclepiadea* for

the second, and *Amarella* for the last. The first is, as a
rule, the most beautiful, the second the best-tempered,
the last is neither cultivable nor desirable.

G. acaulis is a Protean species, whose varieties I will
now enumerate before I go any further, as they are too
often given specific rank in catalogues, to the confound-
ing of the unwary. *G. alpina* is a rather smaller form
with obovate leaves; *G. Clusii* has very dark-blue flowers
and lanceolate leaves—I rather fancy it is a limestone
form; *G. kochiana* has large, black-spotted flowers and
elliptic foliage. As for charm—well, botanical zeal may
revel in these varieties; if the ordinary cultivator possesses and succeeds with the old English Gentianella-
form of *acaulis*, he has got a finer, healthier, more
beautiful plant than any of them, a better plant even
than the type of *acaulis*, which is sometimes slaty in
tone, dull, and almost ugly. The named sub-species are
indeed beautiful and interesting—my own favourite is
Clusii; but they none of them touch the Gentianella,
which somehow during years of cultivation has evolved
itself into such a glorified version of the plain *acaulis*
which it once was, many generations ago. There are,
besides, colour-variations of *acaulis*. There is a very beautiful paler-blue *acaulis coelestina*; there is what is called a
rosea form, and there are two albinos, one very poor and
small and slow-growing and shy-flowering, the other fine
and robust, in its best developments gloriously delicate,
with green-spotted snowy trumpets. But somehow
albino Gentians are not, as a rule, quite a success in my
eyes. The lost original blue is so splendid that nothing
could improve upon it; nor is the white they indulge in
either pure or clean in tone. The most lovely colour-
form of *acaulis*, I give notice to the curious, is still, for
all I know, sitting up on the Little Scheideck, about two
hundred yards from the hotel. It was of a most haunt-

ing azure, very faint and frail and exquisite, with little, seraphic, pale-green spots. I saw and worshipped it in the far days of my childhood, long before I had a rock-garden, while I was making my first tour in Switzerland, with several languishing Gentians and a *Soldanella* tied up in my sponge-bag, on the off-chance that they might live when I got home. In spite of my consideration in giving them air every Sunday afternoon, I regret to say that none survived.

As for the cultivation of *G. acaulis*. I can only repeat what I said before; if well, well; if ill, ill. However, if you have difficulties with it, you might at least try the effect of making it a good deep bed of cool, moist loam, well-drained, with stones to help it. But I am afraid you will always find that country air, undefiled, is necessary. If it grows fond of you it will flow over the garden like a wave of sky; if it does not like you, or disapproves of your living near a town, it won't, probably, die, but it will live sulkily, grudgingly, peevishly, until you long to pick it up and throw it away, being tired of such an ungenial pet.

We now come to *G. asclepiadea*. And I must pause to rhapsodise on one of the most splendid and kindly of all the Gentians. *G. asclepiadea* is a sub-alpine, being only found in marshes on the highest limit of the mountain woods. I shall never forget my first sight of it in the meadows above Rosenlaui. It makes great bushes three or four foot high, bearing, from July onwards, long arching wreaths of the most glorious deep-blue flowers. It takes very eagerly to cultivation and lives for ever, growing finer each year in bed or border. All it wants is good loam or peat, and plenty of moisture. Be careful, though, in getting it, to get a finely coloured form. The type is lovely, but I have been heavily deceived at times in this matter. I found myself unable to cope with the huge old clumps of Rosenlaui, so I decided to wait till I could find younger specimens, more amenable to the trowel (dynamite would hardly stir an established mass of *G. asclepiadea*). It was not till I got down to Iseltwald on the lake of Brienz that I found plants small enough to please me. By then the Gentians had long passed out of flower; but that, of course, made no difference; I grubbed up my little pieces, brought them home, and was happy. Alas, they all turned out to have flowers of a dowdy deep slate colour, such as I have never seen anywhere, before or since, in *G. asclepiadea*. And there they now are in my garden, growing fatter every year; and I feel it would be ungrateful to remove the poor souls; so there they must stop. However, I was indemnified next season, for I found at Rosenlaui, one day as I was going up to the glacier, two plants of the loveliest *asclepiadea* that one could imagine, even in a dream,—with blossoms of the purest, palest azure. As I had a long, heavy day before me, I decided to leave them untouched till I returned. So on I went. When I came laden back that evening,—they were gone! Some German tourist had seen them, and had appreciated them as much as I. Picture my anguish! I cried to the gods for help, and hurled myself prone to earth like great Achilles on the shore. Not grief alone was my motive though. I grabbled and grabbled among the grasses until at last, with infinite labour—it really *was* rather a feat—I discovered where the stalks had been plucked. I then devoutly dug up a root, and now as *G. asclepiadea phaeina*, my pale-blue plant is one of my most cherished glories. *G. asclepiadea* also rejoices in an albino form which I think far the best of all the white Gentians, and which is really a very pure and perfect flower.

G. bavarica is a beautiful little blue devil,—so blue, and so beautiful, — and such a devil! The mighty

Mr. Robinson commends it recklessly ; so do I—as St. Augustine (wasn't it ?) commended all good women—to Heaven, without having anything to do with them oneself. In plain, humiliating words, I have failed so often and so completely with *G. bavarica*, that I won't advise any one else to grow it, for fear they might meet with worse failure,—or more success,—than I. It is a glorious little plant—a marsh-frog of marsh-frogs, growing only in the very soppiest of places, and climbing high upon the mountains, where it thrives so rollickingly that one at once concludes it will be perfectly happy in any cool garden. I always imagine it to be a higher Alpine than *G. verna* ; but that may be simply because, at the season when I have always seen it, *G. verna* has been over, and *G. bavarica* in full bloom on the bogs at great elevations. It is a tiny grower, making dense masses of its little box-green, box-like shoots,—from which come flowers as large as, or larger than, those of *verna*, with long calyxes, and of a very intense dark sapphire blue. The only really hopeful way, I believe, to keep it in health, is to use it as a bog-plant for very wet places. I myself have never found it really permanent out of doors, and, with me, the Gentians hate pot-culture, all of them. Backhouse grows it—or grew it—in almost pure, wet, silver sand, but all who embark upon this problem must buy their own experience, and rise on corpses of dead Gentians to higher things. In the same category as *bavarica* come *pyrenaica*, too, and *imbricata*, both of whom are beautiful, both of whom are damp-lovers, both of whom I have tried and lost so frequently that I will hurriedly pass by these skeletons in my cupboard.

G. brachyphylla is rather better-natured than the foregoing. It is, I think, close to *verna*, perhaps a very high Alpine development of it. You only begin to see it when you are nearing the eternal ice ; it breaks into celestial patches on the topmost alps and moraines—a tiny little, tidy mat of the most startling brilliant blue, a shade paler and clearer than *verna*. It is a brave creature too— and, though I cannot give it an absolutely good character in cultivation, yet I can give it a relatively good one—a good one for an Alpine Gentian. It will live, with care, and if you suit it, in open stony places, for two or three seasons. Nor has it any desire to be treated as a semi-aquatic. It bears, on the Alps, the most terrific elevations, for it runs a neck-to-neck race with *Eritrichium*, and I shall not forget in a hurry, the beatific close of my great Blue Moss Day, when I sat, my labours crowned with glory, on the summit of the Meiden Pass, while all about me were dazzling mats of *Eritrichium nanum* and a minute stunted form of *Gentiana brachyphylla*. Poor darling, at that awful height, well might she be stunted. Very, very far away below was the rim of the lower alps that dipped into the valley of St. Niklaus. But the valley itself was quite unplumbable—a creek of darkness in that infinite gulf of distance. And then beyond, high over everything, the tumbled, terrifying mass of the Mischabelhoerner, away up in the clear blue, rosy-white in the distance, and wound about with curls of pink and white cloud. (I do not know, by the way, whether they really were the Mischabelhoerner; nor, I may add, do I care. I have no pleasure in naming mountains when I see them, nor for tracking them down on a flapping map; if they are beautiful, well, beautiful things, in the eternal fitness, can never have a name that really belongs to them, no mortal word being good enough; and, if they are not beautiful, who cares whether they have a name or not, or wants to know it if they have?)

G. ciliata—or *detonsa*—is a notable beauty, but who is there that can grow it? It is a lowlander, rather than an alpine—you find it by pathways and on open places in the valleys; and I strongly suspect it of either parasitic or biennial tendencies, or both. It has very large flowers, divided into four; the colour is of an indescribable rich pale porcelain-blue of that shade which, for some obscure reason, has been called electric; and each segment is fringed with soft, silky, blue hairs (I once found a lovely albino : long since, of course, defunct). I have tried this plant again and again and again; I have never met with the faintest glimmerings of success. It is near akin, I imagine, to the American *G. elegans*, whose beauty Catalogues commend, adding that it is 'well worthy of the extra attention it requires.' When a Catalogue admits that a plant requires 'extra attention,' look out for squalls. Catalogues do not usually err on the pessimistic side. However, now I have got a whole panful of *G. detonsa* seedlings, so that if the sender's *detonsa* is really *ciliata*, as it should be, and the little plants come on properly, I hope to surmount my troubles with my autumn-blooming Swiss friend.

G. Bigelowi, bracteosa, brevidens, saponaria and *siphonantha* are species, for the most part, of which I have had no long experience. If they answer to their descriptions, one ought to be satisfied; they are large-growing kinds, after the following of *G. asclepiadea*; and all I can say of them is that *G. bracteosa* and *Bigelowi* are the only ones that show any healthful inclination to become established, and that, even so, they have never yet flowered nor earned my praise. In justice I must add that *brevidens* and *siphonantha* are at present but seedlings, so perhaps I ought not to mention them so invidiously—especially as *brevidens* is a form of the glorious and worshipful *Kurroo*, of whom no harm must be prematurely spoken. I will therefore pass over my other seedlings in silence, until I can tell of them with more precision.

DAPHNE CNEORUM

G. scabra Buergeri is another dark horse of mine who arrived unexpectedly from Japan last year. It only grows about ten inches high, and so far seems very robust and healthy and late blooming. I cannot fix it in my memory among my Japanese recollections. There certainly was a most adorable little wee, wee pale-blue annual Gentian who appeared everywhere in the early spring, and was especially charming on the roadsides skirting the Aoyama Palace, just above my little house in Tokio. But *G. scabra* is clearly an autumn-flowering perennial, so I must wait awhile before I can decide on its merits.

G. cruciata is a very stout little creature, of the easiest possible culture anywhere, with clusters of bright blue, cross-shaped flowers. But the flowers are small and the plant leafy, and I have always thought it rather dull, and have never been able to love it. And now that I am on the Uglies, I will go valiantly on and deal with them, cloaking nothing of my opinions, however irreverent. *G. lutea*, the big medicinal yellow Gentian, I must honestly confess I think hideous. It is dingy and coarse and cabbage-like and gigantic. M. Correvon, I think, lauds it as being a plant '*à formes architecturales.*' Heaven bless me from such architectural adornments! Others very near akin to *lutea* are *purpurea*, a rather terrifying, splendid tawny-brown ; *pannonica*, dull purple ; *punctata*, very similar ; *gaudiniana*, a hybrid (of which there are many, and differing in form and colour) between *purpurea* and *lutea* ; if people like these gawky creatures, they are all very fairly miffy in any deep, cool loam or peat. *Gentiana thibetica*, so frequently advertised, is a not very pretty or brilliant species of a *cruciata* description ; so are *Kesselringi*, *daurica*, and *dinarica* ; *macrophylla* is larger, and very lumpish, with little flowers, though the variety *cyanea* is reported to be a fine thing ; I have one plant out in the open which seems to be thriving vigorously. But I must confess that when a Gentian grows to more than a foot high, I have no further use for it, as a rule; *asclepiadea* and its cousins are splendid exceptions. The dwarf brilliance of the Alpine kinds spoils us for the robust dowdiness of the bigger species in Gentiana as in Ranunculus and Dianthus.

G. algida and *G. gelida* have often been ardently recommended to me. As recommended, however, they are never the genuine plants, but only forms of *G. septemfida*. The true *gelida* is a dingy, cluster-headed Caucasian, and the true *algida* a Siberian species, rather like a spoiled and bloated *Pneumonanthe*, whose colour has run. For a long time, too, I was excited by the name of *G. frigida*, which sounded like a cream-coloured *acaulis*. *Frigida* is a rare and exceedingly difficult species from the granitic Alps, and, from what I have seen of it, I very much doubt whether its beauty is commensurate with its ill-temper. *G. excisa*, again, is hardly distinguishable (indeed, from a gardener's point of view is indistinguishable) from *Genttana acaulis* itself,—except by its far greater peevishness and perversity of disposition; *G. Froelichi* is rather beautiful, with narrow leaves, and narrow, bright blue flowers; *augustifolia* is simply another finely-coloured variety of *acaulis*, and *arvernensis* of *Pneumonanthe*.

G. Przewalzkyi.—Oh, these good Russian generals, what a debt we owe them. But I wish we did not try to pay it by imposing their names on plants. *Przewalzkyi* is impossible even to spell; is it to be believed that there is any one in the world who can pronounce it? It is indeed bad luck (though I bow to General Przewalzky for having, presumably, introduced the plant) that one of the loveliest of Gentians should be damned by so impossible a name. (How do footmen manage to announce the General, I wonder?) One simply cannot talk about it. One has to burke it as if it were something improper, and work round to it by periphrasis. Well, the Gentian of the Russian General is a very lovely, easy-going person, whom every one ought to have. It is akin to *Pneumonanthe*, but smaller and prostrate, with few-flowered clusters of the most splendid big azure goblets. As for *Pneumonanthe*, this dear little native plant is far too seldom seen in gardens. It is local, rather than rare, occurring on marshy moors all England over, from Wareham to Ingleborough. Yet, in this country, I only know of two stations for it; and one of these is but a very recent colony from the other. In the original habitat about an acre of moor is covered with the lovely, deep blue trumpets of the Gentian, standing stiffly up on their little, wiry stems; but a stone's throw further on you will find none, and no more for I do not know how far, though every yard of moor seems just as suitable as the place it grows on. *Pneumonanthe*, like *arvernensis* and *Przewalzkyi*, is grateful-tempered, and thrives quite happily in any cool peat or peaty loam. There is an albino which I have neither found nor grown.

G. nivalis, more than any other, may be called a living jewel. When you first see it you notice no plant, no leaf, no stem, just one tiny speck of the most furious blue you ever saw. Slowly the rest of the growth dawns upon you, and you have found *G. nivalis*, one of the true high alpines, and, also, one of the rarest of all our natives, occurring annually here and there in one or two places in the Highlands. Alas that the shameful secret must out: *G. nivalis* is an annual; so are its cousins, *tenella*, *prostrata*, and *utriculosa*. This is, of course, very uncommon among the high mountain plants, which, as a rule, ensure their propagation by insisting on many years to achieve it in. And I wish I could say either that I have found *G. nivalis* generous in coming from seed as any right-minded annual should be, as some slight reparation for his wickedness in being an annual at all. I dally with the dreadful truth. Despite the efforts of many years, I have never succeeded in raising a single seedling of *nivalis*. Let others crow over me in this, if they are more fortunate. I myself believe that the Snow Gentian has a touch of the parasite about it, which at once excuses one for not being able to do anything with it. Really, the colour is the one good thing about the plant; its flowers are very minute, its stem and leaves, therefore, disproportionately large. It is the best of its kindred, but, when all is said and done, not a very well-bred-looking little creature, though unspeakably glorious as you see him jewelling the last fine lawn below the moraines, that smooth and velvety tennis-court of colours, built of small prostrate willows, *Azalea procumbens*, *Phaca frigida*, *Oxytropis montana*, *Trifolium alpinum*, *Dryas octopetala*, with the Gentians *verna* and *nivalis* for brightest notes in the pattern.

G. decumbens is a beautiful species, prostrate with heads of fine big blue flowers, which seems fairly amenable. But *G. decumbens* must always yield to *septemfida*, and *septemfida cordifolia*. These are the most glorious people, very robust and cheerful and easily pleased, flowering too in August, which makes them doubly delightful; and content with any cool, moist loam. Their stems flop about under the weight of perhaps six to eight enormous ten- or five-cleft flowers, of the most brilliant clear azure.

G. Favrati is a most interesting species, a natural hybrid of *verna* and *bavarica*, which, I really think, is more beautiful than either of his parents. He is rare, even in his native land. You will find him all round the summit of the Gemmi, and I believe he also frequents the Jura. But he is none too easy, and I have not yet made very much of him. His flowers are a little looser in build, and larger, than those of *verna*, and their blue is

distinctly lighter. Similar treatment will suit them
both, probably—at least I have a strong feeling that,
as *Gentiana Favrati* is a limestone plant, he will thrive
in a limestone country, and from his general appearance
I should say he might make quite a fair garden plant, if
only we could ensure perfectly sound plants by raising
him from seeds (if, indeed, he produces any).

But *G. verna*, of course, is the type and glory of the
high alpine section, the splendour and triumph of all
Gentians. The rock-gardener *must* grow *verna*, if he
turn grey and bankrupt in the process. To see this
plant in flower on the Alps for the first time is to have
your breath knocked clean out; or glimmering here and
there on Cronkley or Widdy-Bank in Durham among
the great purple pansies. Great as my love and venera-
tion are for *Arenaria gothica* and *Primula farinosa*, I
admit that *Gentiana verna* takes rank right at the head
of our English native plants. He does not, I believe,
occur at all in Scotland either, which is such a mercy!
He haunts the fells of Cumberland, Yorkshire, and
Westmorland; and then crosses to the Irish mountains.
He has been reported to me from a fell at the back
of Ingleborough. But I have my doubts, though I am
sure I do not know why I should. (Yet reports are
risky. A curate, capable, like the prophet Habakkuk,
of anything, has even reported *G. acaulis* as wild on the
Cumberland moors. And I have so often been beguiled
by false tales of discovery.) *G. verna*, as I have said,
is a little beast to transplant, and therein lies half the
difficulty of his culture. For he hates pots; so how is
one to get good established clumps? However, when
one has, half the battle is over; good air, good water,
good, limy loam,—and evil spirits must be about you if
you cannot grow *G. verna*. And if you live in torrid, dry
counties, or foul atmosphere, I am afraid success may be

long before she looks your way.   *G. verna* has an albino, to which I have been allowed to give the name of *chionodoxa*.   In point of fact it hardly deserves quite so high an epithet, being thin in substance and not very startling in brilliancy—like a jasmine flower.   The only other coloured form I can tell of from experience is *verna coelestina*.   I found it above the Læmmern Gletscher, opposite the Gemmi-Kulm.   As I wandered over that vast, sandy river-bed, carpeted with *Linaria alpina*, I saw afar off an unplaceable blue.   Not a Gentian, evidently; not a Myosotis; certainly not *Eritrichium*, so low down, and on those rocks—what could it be?   At last I got near. It *was* a Gentian; it was a pale, sky-coloured *verna* of the tenderest, most poignant loveliness.   I gathered it up with huge sods of earth, to make certain of having every morsel of root.   And now—oh me!—I think the dear creature is still alive, but that is all I can say for it, and I hope that does not involve too great a stretch of courtesy.   The other colour forms—*grandiflora*, *atrocoerulea*, *rosea*—I have grown, but they leave no deep impression on my mind, either of vigour or beauty.   It is with *Gentiana verna* as with *Primula rosea*—the type is so inimitably beautiful that one's heart does not hold a super-superlative of worship for the varieties.   But *G. angulosa* is a notable kinsman of *verna's:* so close that my stock was originally sent me as *verna*.   *Angulosa*, however, is much larger, stouter, more tufted, and tall in growth, with great, angular, swollen calyces containing flowers even more darkly brilliant.   And *angulosa* is as solid a grower as any daisy, so that it ranks as quite the most recommendable of the smaller Gentians—robust in constitution, and not only glorious in bloom but almost perpetual flowering, too, making its main display in spring, and then continuing mildly through the summer to a minor display in autumn.

CHAPTER XV

Some Isolated Treasures

Now that I am emerging from the largest blue and pink clans that the garden offers, I must pause for a sigh of mingled relief and exasperation. For no race of plants has suffered worse than Primula, Campanula, and Gentiana at the hands of the illustrator. But, indeed, the rock-garden is very poorly off for good illustrations. Guidebooks and handbooks alike are all deficient—bad either in drawing or colour, or both. As for Nicholson, he does not aspire to colour, and the drawing of his plates is often so bad as to be merely ridiculous. Look at his *Saxifraga aeizoön*. Then take the little manuals of Schröter : they are invaluable to the anxious tourist in the Alps, but in design and painting they are crude and coarse to the last degree, only giving a rough working notion of the distincter species, and quite useless to any one who wants to distinguish, say, between *Campanula valdensis* and *Campanula linifolia* without wading through all the hideous jargon of barbarous Latin in which botanists clothe their mysteries. M. Correvon has, of course, produced the best attainable pictures of mountain plants in his admirable *Atlas de la Flore Alpine*, while the same author's *Flore Coloriée de Poche* is very bad in drawing, though effective as far as its colouring goes. But even in the *Atlas de la Flore Alpine* there are many terrible lapses ; some plates are figured by some new process from coloured photographs of living clumps ;

P

these are a miracle of fidelity. But on the next page you will find a very inferior sketch by some one who evidently could not draw. Nothing better has ever been done than M. Correvon's figure of *Androsace glacialis*—a tuft pulled from the glacier and simply flung down on the page before your eyes (not necessarily artistic, but absolutely vivid and true); but nothing worse has ever been perpetrated than the neighbouring libel of *Androsace imbricata*—a mean little scribble, utterly unlike the plant it blasphemes. Let us ostracise all the worthless scrawls that disfigure Alpine botany books, and plead with a right-minded millionaire to help the struggling world with a *magnum opus* on the mountain flora, adorned by clear, copious, and trustworthy illustrations. Why, even Parkinson is better than M. Correvon every now and then! And Nicholson's awful illustrations yield to those of Princess Anicia Juliana, that long-dead lover of these delights, who floats like a phantom in the last agonising darkness of the Western Empire. One wonders why botanical plates should consider it so necessary to be either showy and incorrect, or faithful and arid, sometimes making an unhappy compromise by being both mean and false. Years ago Mr. Druce showed me in the Oxford Library the originals of the *Flora Danica*, and such exquisite work I have never seen, although the reproduced plates were both dry and flat. But the originals were really marvellous: every hair, every minute wart on the plant given its fair prominence, and yet the whole so sympathetically wrought and shadowed that the specimen, whatever it might be—Harebell, or more tedious Hemlock—seemed actually lying there on the page, not dried, nor even flattened, but in all the carelessness of Nature, so that you felt that if you put your nose down to smell the flower the leaves would tickle it, or the anthers make it yellow with their pollen.

Far, far has my prophetic wrath carried me from *Lobelia radicans*, that lovely cousin of the Campanulas which is so utterly distinct in all its ways that I could not include it in the Harebell's chapter. *Lobelia radicans* is a prostrate Japanese which roots about all over the place in the fat, damp ground by the rice-fields and streams. When you see all the plains brilliant lilac with it in March you think it must be a *Linaria*, so amazing is the mass of its blossoms. There are superior forms too, larger, bluer, redder, or sometimes white. My *radicans* all comes from seed—two plants only from a packet. But these are now established quite happily in the stream-channel, and root about with perfect readiness, resisting any winter. But they have not yet flowered, I regret to say, and must confess that I am beginning, perhaps early in the day, to have a qualm as to whether they will ripen sufficiently here in the season to show their proper profusion of blossom in the next. However, I cannot pass any verdict yet; and, even if *Lobelia radicans* fails to bloom here, there are scores of places in England where it could certainly be made the brilliant lovely weed that it is in its native country—as common there, and probably as much disliked by the agriculturists, as the creeping thistle is with us. The other larger Lobelias, the gorgeous *fulgens*, *syphilitica*, *cardinalis*, and their hybrids, are, of course, tall and splendid for the bog-garden; and *Lobelia Dortmanna*, from shallow mountain-lakes, as I have found it in North Wales, would certainly be a delightful thing for little ponds, with its subaqueous tufts of fleshy narrow leaves, and its loose spike of pale blue flowers that just rise above the water. But it is long since I saw it, and in those days I had no garden; now, among my other energies, I have never concentrated any determination on securing it for my pools.

The two tiny Andromedas, luckily, are quite good and happy here, which gives me a great deal I ought to be thankful for, as Emmy Sedley would say. The best for ordinary purposes is *Andromeda tetragona*, which grows abundantly in the Canadian Rockies, and develops into wee bushes like some minute Cypress or Lycopodium, with four-sided, hard little boughs. From these, quite paradoxically, come poking great snowy flowers exactly like those of Lily of the Valley. And this treasure of a plant thrives with me quite unperturbed from year to year, making masses of green on the peat-bed. Rather more delicate in growth and fragile in development is its twin species *Andromeda fastigiata*, which you may easily tell by the silvery rim of chaffy scale that intervenes between each closely-lapping, unleaf-like leaf on the quadrangular twigs (I am said to have collected this inadvertently among *tetragona* in the Rockies). This plant is larger than *tetragona* in its flower, and even more brilliant, though much frailer in habit, and requiring, I find, a good deal more attention also, and very rough, cool, gritty peat, never allowed to get sour or parched. *Andromeda hypnoeides* is a very rare plant, I think, and extremely hard to procure or keep alive. I have seen it at Kew, looking rather peevish, but I have never grown it myself, nor even tried to—a querulous Arctic species, like a wee moss with white flowers, clamouring for grit and moisture and partial shade.

I will not enlarge on Rhododendron and Azalea, which both dislike my soil irremediably. Not so, however, that jewel of jewels, the little Tyrolese Rhododendron, properly called *Rhodothamnus Chamaecistus*. This amenable treasure forms into neat wee bushes, literally covered, in their season, with large salver-shaped blossoms of glorious pink. If you want to imperil your soul with covetousness, study the Royal

Horticultural Society's *Journal's* photograph of this as it bloomed in Mr. Hindmarsh's garden at Newcastle. The plant has rather a notorious reputation as a bad doer, which, for my own part, I am bound to deny. In my garden this delight has made an excellent little shrub, nearly a foot across, and increasing steadily in vigour from year to year. Nor has it any attention either, beyond peaty soil and then a salutary policy of let-alone. Controversy rages round the question as to whether *Rhodothamnus Chamaecistus* loves lime or hates it. Some wise people say one thing; other wise persons, as the habit of wise persons is, say quite 'contrary.' My own mild word is to go on never minding, but on principle to put all Ericaceous plants in peat, and then let them alone. And this treatment answers here for *Rhodothamnus* quite as well as for the commonest *Calluna* that was ever shoved into a border on a peat-block and then left to look after itself. But one must not be disappointed if the Rhodothamnus is a little erratic about flowering. Its way, judging even from Mr. Hindmarsh's specimen, is to grow on for years, and perpetually hang fire in the matter of blossom ; then, one season, for no apparent reason, to make a nerve-shattering display of beauty ; and, after that, to rest on its laurels for a bit and do nothing very particular for the next spring or two except grow. My own plants continue to grow most excellently, but so far they have never felt themselves equal to any great floral effort ; however, all the growth they have gone on making cannot be useless, and each year I await with rekindled hope the marvellous things they are certainly going to do for me one day or another, unless I happen to die of old age before their prologue has been accomplished.

Bryanthus erectus is a very well-born hybrid, report assigning *Rhodothamnus* for one of his parents, and

Kalmia glauca for the other. *Bryanthus erectus* makes a frail, stiff little bush of branches, like a pale green Yew, crowned with large intermediate flowers of a lovely pink, like shallow cups. This rare beauty thrives in any good peat; but his cousin, *Bryanthus taxifolius* (or *Phyllodoke taxifolia*), is, under the third synonym, of *Menziesia coerulea*, one of the rarest of all our own alpines, being found here and there among shale slopes on the Sow of Athol, in Perthshire—a tiny, wiry wee bush, with Yew-like leaves, and bluish-lilac bells of blossom. I have only had *Menziesia* once, and now have lost him. The plant is almost as uncommon in gardens as out of them, and seems a capricious, rather feeble person, hardly worth any great attention; his cousin, the brilliant *Menziesia empetriformis*, being so incomparably better—a splendid dwarf shrub, loose and sturdy in growth, with clusters of bright rosy flowers, very freely borne. (How, by the way, ought one to pronounce a tricky Scotch name rendered into Latin—*Menziesia*, or *Mingiesia*? Imagination boggles at either, and Euphony covers her afflicted ears and flees away. Botanists should really have more discretion.) I have collected *Menziesia empetriformis* in the Rockies growing rarely among *Andromeda tetragona*; and, in cultivation, the Andromeda itself is hardly more pleasant to deal with.

The Kalmias are blank black failures here; all of them, alas! from the lovely big *latifolia* (with its dreadful wicked way of poisoning all honey that it helps to make) to the precious little tiny Alpine form of *angustifolia* which grows in the Rockies round Laggan, where I collected it with immense pains and difficulty years ago, and ever since have been coaxing along into some sort of pretence at vitality. And now, if my one American bed-plant is still alive, that is all the doubtful praise I can give it. With the Ground Arbutus, on the other hand, a plant of worse reputation, I have at last achieved success. *Epigaea repens*, I find, will only succeed if you give it the very densest possible shade, where neither light nor wind nor rain can ever penetrate to it through the thicket of overhanging boughs. For years whole hecatombs of Epigaeas died on my hands, as on those of so many people, I imagine, until, some time since, I lost patience and, in desperation, clutched my best nursery plant, and hurled him out in the Old Garden, on a peaty bank, just at the root of a big *Erica arborea*, whose trailing film of boughs makes a close cover all over the surface; and there, helped by the Heath, no less than by the autumn leaves that drift in and pile themselves up there, *Epigaea* has gone ahead like anything, and seems to be perfectly satisfied with its situation, peering out here and there among the sere deadness in a heartening, evergreen way. Whence follows the rather annoying paradox that if you want *Epigaea* to succeed you must put it where you will never be able to see it except by accident. For, until the plant is well embowered in leaves and branches, it will not be happy; and then, in the nature of things, only a routing about on your part, or else some fortunate coincidence, will give you a glimpse of those oval, flat pairs of leaves, or those starry, rose-white flower-clusters, with their exquisite fragrance.

In our Native Flora the Diapensiads have no place, but the few species of this race are all choice, beautiful little creatures—and, for the most part, exacting little creatures too. *Diapensia lapponica* itself I have grown and flowered successfully, but have now lost; it is a rare Arctic and North American species, making great lichen-like mats of foliage, and then from each tiny rosette sending up a cup-shaped pearly flower. Damp, gritty soil is probably what it wants. For it is atmosphere rather than soil that is so hopelessly trying in our gardens to these plants from very high places and latitudes. The Pine Barren Beauty is a beauty indeed, from New Jersey, haunting the loose sand among the trees, where it makes masses of foliage like a wee reddish-green *Hypnum*, with abundance of pinky-white stars sitting close upon them. But *Pyxidanthera barbulata* has been an utter failure here, if I must speak the humbling truth; although other cultivators taunt me with their successful cultivation of it in very moist sand. My own impression is, that for this climate of the North, rather warm sunny sand is needed to suit the *Pyxidanthera*. However, some day I hope I may solve the riddle, for the plant is too lovely to abandon. Next comes *Galax aphylla*, a North American, with rounded, pretty leaves on long thin stems arranged in a loose rosette. The flowers are white, carried in thin stiff tails about six inches high or more. But it is in the leaves that the charm of the plant chiefly consists. For these turn of a most gorgeous scarlet if planted in some fairly exposed situation, and altogether Galax is one of the best and easiest of his race for the peat-bed.

But of the Diapensiads the special glory are the *Shortias* and *Schizocodon soldanelloeides*—two species very closely related and almost synonymous. *Shortia galacifolia* is a North American, discovered years since in Carolina, then lost, then rediscovered, and now, I am told, becoming extremely rare. It grows in loose woodlands with *Galax*, and very closely resembles the Wand-flower in growth, though the leaves are much more solid, the stalks thicker, the whole growth of the rosette denser and more stocky. The numerous flowers, five-cleft and single on their stems, are vaguely like very large and much more beautiful Soldanellas—ragged,

pearly-pink, and altogether most exquisite; the plant
is a splendidly good-tempered one, too, on any peaty
bank, sunny or shady, in light, well-drained stuff;
while in either situation, but most in sun, the leaves
and their stems turn of a dazzling crimson-scarlet most
startling to behold. There is also a dainty, rosy-flowered
form of this *Shortia*, which, take it all in all, has turned
out one of the most important additions to the rock-
garden. But for years a dim rumour floated of another
Shortia existing in the Alps of Japan. Some asserted,
others denied; some called the Japanese plant a synonym
of *galacifolia*; others sniffed at it altogether, until at
last, to confound all Betsey Prigs, *Shortia uniflora*
turned up in all its unmistakable beauty.

Shortia uniflora is exactly—but exactly—like a tiny,
straggling little *Galax*, with the same thin leathery
leaves, and everything. Yet, though the plant is so
much smaller than *Galacifolia*, the blossoms are even
larger, fringy great nodding bells of soft pink. Mr.
Hindmarsh of Newcastle has done more, I believe, than
any man living to wreck the Tenth Commandment, and
in his garden you will see the *Shortia* thriving like a
groundsel—look at the photograph in the Royal Horticultural Society's *Journal* if you doubt me. The plant
is decidedly difficult, I am afraid—a melancholy, shy-
rooting species. The trouble with these Diapensiads
too often is that they have very few, wooden, wiry
roots, and are extraordinarily reluctant to set about
making any more. However, now I have got a superb
importation of *Shortia uniflora*, hundreds of them, from
Japan, which arrived looking as if they had been packed
yesterday, and are now beginning to push new growths
with a pleasant appearance of happiness (though I fear
the plant is sometimes liable to collapse suddenly and
unexpectedly, without cause or cure), and the strongest

of these have been put out in very elaborate lily-beds and so forth—places where the soil is deep and rich and light, well mixed with crock, and with violent drainage far down below, two feet or so; there I had a justified hope that they might thrive. In Japan I never saw *Shortia uniflora*; but one day at Shoji the hotelkeeper pointed me out a patch, six miles or more across the country, in the dense pall of jungle that flows so royally down the western slope of Fuji-yama, and told me of a plant there which can have been nothing else. As to *Schizocodon soldanelloeides*— the name is daunting, but veracious, even if inadequate —that also I never collected, well-known high alpine though it be. I knew of the plant, and was bitterly disappointed never to hap upon it. But one evening I sallied forth from my little house in Tokio, to one of the fascinating night fairs that are for ever occurring in one street or another; and as I passed from stall to stall of delights, I came at last to the plants and toy-gardens. And there, before my eyes, in the streets of Tokio, shone the high alpine, unmistakable — stout rosettes of leathery, Galax-like leaves, and tall stems each carrying a dozen flowers or so—nodding great fringy bells, rose-pink, and marbled with crimson—far more dainty and more gorgeous than any Soldanella that ever pierced the snow. Of course I fell upon the treasure (so utterly different from the stunted little miseries that so far had represented *Schizocodon*'s best efforts in England) and ordered hundreds. They arrived next day—stalwart, tall-growing, splendid clumps, costing twopence each or so. My heart was filled with joy, and I sent them off to Yokohama to be packed for home. And there, in the summer heats of that unutterable place, they all sickened and expired. However, now I have got another lot of excellent plants, and am already beginning to look upon them anxiously. They were stout and luxuriant when they came, but their new growth has been wretchedly poor, and again I find that the plant is very shy about adding to the number of its few woody roots. However, in careful, well-drained beds with *Shortia uniflora*, I hope that it may do fair things, though already I see that it does not so far mean to emulate the cabbage - like development it affects in Japan ; while the poor stunted flower-stems that I have seen here, and in botanical gardens, show the high-water-mark of its ambitions, as against the sturdy, foot-high stems that it throws up in Tokio.

Of Ledum and Daphne I will first specify the dwarf little *Ledum buxifolium*, which makes dense, tiny, box-like bunches, with innumerable pink and white stars, and is invaluable for the choice peat-bed. Then there is the larger, and still neat, but much less attractive *Ledum labradoricum*, which, I remember, covered all the scabby quaking crusts about the awful Solfataras of Noboribets' in the Hokkaido—the most venturesome of all plants, daring the last limits of so-called solid ground, and venturing out even on to the volcano's recognised territories. Of the dwarf Daphnes it is impossible that I should speak without sorrow. With one exception they do not naturally like me, and though I grow them, and insist on growing them, whether they will or no, these glorious little plants are always more or less at war with me and my soil, so that our connection is rather a stormy one. The sole lime-lover of the race, so far as I know, is the rather rare *Daphne alpina*—a straggling, woody little gnarled grower with white flowers, which I have raised from seed and now possess at least one flourishing bush of in an unlikely dank corner of the Old Garden. Then comes *Daphne cneorum*, loveliest and sweetest of dwarf shrubs, with its abundant, bright-pink flower-heads, and its intoxicating fragrance. But, though *cneorum* haunts the limestone, I am told, quite happily at times, and though in Leeds I have seen it thriving like a weed, with me the plant is seldom satisfactory for long, and my growing of it is often an uphill tragic matter. And then, in a garden ten miles off, it will flourish like a bay-tree. It is true that some of my newer plants are looking perfectly satisfactory, fresh growth and all, in carefully built peat-beds, but how long this apparent prosperity will last I cannot tell, and of all things on earth what is more depressing than a gradually ailing, dying shrub? As for the new much-advertised *Daphne Verloti*, I purchased a lot of it when it was first proclaimed, and my own impression is that it only differs unfavourably, if at all, from *Daphne cneorum*. I have lost all my plants and shall never replace them. *Daphne blagayana* has been quite good with me ever since I realised that all the plant really wants is to be perpetually stoned with stones like the tomb of Absalom. Plant this lovely trailing Tyrolese Daphne in rough peat, and then, every time you pass, hurl a mighty rock on top of him, and pin down all his branches under boulders. And then he will break up through every interstice, and in time will make you a mass many yards across, as at Glasnevin, producing untold abundance of large creamy-white flower-heads, scented like nearly all his race. *Daphne rupestris* is the last, the wee-est, the most difficult of the Alpine Daphnes—a tiny, almost microscopic shrub, with waxy great pink flowers, far larger and more lovely even than those of *cneorum*. *Rupestris* is a Tyrolese, and in cultivation wants stony peat and a good deal of fuss. My own experience, however, has been entirely with grafted plants, which are infinitely more vigorous than own-root specimens, and fifty times more easy to grow. *Rupestris*, grafted on

DAPHNE RUPESTRIS

(*Award of Merit, Temple Show, 1906*).

seedling *Laureola*, makes a minute dense bush, quite robust and healthy, and never (or very, very rarely) breaking below the graft. Thus treated it flowers amazingly, and thrives in any sunny, peaty soil, making sturdy short trunks that increase each year. My famous plant lives in a pot, and receives daily homage—the finest specimen possibly in the world, started years ago by Dr. Stuart, and grown on here from season to season, till now it is a rounded tiny tree about eight inches high and as many across, which flowers so profusely that one cannot see the leaves. At each Temple Show this glorious little veteran appears, never suffering from the jaunt, nor failing to be ready in time. The worst of the matter is that his appearance precipitates such a demand for *Daphne rupestris* that all the mountains of all the world would hardly be able to supply it.

Of the Pyrolas no one needs to be reminded who has seen the big Lily-of-the-Valley-flowered spikes of *Pyrola rotundifolia* on open grassy shoulders of the Alps—a long-fibred, straggling thing, with rosettes of round leathery leaves, which, if you give it time, and make certain of soundly rooted plants, is perfectly easy to establish in any peaty corner of the rock-garden. My own best plant was brought years ago from the Dolomites, and by now has made himself perfectly at home, and runs about all over the place, flowering each season from his strongest rosettes, and perpetually sending up more in the most unexpected corners among *Gentiana Asclepiadea* and *Rosa alpina*. The one thing to remember about this Pyrola is that he is exceedingly difficult to collect, as his sparse root goes rambling underground for ever so far, and never forms into any nice compact tuft of fibres. (Notice this tiresome weakness in all these leather-leaved species of the Copses.) The other varieties of Pyrola are, to all intents and purposes, lesser variants of *rotundifolia*, and, having the one, I have never troubled about the others. But *Pyrola incarnata* stands away from them all in a splendid isolation of loveliness. Imagine a *rotundifolia*, pure and simple, but with flowers of a soft carmine-rose. This is *Pyrola incarnata* as I found and adoringly collected it in the Canadian Rockies some years ago. Other kinds of *Pyrola* were abundant, but *incarnata* only occurred here and there; and I removed whole wads of the world—great rotten masses of leaf-mould and wood—in my reverent zeal to get its roots intact. And I have been rewarded, in that my plants have all survived. But they have done no more. They have survived, and survived in unimpaired health, too; but they have neither gone ahead nor thriven, which seems rather ungracious of them. In all these seasons I do not think I have ever seen those rose-red bells again, though every attention in the way of loose spongy, peaty, leafy mould has been prepared for the thankless plants who ought to be their bearers.

Pyrola uniflora is, properly, *Moneses uniflora*, I believe —a most lovely and most awfully difficult species, which occurs in damp mossy woods all over the northern mountain-chains—even, rarely, in Scotland. I have found it in the Rockies and in Switzerland, and collected it repeatedly, but never with any permanent success. From the flat, glossy little rosette of leaves springs one flower-stem, carrying a single very large flower, like a nodding Grass of Parnassus, with a great projecting stigma, and the most exquisite, poignant fragrance. But you only have to look at the plant to see that its growth promises no vigour. For my own part, I believe that it is either saprophytic or parasitic—that those tiny, threadlike, white roots are dependent on some dead or living host for their nourishment. Anyhow, do what I will, it only languishes here—blooming one season, perhaps, with great care, and after that dying with prompt decision.

And now comes *Tiarella*, a plant whose appearance follows Spiraea. And this is no pretender, for Tiarella belongs to the Roses, as Spiraea does also—for some sacred, esoteric reason. *Tiarella cordifolia* is no less valuable than common—a splendid plant for any shady bank, making carpets of handsome Heuchera-like foliage, russet-red in autumn, with innumerable fairy-like little plumes of white in early summer. It roots freely as it goes, and makes great masses in no time; so that it is a treasure of very high rank. And then comes my own particular marvel—a plant which was found by my Manager in an old Yorkshire garden, where it had been grown for more than a hundred years without name or history. Its name was long doubtful, in fact, and we have shown it under many vacillating but enthusiastic titles—as *grandiflora*, *superba*, *rosea*, and so forth. Now at last I have definitely ascertained that it is the almost unknown third species of *Tiarella* (the other is the pretty but not very wonderful *polyphylla*, and I will not talk of dowdy things like *Tolmiaea* and *Tellima* in this connection), the true *Tiarella unifoliata* of Asa Gray. This North American may be briefly described as an enormous version of *Tiarella cordifolia*, with foliage that forms into a dense clump, and takes the most splendid bronze and crimson tones as the year gets old. The plant, however, throws no stolons or offsets, though it can be easily divided, and the flower-stems are sent up two feet or so in such abundance as sometimes, in very wet weather, to clog and rot each other—the plumes being long and very graceful, creamy-white, each flower having apricot-coloured anthers that give a delightful rosy tinge to the flower-spike. The plant is a perfect grower in any deep, fairly rich soil on border or rockwork, never ramping about like *cordifolia*, but always sitting still in the same place, and giving profusion of white foam-flowers, as fine to look at as they are to pick. It will appreciate any amount of richness, though, in the soil of manure and leaf-mould.

The Natural Order of the Bignonias—a paradox, seeing what fearful tropical climbers and Lianes are Bignonia and Tecoma themselves—provides the garden with what, when all is said and done, remains, probably, the most important introduction of the last fifty years. I do not think that, considering its brilliancy, its size, its extraordinary hardiness and vigour, this award is any too high for *Incarvillea Delavayi*, that splendid find of Abbé Delavay's, which, in itself, is almost enough to reconcile oneself to the existence of missionaries. If only all their actions were so productive and beneficent! Nowadays every one knows *Incarvillea Delavayi*, with its magnificent Acanthoid foliage, and its tall spikes of great pink Gloxinias. Every one knows, too, that any deep soil with fair drainage suits the plant absolutely; so that I will only say that for border or rockwork nothing could well be more stately or admirable. My only ambition is for a white *Delavayi* to appear among my seedlings, for, to confess the great shortcoming of the plant, its colour has a horrid tang of impurity—a taint of chalk or lilac in its pink. For the rock-garden, even more important is the newer and still rare *Incarvillea grandiflora* — a truly superb thing, like a miniature *Delavayi*, making a small, flattish tuft of leaves, with stem of about six inches height or less, each carrying one or two blossoms quite as large as, if not larger than, those of *Delavayi*, with far more brilliancy of colour, and bright definite markings in the throat of their trumpets. *Grandiflora* turns out in my garden to be as satisfactory and trustworthy in every way as *Delavayi*, and, altogether, is one of the most splendid dwarf plants that one could possibly have. Of *Incarvillea compacta*, rather similar in appearance, my experience has not been long enough to let me speak. But I cannot conceive that it will rival *grandiflora*. As for *Incarvillea Olgae* and *Incarvillea variabilis*, my experience of them, in every soil and situation, has been that they are invariably half-hardy in constitution, and not very satisfactory either in growth or flower—to flower, in fact, they seem to have a great reluctance. I have long since given them up.

Of *Cyananthus* there are two species, but only one, I believe, is in cultivation. *Cyananthus lobatus* is a very brilliant and perfectly hardy trailing alpine, which has the rare and splendid merit of blooming in the autumn. The whole plant is rather fleshy, with a quantity of prostrate branches that break up anew each spring. The flowers are produced in great abundance, and for a long period; they are large, and of an almost cold steely blue, vaguely like very starry deep-coloured Periwinkles. They have huge inflated calyces shaggy with black hairs, which too often, by retaining the autumnal rains, rot the seed-capsules unless you strip them away. With this one caution, the plant has a perfect character here—quite hardy and trustworthy in every way, though you should plant it rather high and dry so that its dormant root-stock may not be annoyed by excessive or stagnant damps in winter.

The Potatoes only give me one plant in the lovely *Nierembergia rivularis*, which, in rich cool soil, makes a deciduous carpet of ovate glossy leaves, amid which nestle freely its huge pearl-coloured cups. *Nierembergia frutescens* is a delicate, exquisite sub-shrub, not hardy, with long fine branches like those of a Linum, and big bluish flowers of extreme beauty.

The Polemoniums lead off with the common Jacob's

Ladder, so abundant in every old garden, and a rare
native in this country, being found in our own valley,
and again round Malham. *Sibiricum* is a more or less
synonymous form. *Polemonium reptans* is a very valuable
plant for border or rockwork, making great bushes more
than a foot high, starred with countless bright blue
flowers. And *Polemonium humile* (or *Richardsoni*), with
its variety *pulchellum* (or *pulcherrimum*), are charming
choice dwarf plants, for much more prominent select
corners than the bigger-growing kinds. Then comes
the rare and lovely *flavum*, which I had seed of as
pauciflorum—most attractive, with long pendent trumpets
of soft yellow. But the aristocrats of the race are *confertum* and its variety *mellitum*. The leaves in both are
downy and very densely pinnate—so densely, indeed, that
they look quite like plumes; the spikes rise to eight inches
or so, and are thickly set with large flowers, which, in
confertum, are of a brilliant soft blue, while in *mellitum*
they are of a skim-milk white. Both are lovely, but
confertum, the type, is to me far more lovely than
mellitum—a most delightful and fascinating plant. Not
to mention that *mellitum* has such an awful smell of beer,
that when I show it I find all friends of temperance principles looking upon me with a suspicious eye. They are
both, though North Americans, quite happy in cultivation. Some people find them miffy, I hear; with me,
however, they are perfectly trustworthy—remembering
always that they want a high, drained place, where they
will be safe from undue damp in winter. They die down
and disappear as autumn draws on, but can almost invariably be trusted to perk up again with the spring,
unless stagnant moisture has been too much for them in
the resting season. All the other Polemoniums are as
hardy and easy as the native one, and every species seeds
with laudable fidelity and freedom.

Passing over the washy-coloured Thrifts (none of whom can I love) and the brilliant Acantholimons from the sunny East, we come to Gesneraceae and a group of rock-plants before whom we ought to go down in gratitude on our knees. Long, long ago, Parkinson loved *Ramondia pyrenaica*, and described it with his usual accuracy, though, with the limited knowledge at his command, he included it among the Alpine Primulas. And, indeed, the great crinkled, hairy, flat rosette is not unlike some Primulas, and the big blue-lilac flowers also have something Primulaceous in their look, though now we can easily see that they are something quite different, with their overlapping lobes and the lovely gold-eyed ' Pointil,' as Parkinson would call it, sticking out of the middle. On any rockwork, in any cool or peaty soil, on the sunless side *Ramondia* thrives splendidly, and seeds, too—the seedlings very often proving albinoes; though, for my own part, neither the white nor the *Rosea* Ramondia pleases me nearly as much as the ordinary form from the Pyrenees. The plant can be multiplied, too, I have found, by striking leaf-cuttings, as with Begonia, though this is a slow process. *Ramondia serbica* is a closely allied plant, in some ways even prettier, with smaller and more numerous flowers of a brighter blue, and generally four - lobed, and therefore cross-shaped in appearance. Much more beautiful, however, than either of these, to my mind, is the Queen of all Ramondias—Queen Natalie's Ramondia. *Ramondia Nataliae* is glossy in the leaf, and wonderfully free in the flower. Otherwise it closely resembles *pyrenaica*, but the flowers are rather larger, earlier, and infinitely more bright and delicate in the tone of their lovely lavender-blue; a clump of *Ramondia Nataliae* in good bloom beats every other beautiful Ramondia quite into the background. *Pyrenaica major* is fine, so are *serbica* and the hybrid *permixta*, but nothing can compete with *Nataliae*. Years ago, too, at vast expense, I imported a mass of it from the Balkans, on the promise that the batch contained an albino form. Out of all that high-priced bale, only one plant bore me true white flowers. But the snowy *Nataliae* is indeed an exquisite thing, solid in build and pure in tone—not feeble and ragged as the generality of albino Pyrenaicas. And *Nataliae*, too, simply requires the same treatment as any other Ramondia. They all like cool, peaty chinks, and, these granted, nothing in the world is easier to grow than the Rock-Mulleins. As for *quercifolia*, *leucopetala*, and *peregrina*, these are new species, of whom I have no startling news to tell, except that they are nothing but minutely differentiated varietal forms of the ordinary *pyrenaica*.

Close to Ramondia comes *Haberlea*, the delightful little mountain Gloxinia from Rhodope, whose foliage is like that of a narrow-leafed *Ramondia pyrenaica*, and whose abundant flowers are carried on six-inch stems in little loose heads, and are exactly like those of a wee *Streptocarpus*. This charming plant is quite as easy to grow as the Ramondias, requiring exactly the same treatment. As for the albino form that I managed to import last year, I should want to rhapsodise like Ruskin before I could do justice to its fine snow-white trumpets with the stain of pure yellow in their throat. It took an Award of Merit at the R.H.S. this year. A near cousin of this is one of the worst reputed of all alpines—the silver-leaved *Jankaea Heldreichi*, which sometimes masquerades as *Ramondia Heldreichi*, except when it takes it into its head to be called *Haberlea Heldreichi*. This true rock-plant makes flat rosettes of rounded leaves that are brilliantly silvery with a felt of fine white down. This at once shows you where difficulty lies. The plant is utterly, absolutely opposed to any surface moisture whatever. It must be planted where no drop or drip can ever get to it. After I had failed many times my Manager discovered such a place on the rockwork, four or five years ago, and there, in a cunning cavity which you have to bend down if you want to see, my best *Jankaea* was stuffed with plenty of rough peat, in such a cavern that no shower could ever worry it. And there this 'miffy' subject, as even Mr. Robinson calls it, has thriven and increased in the most heartsome way, adding yearly to the number of its crowns, and simply flashing with the untarnished silver of its rosettes. As to the flowers, they are of a rare and marvellous loveliness; on each stem several open bells, much larger and rounder than *Haberlea rhodopensis*, and of a very, very pale violet, almost verging towards white, whose charm is enhanced by the consistency of the flower, which has that crystalline solidity that you get in certain Orchids, so that the whole blossom, if you see it in the sun, glisters all over with innumerable crystal points, and seems to be carved out of lavender-tinted snow.

Conandron ramondioeides is the last of our noble Gesneriads — a puzzling Japanese which ought to be perfectly hardy, and yet, somehow, is not. *Conandron* makes immense pointed, Begonia-like leaves, crinkled, glossy, and pale green, with half a dozen flowers or so on stiff, short, fleshy stems. The blossoms themselves are very fascinating, like large potato-flowers, with a golden eye. This plant goes far into the high Japanese Alps, where you find it creeping over the face of mossy, unsunned precipices, with no soil to grow in except a tiny cranny here and there. As you enter Nikko you see it above you, just as you are crossing the bridge which now occupies the place of the Holy Red-Lacquer Mihashi; and again, on fully exposed sunny cliffs by the Kenchoji at Kamakura, I have seen *Conandron* making the whole precipice a curtain of its shining leaves. But here, in

England, the plant seems doubtful, resenting something in our treatment, either damp, or sun, or shade, or drought, or exile. I have not yet solved the riddle; so far, all my attempts in the open, under rocks, and so forth, have ended in failure. But I do not mean to be baffled by a Japanese alpine who has no sort of excuse for being half-hardy, so I intend to continue until I have found out what it is that *Conandron* really does require in our gardens.

Of the Mertensias all, as far as I know, are royally beautiful, and most are quite successful here. *Primuloeides* has not done well, and I regret this the more, that I have always thought *primuloeides* so much more pretty than *echioeides*, which prospers and spreads delightfully, and is a treasure. *Primuloeides* is but small and frail, with heads of flowers that change colour as they open, so that on one head you will see ruby, sapphire, and deep amethyst blossoms all at once, with others fading by turns into each shade. *Echioeides*, that unexacting Himâlyan, likes loose peaty soil, in which it does not seem to want any further attention. Indeed, I now believe that it will thrive in any ordinary fair loam. My only loss with it was of one plant that died of sunstroke one hot day; but the others, in cooler corners, go on thriving of their own accord, and never mind my winters. The Virginian Cowslip, the rare and glorious old *Mertensia virginica*, is splendid for very fat, peaty, manury soil in some sheltered place where winds cannot annoy its lovely glaucous and bronzy leaves. The plant is of rather poor reputation, and slugs love it. But really, with good deep soil and perfect neglect, it is absolutely hardy and easy to do with; while, as for its almost synonymous cousins, the only slightly less beautiful Mertensias, *ciliata* and *sibirica*, they will thrive anywhere, and increase mightily, and sow seed of themselves. *Mertensia alpina* is really *Mertensia*

lanceolata, a comparatively small - growing alpine, very
choice and rare; while similar, and of extraordinary
attractiveness, even among Mertensias, is *elongata*, far and
away the very best of all, with narrow, blue-grey leaves
and the most heavenly pale blue bugles, with rosy-red
buds. This I have grown on from seed, and now find
perfectly easy and precious in any sort of soil or aspect,
the least exacting of its race, and quite the loveliest.
Finally, our own native Oyster-plant, *Mertensia maritima*,
is both interesting and attractive. I succeeded once in
getting seedlings of it from the sea-sands above the
Isle of Walney, and now it grows as happily and stoutly
in ordinary garden loam as if it had never even heard of
the sea. Each season it sends up its pinky-blue glaucous
leaves, that are soon trailing about all over the place,
bright glaucous grey branches, with countless rather
small flowers of a brilliant, and brilliantly contrasting,
azure. It is a perpetual wonder to me that this exact-
ing-looking sea-board plant should prove so vigorous in
a mere heavy loam, unhelped even by peat or sand.

In Omphalodes the Borages give us another of their
notable contributions to the list of Alpine plants.
Strange, that so large and hot and hairy a race should
yet give us some of the very choicest of small difficult
plants. But no one will dispute the claim of the Forget-
me-nots, of *Eritrichium nanum*, and of *Omphalodes Luciliae*. The Omphalodes include, too, Blue-eyed Mary,
the invincible trailing Forget-me-not that is so invaluable
for rough shady places in poor soil — a simple azure
woodlander, artless and rustic enough to have become,
so they say, the favourite flower of Queen Marie-Antoi-
nette. There is also the pretty annual *Omphalodes linifolia*, and the very rare, and, as rumour has it, most
beautiful *Omphalodes nitida* or *lusitanica*, which I have
never yet succeeded in getting living plants of. How-

ever, though my pot-plants of *Omphalodes Luciliae* seem but poorly, this notoriously capricious little beauty is now quite pleased with life on the moraine, and its lovely grey leaves are already in such good evidence that before long the large, flat flowers of pale blue should be appearing. In fact, one tried to appear the other day, but a frost interfered and said 'No.' However, the plant is clearly established, which is one comfort; and my idea seems sound that soil, in this damp climate, can easily be too lavishly applied; while there is far greater chance of establishing Lucilla's Omphalodes (whoever she may have been. Mr. Wolley-Dod told me once, but I have forgotten. She owns the Glory of the Snow as well, the grasping Lucilla) in light, warm, poor stuff, than in any heavy loam or peat. Slugs eat it, too, with passion, so that on all hands this lovely plant requires all the care that tradition declares is necessary for it. It has very sensitive roots, I believe, that resent disturbance, which is another addition to the difficulties attending its culture, though one reads of favoured places where, in light ground, it makes a weed of itself. This Omphalodes hails from Greece and Asia Minor, a rock-loving, sun-craving mountaineer, impatient of damps and dulness.

As for the Forget-me-nots, they come under the wing of *Eritrichium*, and *Eritrichium nanum* is so distinctly and essentially what Edelweiss pretends to be — *the* typical high alpine—that this patron saint of my book must have a chapter all to himself, a full Odyssey of his finding and reception in my garden. So now I will only say that *Eritrichium strictum* is a dear little annual blue thing, like a wee Alkanet, who has the meek charm and amiability of some inconspicuous pretty sister to a spoiled haughty beauty.

CHAPTER XVI

A Hunting Day and Eritrichium nanum

In and out of all the great mountain - chains lives *Eritrichium nanum*, but high, high up, far above the highest of the Androsaces—so high that, except with luck, the mere walker can rarely hope to meet with it. Into chinks of the great granite precipices it makes its little cobweb cushions of down, that, in their time, are hidden by the dense mass of its dazzling sky-blue blossoms. The plant's range is extraordinary; in all probability it is essentially an Arctic, rather than an Alpine species. For, while in the mountains it is only sporadically found, and always at very high elevations (seldom does it appear till you are at least 10,000 feet above sea-level), yet, as you get north towards the Pole, it comes lower and lower, carpeting the ground, until at last, in some of the Aleutian and Antarctic islands, it is reported as coming right down to the water's edge, where it is for ever soaked with the salt spray. In the Alps it occurs along the whole chain, but always seems to avoid the limestone. But throughout the granitic mountains you may usually hope to find it, if you go high enough; while, in the Tyrol and Engadine, there are blessed peaks where the mule-track leads you over beds of it.

For years of misfortune had I hunted it, never succeeding in my quest. My search had been made along the Bernese Oberland, where, I believe, it does not, as a matter of fact, appear at all—anyhow, is not readily attainable. And I am not a mountaineer, to go tight-roping along arêtes, or daring the horrors of the mountain world; I am a mild and modest walker, and will walk anywhere for a plant. Therefore it was an important point with me to find some place where *Eritrichium* should come to meet me half-way on neutral ground, instead of leering derisively down at me from unattainable heights. And often, from the Gemmi, had I longingly scanned the great wall of the Valaisan Alps far away across the invisible bed of the Rhone, five thousand feet below. For the distribution of *Eritrichium* can hardly be said to begin until you reach the southern and the easterly ranges, and I knew that all along the Monte Rosa chain the high, high crevices of the rock here and there yield *Eritrichium*, not to mention *Androsace imbricata*, and sometimes the rare, lime-craving *Saxifraga diapensioeides*. *Eritrichium* had been specially reported to me from above the Schwarzsee, over Zermatt, and several climbers had told me of having seen its celestial tufts huddling into the rock as they wormed their dreadful way up the crevices—the climbers, not the *Eritrichium*. So for long I coveted leisure to search the southerly valleys off the Rhone, and went about to hear of a pass where *Eritrichium* might be got without imperilling one's days.

And at last I got both the leisure and the direction. M. Correvon gave me news of a little cul-de-sac called the Turtmann Thal, between the valleys of Zinal and Zermatt. From this gully between the hills, was his tale, you climb and you climb and you climb until you come to the summit of the Meiden Pass that leads over the mountains and down upon St. Niklaus in the Zermatt valley. And near the crown of the pass sits *Eritrichium*, said he, in a happy abundance all over the slope. This rosy prospect was confirmed at Kew, and so, in a few days, I packed up my best trowel and set off.

It was a steaming hot morning when I and my party alighted in the Rhone valley, that Turkish bath of prostrating heat. And immeasurably far above rose the awful mountains. Is there any weak vessel who will sympathise with my feelings of crushed despair when I stand at something like sea-level, and gaze with craning neck up, up, up to those peaks ten thousand feet or so straight overhead? The whole thing is so Titanic; my mind is reduced to a feeble wonder as to how it can *ever* be possible to get anywhere near such fearful elevations. Then one sets off, and in about five or six hours the job is done. But it is a fearful pull up from Turtmann to Meiden. As with all these mountain gullies—relatively tiny little channels worn deep between the hills by torrents from the upper snows—you have first a breathless scramble of a thousand feet or more, till you have reached the mean level of the upper valley; and thence your road goes on ascending, steadily, indeed, but without truculence, until you have reached your destination, above which, up another fierce climb, lie the upmost mountain glens that each feed the valley with a stream. The Turtmann Thal is wild and very little trodden, and very beautiful. To a gardener it is especially interesting as being one of the few westerly habitats of *Linnaea borealis*, which, at one turn of the path, rather more than half-way up, is seen trailing freely about among the moss and boulders. But, oh, it's a weary way! I must evidently make a clean breast of it here, or the shameful truth will leak out. I am lazy. I can walk, I suppose, as well as most. On the open fell I can go on perpetually without much food or fatigue. But I don't really like walking for its own sake; I had rather not walk. I walk only when there is something to be got by walking that

could not be got in any other way, and never for the
mere sake of the walking itself. I regard the British
craze for exercise as a superstition, and, of all Mr. Cham-
berlain's ideas, am proud only to share one, in our common
prejudice against unnecessary exertion. Therefore, it will
easily be seen how hard a fate it is that has dowered one
so sedentary with a passion for plants. Walk I must,
and walk I do. But, whenever I needn't, I frankly don't.
I have no shame whatever in availing myself of any
funicular that may happen to be handy; and when there
is a railway up the Matterhorn, I may faintly deplore it,
but I shall certainly go up in it. And so will many
others who virtuously declaim against any such unpic-
turesque concession to idleness. Accordingly I rode up
to Meiden upon a mule, an animal for which I have no
love, but which is preferable to avoidable pedestrianism.

Meiden and its hotel—in fact, the hotel is about all
there is of Meiden—sits up near the end of the cul-de-sac.
The high snows are quite out of sight, hidden, on either
hand, by the most fearful ramparts of forests. Up and
up they go, those walls of woodland, till you think that
nothing can possibly stand above them, for surely they
are the pillars of Heaven itself. And yet, above them
again, and dwarfing them to molehills, go soaring the
real giant mountains. Every one of these mountain
glens has its great peak, whose snow-bred torrent it is
that has carved the valley out. Evolena has the ghastly-
glorious Dent Blanche, Arolla has the Mont Collon, Zinal
has its Roth-Horn; as for Zermatt, it has the Mont Rose
and the Matterhorn, not to mention many others. The
mother-peak of the Turtmann Thal is the Weisshorn—
that stark pinnacle which is so appallingly impressive
from the heights of the Furka, I should not like to say
how many miles away. From the hotel at Meiden you
get no hint of its dominating presence, but scramble

along the steep woodland above the old burnt hotel, across the stream, until you have turned the intervening shoulder of the lower hills, and there you see It, the dreadful, splendid It—the peak of the Weisshorn, from this point crooked and taloned like Death's beckoning finger.

The first part of my climb, from the hotel, is pure treadmill. Up one goes, through the steep woods, up and up and up and up eternally. No mules here, no adventitious aids; nothing but trudge, trudge, trudge. But—and far sooner than I had dared to hope—the woods are surmounted. My favourite method of progression on such occasions is by alternate rushes and panting stops. This method is utterly derided by my friends. But it certainly covers the ground quickly, and does not, at least in my case, produce any ultimate fatigue. At last the stifling valley (Heaven be thanked that, our slope being an eastern one, the sun has not yet come over the Meiden Pass to embitter it with his beams) is left beneath us, and already the clear air is beginning to sing in our ears. Below us the hotel (almost straight down, it looks, beneath our feet) is a mere hut. 'There are many wonderful things,' says Sophokles, with his usual acuteness, ' but there is none more wonderful than man.' From below, that slope had looked infinite. Yet in half an hour it is conquered. Appalling as is the vastness of the hills, the flea-like little speck of humanity is able to devour so great a slice of them in so little time. Mountains, be humble ; man, be set up ! We can get to the top of you in time for lunch—yes, and be home again in time for dinner !

Now the last trees, the last little juniper scrubs are left behind, and left behind the muddy agglomeration of huts which marks the upper cattle-station. When you come to this, you always know that you are on the lower limit of the Alpine vegetation. The track leads upwards for a little, and then debouches into the upper glen, which now stretches away before us, level and smooth, right away to the peaks themselves. A dark notch against the sky shows where the pass is, the one break in the wall of ice and rock that goes jagging viciously across the clear blue. The Weisshorn is out of sight, towards the right.

And as we go, the pure little people of the mountain begin to throng around us. I would not for the world do injustice to the flowers of the lower world, but, once up in the hills, I cannot believe that any lowland plant has quite the luminous glory of these untainted creatures that make colonies of brilliance up here amid the sunshine and the mist, far across the twinkling expanse of grass. The first to appear is an early *Aster alpinus*—a fine clump of him, brilliant purple, far deeper than usual. And then, if my memory serves me, he never appeared again all that day. *Arnica* soon comes into sight, gorgeous with his orange blossoms; and then, later on, *Senecio Doronicum*, even more beautiful in the fiery colour of his deep-golden flowers, contrasted with his grey-and-silver leaves.

The track now takes us across lawns of fine grass that are almost hidden by *Viola calcarata* in every shade of purple, by *Primula farinosa*, *Myosotis rupicola*, and *Gentiana brachyphylla*. No one could imagine the beauty of it all, the dainty riot of glory. The big Alpine Pansy is one of the plants that simply shakes hands with you, and insists on doing so. There is no resisting its friendly little face, and the way its black-lashed eye winks and twinks as it looks at you. Nor is such an appearance deceptive. *Viola calcarata* is a real robin-plant, a friend of man, and delighted with his company. I have grown innumerable plants of him, and they all smile at me as happily on the rockwork,

Myosotis rupicola and Saxifraga cochlearis

even in autumn and early winter, as they do in July on the Alpine meadows. Far otherwise is it with the almost undistinguishable *Viola cenisia*, which I have many times collected and never succeeded in making friends with. About *Myosotis rupicola* I must go cautiously. The name is doubtful; in fact, few people seem to know what *Myosotis rupicola* really is, and fewer people still to possess it. The origin of the name too is rather 'wropped in a mistry.' Certainly one *rupicola* was named from the British high-alpine form of *Myosotis alpestris*, which occurs only on Mickle Fell. Thus *rupicola*, of gardens, should be a dwarf stunted, big-flowered version (if a plant loses in length of stem, it generally increases in size of flowers) of *Myosotis alpestris*. And the common form that one gets on these Alpine meadows is certainly faithful to that description. It is *alpestris*, large in the bloom and short in the stem. But dim rumour whispers of another plant to which the name of *rupicola* has been given; and the contradictions of nurserymen on the point are endless. As often as not, what is sent out as *rupicola* is nothing like this beautiful little Swiss dwarf which I grow for *rupicola*, and shall, *salvâ veniâ*, continue to call *rupicola*. The true *rupicola*, then, to beg the question, is singularly lovely, but it has not a very good constitution. It likes a sunny, well-drained corner of the rockery, but intensely dislikes excessive damp in winter (on the Alps, you see, it would be dry under snow all the resting season, and, of course, has the characteristic hairiness that makes alpines so impatient of surface damp). My oldest, finest clump went to its long home this last winter, after four years of glorious life. It was grown from Mickle Fell seed, so must certainly be *rupicola*. As for *Primula farinosa* and *Gentiana brachyphylla*, I won't pause on them now, except to tell how I found among the rest three little snow-white flowers of the Gentian, like big Jasmine blossoms.

So the way carries us on and on over meadow and marsh, till at last we are passing sodden hollows from which the snow is just gone, and where *Soldanella* is peeping up, and *Draba aeizoeides* already bearing its little yellow blooms.

No song of praise is needed for Soldanellas. But— they are not everybody's plant. They will grow in any cool, fair place; but in many gardens they sternly decline to flower. And nothing is more exasperating than to see a plant derisively making innumerable fat leaves at you, when you know that it means to refuse you even a bud of blossom. Of the species, I have found *Clusii* and *pyrolaefolia* the best in this respect, where all are bad. These two are handsomer than most, and more free-flowering. *Alpina* is not quite so good in any way, and *minima*, exceedingly wee and dainty, has the double advantage of being a shy flowerer and also rather a miffy little doer. I have got one clump in the Moraine Garden, however, which seems to be thriving and flower- ing. Otherwise I have no very good character to give with the plant. But it is worth noting that a way of coaxing all the species to bloom is to put a good pane of glass over them in the winter. I forget who gave me the tip, but I have found it answer admirably. The idea is that, to ripen them well over the resting time, it is necessary to provide some substitute for the snow that keeps them so snug and dry through the winter in their native hills. Look how briskly they spring up after the snow, or even pierce through it. They evidently require a sharp rest, and then a brisk, rapid awakening. And yet I have heard of unfussed-with Scotch borders where *Soldanella* not only grows like a weed but flowers as freely as any Pink!

Now the track begins to lead up over humped ballast-hills of tumbled stone and shingle, with streaks of moisture running here and there. Here and there glows *Ranunculus glacialis*; and great mats of *Saxifraga oppositifolia* begin to shine at us, and show, by the fact that they are still in flower so late in July, that we have reached a very considerable height, certainly nine thousand or more. Ah, *Eritrichium* is near! Down, beating heart! I suppose all collectors have that same trepidating glory which a gardener feels when he is drawing close to the place where he expects to find a treasure,—the tremendous thrill of excitement, of ecstasy, of doubt, of terror. How we con all chances—whether the place be right, the season propitious, our informant trust-worthy; how our spirits flutter lest untoward chances—cattle, storms, landslips—have obliterated our heart's desire. How the minutes pulse agonisingly by, growing into a sort of abscess of suspense, to break in a moment into the full rapture of relief, or, inwardly, bitterly, with the dreadful gall of disappointment! But, at least, we gardeners have advantages over other collectors. For we have not to buy or bargain for our pleasure, like collectors of stamps or curiosities. No fluctuating markets can pull down the value of our joy; above all, our joy, once found, is there for us to take. Think of the poor sportsman, the poorer entomologist. The Okapi, the Camberwell Beauty discovered, away they flee. An unlucky shot, a futile sweep of the net, and all glory of the delusively successful quest is dust and ashes. At the best, your entomologist has to run sweating over the country after his prize, while we, we blessed ones, may sit down calmly, philosophically, beside our success, and gently savour all its sweetness until it is time to take out the trowel after half an hour of restful rapture on our laurels.

R

Already I am beginning to feel rather tremulous.   For
we are very high up now, and the crown of the pass is
straight above our heads, four or five hundred feet.
Somewhere in that four or five hundred feet lies radiant
triumph or blank disappointment.   But hitherto nothing
in the least resembling *Eritrichium* has been seen, and
the precipitous jumble of *débris* that leads up to the Col
is clearly not the place to expect any interesting plant,
least of all the Blue Moss.   At best it will only yield
Saxifraga oppositifolia here and there.   Qualms beset
me; can I have missed my treasure by the way?   Yet
no; impossible; such a thing as *Eritrichium* is not easily
missed.   Even if it were out of flower?   Well, he's but a
poor botanist who requires the help of the flower before
he can recognise a plant.   Many bad moments have I
had already, thinking I saw the soft grey mats of my
ambition.   Every valuable plant seems to have a common
counterpart, and there are some odious little high-alpine
plantains which make silvery rosettes not unlike those
of *Eritrichium.*   Upon these have I darted again and
again, only to fall back in disgust.   Black despair begins
to hover round me after many such rebuffs, and oh, how
high and unapproachable looks that horrid pass above us!
Shall I ever drag my disheartened limbs up that pitiless
final ascent?   Now the path is skirting the sunless inner
slope of a great mountain of rubble that has formed in
front of the Col.   Our track has to climb this slope, then
take a sharp outward turn over the shoulder of the
hump, and so slew round again and inward, a hundred
feet above its present level, on the last steep slant that
leads up the Col.   Where we are is shade and snow-
banks, and a dark, dank depression.   And across that,
over a late snow-bed, the sunny final acclivity of the pass.
And our present track is quite clearly no place for
Eritrichium; no sensible plant would grow in so gloomy

a dell. Only *Aronicum* peers out here and there among the bare blocks, but even *Aronicum* cannot flower in so unpropitious a corner. However, at last we reach the top of the shoulder, and our path comes out of shadow into the light of the summit. It is the change from Hell to Heaven. And what a Heaven, fallen in splashes on the earth! A dry, sunny hillside, dropping down, down, down towards the lower levels, and over it everywhere, amid soft stunted grasses, tiny blots and patches of blue sky—Woolly-Hair the Dwarf!

One pause, just to make sure of the bliss which is so hard to believe. Yes, this is no delusion, no silly *Myosotis*—it is *Eritrichium* itself. A calm glory of destiny fulfilled descends upon me. In another moment I am on my knees before the nearest tuft of blue, babbling inanities into its innumerable little lovely faces. Then I look up at the Col. Bless me, how close and easy looks the climb! I return to *Eritrichium*, and begin wandering up and down the slope, adoring each blossoming mass in turn. There is no colour that I know exactly like that of *Eritrichium*. It is blue—the absolute blue. And yet there is a softness about it which sets it far apart from the terrifying brilliance of *Gentiana verna*, or the almost vicious blatancy of *Scilla sibirica*. The very sky, again, at its best has a faint touch of green in its azure that makes it rather fiercer than the tone of *Eritrichium*. As for the Forget-me-nots—well, I can only say that their otherwise lovely blues become harsh, thin and mean beside that of their tiny cousin. I tried then and there; I pulled out a clump of *Myosotis rupicola* from my collecting tin, and compared it with the *Eritrichium*. And the *Myosotis*, otherwise so pure and adorable a colour, lost all its sweetness and turned sour beside the bland blueness of the other. I find that in *Eritrichium* a dash of Chinese white is mixed with the azure, and thus the softer tone is produced ; there is also—and now I must be read with caution—the minutest, minutest touch of crimson,—oh, so little that the very suggestion seems ridiculous, and yet the cobalt-laden brush, after a lick of white, must make the merest feinting flirt across the cake of crimson, if the rich, clear, gentle, perfect blue of the flower is to be finally divorced from any suspicion of yellow. For, into nearly all the azure flowers we know, a suspicion of yellow enters, and leaves a tang of green; only *Eritrichium* is perfect and undefiled in its tone.

Ah, the blessed little creature, how it takes one captive! The first sight of it catches one by the throat. So exquisite, so tiny, this indomitable small soul sits up here on the barren slopes, from age to age, working out its own destiny without regard for any worldly cataclysm. Even the loveliness of it seems almost a heavenly selfishness. Little indeed does *Eritrichium* care whether any one worships it or no! Alone, unfriended, it braves all the everlasting fury of the hills; sits quiet through the long Alpine winters; then, during the short, gorgeous Alpine summer, makes haste to smile at the sun before the dark days return. And what of *Eritrichium* in England? Ah, what? Will any one give me news of any old-established clump anywhere in our islands? Of all the children of the hills this is the most intractable, the most irreconcilable. And yet, it should not be— least of all if, as report goes, it allows itself to be soaked by sea-spray on Antarctic islands. But the mischief, briefly put, lies here. Although the plant is healthy, robust, and absolutely easy to dig up with perfect roots (it comes up in the nicest, neatest balls), yet, above all other wet-hating plants of the mountains, does this one loathe superfluous moisture. Here on this slope of the Meiden Pass it submits to as many showers and storms as the Alpine summer brings. But then, the other days of that Alpine summer are baking and glorious, the sun's beams playing clear and pure through the thin mountain air. Then, in late August, probably, or even earlier, down comes the Alpine winter again with its coverlet of snow, and *Eritrichium* goes comfortably to bed in perfect warmth and dryness, there to remain, a true sleeping beauty, till June begins to attack the frozen heights of the mountains. Compare with this what its life must be in England! The whole plant is densely fluffy with the loveliest silver fur, and it is always this hairy coat that serves the Alpine species so ill in England, though so well in their own homes.

It will be clear, from what I have said, that *Eritrichium* is most likely—one cannot dogmatise even here—to survive if it is given a very long, very hard resting season of absolute, absolute drought. From September to May it should not be within smell of water even, much less within touch of it. Now, manage such conditions in the open, if you can! Yes, there's always our old friend the crevice. Firmly packed, *Eritrichium* may thrive there for a season, but I don't expect he will often live longer. Not only is the crevice rather hard to keep in order, but it is almost impossible—remember I am the victim of a wet-winter climate—to keep away a certain amount of damp in the resting season. Even if the ground is dry, there is rain and rot in the autumnal air. And *Eritrichium* resents this only less than actual moisture surface. As I write there rises before me, like King Richard's ghosts on the eve of Bosworth, a long and expensive train of phantoms—all the *Eritrichiums* that I have loved and lost, despite care and pains unutterable. Frankly, I have found that the best chance in this district is to grow the plant in pots and keep the pots in frames. *Eritrichium* is a tidy rooter, and doesn't resent pot-culture as the Gentians do. With pot-plants in frames you can deal

drastically. You can keep the frames almost hermetically sealed for nine months of the year if you like, and
you can ensure your Blue Mosses against the least possible whiff of damp. Even so, the plant is rather a terror.
I sent home from the Meiden Pass about fifty splendid
little clumps. Not one of them failed or flagged. They
all came through the winter triumphantly, and in the
spring they bloomed so gloriously that, when they were
shown in a mass in London, gardeners of long standing
almost wept for joy. But, the next winter, this last—
what? Well, I don't know. I am sure a great many
are dead, and I only hope there may be a few survivors
among those withered, woolly little mats that look so
dismal in their pots. But appearances are deceptive in
the case of *Eritrichium*, and I have seen resurrections
before now. The fact is, the plant is in a way deciduous.
That is, the season's leaves die off, turn ashen and dead
under the snow, and nothing more happens until the new
silver tufts push next spring. But in the garden one
goes in February or March, and sees only a withered
ball of deadness sitting on the bone-dry surface of the
pot. Ah, think you, another three and sixpence gone to
glory! But, if the plant still feels solid, hope may still
dwell in you, as life still dwells in *Eritrichium*. By April
stand its pot in water to soak (I never give *Eritrichium*
overhead watering in any circumstances myself until the
summer is well in ; it is too dangerous in this climate),
and then, ere long, you will see green dawning through
that deadness, and then, in a little, the silver rosettes are
up, and nestling upon them in another three weeks the
inexpressible blue of the little golden-eyed flowers. And
after that the plant must rest. Some of my clumps still
feel solid at the neck, and I cling to my faith therefore
that out of their seeming death life may yet arise. And
then I should be the blissful possessor of an *Eritrichium*

that had borne two seasons of cultivation in England. M. Correvon, by the way, grows his *Eritrichium* at Geneva in a compound largely built of Sphagnum. And thus they grow superbly, and I have received the most magnificent specimens from him thus potted. But I must now solemnly repeat his warning to all English growers, that in our country—at least in my part of it—such a system is absolutely and almost instantaneously fatal, as indeed is the whole theory of growing Alpine plants in Sphagnum. With M. Correvon it answers excellently, and exactly meets the climate of Geneva, with those appalling torrid summers, and those stone-dry, inexorable winter frosts. Here, in our mild summers and winters, with rain almost persistent through certain months, the Sphagnum acts as a sponge, grows heavy with hoarded moisture, and rots the plant to death in about a week. For dry-hot, dry-cold countries Sphagnum is invaluable for Alpine plants ; in wet-warm, wet-chilly countries, Sphagnum is the deadliest thing you could possibly use. For *Eritrichium* I myself mix very rough sand and grit with a small amount of peat and a good deal of granite dust. Plants of the high mountains are not, as a rule, fond of rich soil ; and *Eritrichium*, of course, particularly dreads fat composts, as they harbour damp around that neck which is as susceptible to catarrh as Mr. Wood-house's.

CHAPTER XVII

From Pentstemon onwards

Pentstemon coeruleus and *Pentstemon glaber alpinus* are the first beauties we meet in the dowdy race of the Fig-worts. As for *Pentstemon coeruleus*, blue it is indeed, but between two plants in the same batch of seedlings there is as much difference as between two children of one family. Often the blue is dull, steely, washy, poor; at other times it is of a brilliancy that is almost impossible to describe, and quite impossible to over-value. One is brought up short at this point by reflections on the inadequacy of our colour-vocabulary. We feel colour far more subtly than we can express; and in this matter our cultivated eyes are hampered by the lagging pace of our speech that still, in the matter of colour, is content with serving the primitive needs of our ancestors. Red, blue, yellow, green, purple—think what an awful field those hard-worked adjectives have to cover—think of all the greens that come under the one monosyllable, all the ranging tones from the Primrose at one end to the Funeral Cypress at the other; why, even among the whites are fifty shades and more that all have to be content with the one word, 'white,' which means so much and yet so little. Our ancestors, perhaps, saw only white or green; we see infinite gradations and divergences that our tongues are unable to hint at, so that in our voicelessness we have to begin moulding double-barrelled epithets—a hateful but inevitable development—or else must needs supply some parallelism which, as often as not, quite fails to convey to another person the same or even a kindred impression to that in our own thoughts. ' Pearl-white,' one has to say, for that faint roseate flush, barely perceptible, subtle, yet so distinct, which one gets in such things as *Oxalis Enneaphylla*, and finds it so hopeless to describe.   However, if we want to avoid the use of half a dozen explanatory adjectives, we are absolutely driven upon pearl-white, knowing well that our notion of pearl-white is not that of Mrs. Smith or Mr. Tomkins, so that our poor attempt at description probably, in the lack of any accepted currency for colour-words, conveys to others a perfectly false notion of the charm that our epithet had been desperately coined to convey.   So that one can only throw up one's hands in despair, confronted at once by the inadequacy of language and by the unending variety and delicacy of flower-tones where no two whites or blues are alike, but all have to be lumped under the one rough heading, eked out by such explanatory qualifications as each separate mind has to hammer out for itself, more in the hope of satisfying itself than of carrying a true picture to others.   Rose-white, pearl-white, ice-white, snow-white, chalk-white, wax-white, are all totally different tones; but as no three people see ice or snow or wax or pearl or rose with the same eyes, or have the same idea of them, the descriptive tag can only be the inventor's own particular little pet view, having no help or authority except for himself. And with this wail of apology I must go back to the best blue forms of *Pentstemon coeruleus*.

And in this, the slight, rather floppy stems, from their rather miffy little stock, are adorned with glaucous-grey leaves, amid which nestle whorls of the loveliest flowers, rather small, but of translucent, very pale turquoise colour, with a soft white throat. Not even to myself, of course, does the hard opacity of turquoise convey a fair impression of the bland soft transparent blueness of the Pentstemon—so perfectly gentle yet so decided in its perfect purity of tone. However, there is nothing better to be done, unless one ventures on the tenderest azure of early dawn for one's parallel, and that, again, has too much green in it to realise the absolute heavenliness of the Pentstemon's blossoms. A good seedling, in good health, is beaten by nothing in the garden as far as colour goes; the clear, mild sweetness of its pale heavenliness is better even than the richer, heavier colour of *Eritrichium nanum*, or the more violent hard splendour of *Gentiana verna*. But, having said this of *Pentstemon coeruleus*, my tide of smooth sayings runs dry. For I find the plant inclined to be untrustworthy—either no true perennial, or no true hardy species. Cold, wet winters, anyhow, seem to destroy it, though in more favoured parts it may very likely grow ahead for ever. Nevertheless it matures good seed abundantly, so that you can continue to raise it; though thus you never have any security that more than a small percentage of the seedlings will have that exquisite colour, without which the plant is as a sounding brass and a tinkling cymbal.

Pentstemon glaber alpinus is larger in growth and flower, with a rather more solid constitution, and with flowers of a fine blue tinged with rose and white, which, however, cannot approach the unique (hateful word, but it *must* be applied here) brilliant gentleness of *coeruleus*.

A great number of the larger Pentstemons (besides being delicate) are undoubtedly inclined to be both gawky and leafy; so that my own attention is always concentrated in the smaller species, of which there are some delightful people whom one finds far up on the Canadian Rockies, quite dwarf and genuine alpines of the most alpine description. Two especially did I collect on the moraines far above Laggan; one a little mat-like bush with ridiculously large snapdragonish blossoms of a rich violet, the other a stiffer creature with small upstanding shoots set with whorls of most beautiful, bright blue-purple blossoms. This last is a stray, and turned up 'unbeknownst,' like Mrs. Gamp's unlamented offspring, among my packages from Canada. However, both these little treasures seem disposed, as one would have hoped—another superiority of these high-mountain species—to be perfectly hardy and at ease from year to year. At least Blue-spike has come up better and better for several seasons; while, though my pot-plants of Purple Bell have either died or been sold off, the American bed-plant made a brilliant show last year and I have every hope that it will do so again,[1] and justify its inclusion in so august a company. For the American bed is an elaborate piece of work—a high plateau in the rockwork where the soil was taken out for two feet or so and then filled in again, on very rugged drainage-stones, with rich, cool, light stuff, suited, like Benger's Food, to the most delicate consti-tutions. And in that bed I now have thriving very happily *Primula deorum*, *Gentiana scabra Buergeri*, *Gentiana Kurroo*, and *Castilleia acuminata*, besides other gems.

Castilleia, however, is the emperor of that bank—almost the only specimen in England, I fancy, for there is something odd about this gorgeous plant. You see him everywhere in the Rockies, growing like a slight *Salvia*, and far more brilliant than even *Salvia splendens*, with bracts and long tubular flowers all alike of an in-distinguishable blazing scarlet. In the valleys he grows two feet or more in height, flaming out of the bushes and

[1] Alas! never more, I fear.

copses as the train carries you by in a stupor as to what
that terrific colour belongs to.   And then, when you get
into the mountains, the *Castilleia* goes with you all the
way, contrary to your expectations, and this apparently
lowland plant makes great flares of vermilion even on
the edge of the last lowest lips of the moraines.   But,
gorgeous to behold, and easy to collect, there is, as I said,
something suspicious and ominous about this plant.   The
practised gardener soon learns to detect the species that
threaten him with biennial or parasitic tendencies, or
some such 'contrairy' fad.   They generally have a certain
unstable look about them ; they carry too few shoots, and
those few too vigorous and leafy for the root or the stock.
In their appearance there is something top-heavy and
unreal, as if they were blossoming stems merely stuck
into the ground.   *Pyrola uniflora* has this warning look,
so has *Gentiana ciliata* ; nor, in their case, is the appearance any fraud.   And there is some similar kink in the
nature of the *Castilleia*, I fear, though there can be no
shadow of doubt that the plant is as absolutely hardy
and as soundly perennial as any weed of our own islands.
But I am inclined to suspect it of being a parasite, or, at
all events, of semi-parasitic inclinations.   It has all that
appearance—that disproportion of stem to slight root.
Anyhow, though I collected abundance of it in well-fibred
clumps, nearly all the pot-plants died off, although they
had borne the journey perfectly, until ultimately, what
with deaths and sales, only the peat-bed specimen re-
mained.   But that, I confess, has surprised me with the
perennial and increasing vigour that it shows, blessing
me last year with three or four fine scarlet spikes (very
gorgeous, if not quite as flaming as where the summer has
more sun-heat), and this spring it is sending up, besides
more than half a dozen main shoots, innumerable lesser
ones which all seem to be bushing up most prosperously.

So the plant is evidently suited and established. Perhaps it had a grudge against me at first because I catalogued it as *Castilleia miniata*, botany books being confused and unhelpful. Now, however, that I have given it its own name of *Castilleia acuminata*, it seems to have withdrawn its grievance and to be thoroughly satisfied with English life.

Another plant which has come round is *Ourisia coccinea*. Probably every one knows and grows this brilliant little Chilian plant, which, against all reason, proves perfectly hardy in England. In rocky, shady places it is supposed to ramp about uncurbed, sending up beautiful, crinkled, green leaves, roughly heart-shaped, glossy, and jagged along the edges, with loose showers of pendent vermilion trumpets, carried about eight inches above the foliage. For years I bought that plant in hopes that it would so ramp. Not a bit of it. It sulked, hung fire, passed away. Few mothers ever made more ado for a sick baby than I for *Ourisia*. I reverently read up Mr. Robinson, made it beds, put porous rocks for it to cling against, constructed every sort of elaborate situation to suit it. And wherever I had it from, in clumps, in crowns, in pots, or from the open, the *Ourisia* inevitably died, like Anne Boleyn, '*sans nul remède.*' At last I sickened of such obstinate ingratitude. No more *Ourisia* for me, said I; let us consider the plant half-hardy, I continued, putting the best face on failure. And so matters stood until one day I had a very cheap wholesale offer of *Ourisia* tufts. Well, I thought, they can but die, and I shan't be ruined, at these rates, even if they do. So I ordered them, rather scornful of my own weak extravagance, and when they came I was inclined to despair. No beds or fussments this time; I had the Ourisias slapped out into the open borders and on to vacant corners of the rockwork, to sink or swim as they chose, unaided. I fully expected those plants, which had sunk even under my tenderest care, to sink with double promptitude when cast thus on their own resources. But not at all. *Ourisia* had quite other views. Never have I seen a plant set to work thriving quite so vigorously. Over beds, over rockwork it now grows, crawling like the worms of Alonzo and the fair Imogene, horrible as such an apt image is for the purple, caterpillar-like feelers of *Ourisia*, so fleshy and fat, that go creep-creeping about with such indomitable robustness, now trailing over and over each other on the level, and then shinning up the bare rocks to find fresh fields. I say nothing of my treatment of the plant nowadays, for the simple reason that it has no treatment, but ramps all over the place without any encouragement, so that every little nose that I break off will set to work again on its own—providing always, of course, that it is put in rich, moist soil in a rock-shaded spot. Some people tell me of *Ourisia* making a weed of itself as a sun-plant; here, certainly, all my success has been in cool corners under walls or in rocky dells.

Wulfenia carinthiaca is a very rare plant in nature, restricted to one range in Carinthia. And with this, again, after years of comparative failure and difficulty, I have at last happed accidentally upon success. Wulfenia makes clumps of tufted rosettes, bright glossy green, of strap-shaped serrate leaves. Then up at the side of the rosettes come spikes, about a foot high or so, of deep blue flowers, individually small, but so numerous and close-set that the general effect is of a rather sober, well-bred brilliancy. For years and years I grew the plant as an alpine, in alpine soil, in chinks and crevices, and so on. I had never collected it, which must be one of my excuses; for one great advantage of collecting is, obviously, that it teaches you precisely how and where your plants like to grow, even though it is not necessary in most cases to bother about reconstructing their circumstances with any pedantic accuracy, most plants being quite content with ordinary treatment of the kind to which Nature has accustomed them—that is to say, a meadow-plant is quite happy, as a rule, with border treatment, and a rock-plant with rock treatment—without any hopeless effort to imitate exactly the meadows or the chinks from which they came. However, although I had not collected Wulfenia, his abundant, greedy-looking roots ought to have warned me; but I took no heed, and therefore met with nothing but failure. All my plants lived, but they neither throve nor flowered, until at last I was in despair. Then, one day, I had an importation of *Wulfenia*, and, for lack of space in the rock-garden, I put them out in a fat-soiled nursery bed. And those Wulfenias immediately opened my eyes, for they set to work growing high and wide and deep and strong, while their leaves, from a sickly green, became solid and lustrous; and, when the flowering season came in spring, vigorous blue spikes came shooting up all round the clumps, and, not satisfied with one display, were so ebulliently happy that they repeated it again in the autumn. At least I have the merit of learning my lessons. All my Wulfenias were hoofed out of their pots and crevices into rich border-soil, and there those poor starved creatures have gone on making cabbagy tufts of foliage each season, with profusion of flower-spikes, until now they are beginning to run about the beds and increase of their own goodwill. The only other Wulfenia—*amherstiana*, from the Himâlya—is a small creeping rock-plant which I have never got.

I only grow two Calceolarias—*polyrhiza* and *planta-ginea*—but I am perpetually surprised at the amount of pleasure given me by these two members of a horrid race

—or of a race which is horrid because Calceolaria too often means the bloated monsters that appear at shows, or the stubby yellow-and-brown frumps that are used in bedding. But no one seems to realise how very graceful and lovely are the species, and how perfectly hardy, and how invaluable in vigour and everything else. *Calceolaria polyrhiza* is a terrific grower, ramping about all over a bed in dense, ground-hugging tufts of hairy leaves, with countless stems a foot or eighteen inches high, each daintily balancing a single soft yellow flower. *Plantaginea*, no less perpetual-blooming, has much larger leaves, glossy and crinkled, with a much slower-spreading habit, and showers of larger blossoms, sparse on their stems and of a clear canary colour. And though these two species are usually recommended with caution, even by catalogues, as rather tender, with me they have proved impregnably hardy, having resisted the most ferocious cold or damp in winter, and that though unfavoured by any sheltered situation. For, instead of being planted on well drained rockwork, they are both turned loose in the perfectly level ground of the bog-garden, where the soil is rich and fat and sticky; yet there they thrive unperturbed, whatever the winter. In fact, these Calceolarias are clearly more or less of marsh-plants, loving rich cool soil that never gets parched or thin.

Linaria, of course, gives us the priceless *Linaria alpina*, the little dwarf orange and violet Snapdragon, whose blossoms are so gorgeous in themselves and contrast so effectively with its fleshy little blue leaves. This is, perhaps, the one annual that must inevitably be cultivated—nor am I so absolutely certain that *Linaria alpina* is only an annual. I have a last year's plant, a big, profusely-blooming clump, whose withered stems moved me to weed it away this year, believing that its day was over; but I found such a mass of young sound-looking shoots underground that I tucked it apologetically back again, and registered a vow never to believe *Linaria alpina* to be dead until the most solemn proofs had been given. This beloved small plant flourishes everywhere in Switzerland on the high moraines, and in cultivation is certainly the better for very poor, gravelly, rubbishy soil, such as it haunts at home. In fat ground it loses its neatness, grows rank and less glaucous, with less brilliancy of blossom and a good deal more uncertainty in winter. I have collected a *rosea* form of it which is pretty, but not so pretty as the type, which has also a *concolor* variety, lacking the orange blotch, and therefore less attractive than the common plant. As for the variety *alba*, it is exquisite beyond belief—a perfect virginal jewel among plants. I gasped incredulous when I found two clumps of it within a yard of each other on the Laemmern Gletscher, above the Gemmi, among acres and acres of the purple form. But, alas! though I collected it with as much reverence as ever a Pope deployed in gathering a relic, that plant died off childless, and bore me neither seed nor offshoot, while all the seed I have bought since that day as *Linaria alpina alba* has turned out to be mere *Linaria alpina*.

Now we come to my two well-beloveds among the Veronicas (space lacking to tell of all the other countless kinds). *Canescens* is a weird little creature, so tiny that you can hardly see his wee leaves and hair-like stems, as he forms carpets in any cool level place, in light soil. What, then, is one's amazement when, suddenly, the bare earth breaks out into big brilliant blue cups, fading to white! One's first instinct is to look up and wonder whence these fallen prettinesses can have dropped. But they are the rightful property of that wee Veronica, and he goes on producing them right away to the end of the season, and matures seed which comes up next year in

s

every sort of unexpected place. *Veronica chathamica* is a particularly charming thing, too, though of quite another persuasion—a box-leaved shrub, but absolutely prostrate, creeping along the rockwork, and following the fall of each cliff-face, with abundance of pale blue flowers, far on in the late autumn. And then, of the same easy growth as these two treasures, is a hybrid called Autumn Glory, an erect shrub, with spikes of wonderful deep purple, so beautiful as to overcome my coldness towards most of the bushy Veronicas—except *hulkeana* (which is hardy here).

Dracocephalum gives us one or two good things, notably *ruyschianum japonicum*, a beautiful and free-flowering herbaceous plant, making solid tufts about a foot high, with profusion of big purple and white blossoms in July and August. *Dracocephalum altaiense* is the proper name of the much-sought-for *Dracocephalum grandiflorum*, a species often catalogued, but almost impossible to procure, spurious Dracocephalums being almost invariably sent out under its name. The true *altaiense* is a dwarf plant, with large blue flowers, which I have always found it as hard to keep as to get. Besides being beloved of slugs to a terrible degree, the plant is a real bad doer, I believe, though perfectly hardy ; my own plants have given me no pleasure yet, but a vast deal of trouble and fuss. What, precisely, it is they want, I cannot find out ; all I can say is that their temper seems thoroughly peevish and ill-conditioned. The loveliest of all is a species I saw in Japan on the way up to Ikao—a few-stemmed, frail thing, with whorls of narrow, hairy, greyish leaves, and a few most splendid big flowers of a soft and lovely blue. None of my plants survived, nor can I ascertain the treasure's name ; but now I go on vainly buying seed of every Dracocephalum that hails from Japan (that is why I got my form of *ruyschianum*), in the hopes that I may at last hap on my friend of Ikao.

My latest speculation is *Dracocephalum peregrinum*; perhaps, at last, my quest may be achieved—but I don't think so, for the unfolding leaves are becoming fiddle-shaped instead of linear.

The Butterwort grows freely about all our marshes, and a charming thing it is, with its flowers like wee violet Gloxinias, and its wicked sticky rosettes of carnivorous leaves. Then, one year a friend brought me over clumps of *Pinguicula grandiflora*, or what she hoped would be *grandiflora*, from Ireland. She planted them in the bog with immense care, and being a deep-dyed gardener of real enthusiasm, she fed them daily on cold grouse and cold minced veal. Whether it was this handsome diet or no, I cannot say, but they all rewarded her by thriving, and now are quite established, if it were not for their tiresome habit of dying away to a sort of corm in winter, in which state they flop about at the mercy of wind and birds and weather. Moreover, I am not yet quite satisfied that they are really and truly *grandiflora*. *Pinguicula alpina*, the white-flowered, I have collected but never made a success of, so that the comfort of my Grandifloras must be attributed to my friend and her lunches of cold grouse—although she omitted the bread-sauce and bread-crumb, which I thought rather aggrieving of her.

CHAPTER XVIII

Orchids, Lilies, Tulips, and Bulbs in General

ORCHIDACEAE does not, as a rule, mean much more than
Cypripedium, as far as the gardener is concerned; for
Orchis, Ophrys, and the others of this most haughty
and noble race are unapproachable, intractable plants in
cultivation unless they happen to have brought themselves there.   Of course, one may specialise on them and
spend a long and arduous life trying to imagine and
satisfy their requirements; but, for my own part, I have
been content to deal with other things, and have not
made myself unhappy over the Orchises.   *Orchis mascula*
has brought himself, and so has *Habenaria conopsea*;
otherwise Orchidaceae to me mean *Cypripedium*—of whom
I have already expatiated on the beauties and good-temper
of our own *Calceolus*, so that I can now go on to deal
with one or two of the rather less easy but even more
splendid sorts from abroad.

Cypripedium debile I collected in the rich rotten woodland soil near the tomb of Yeyas', at Nikko, on the way
to which you will find this, with Trilliums, and Anemones,
and all manner of such delights, in the undergrowth of
the forest on your left.   But *Cypripedium debile*, which is
just beginning to be heard of in England, and advertised
at high prices, is conspicuous only for its extreme incon-
spicuousness, and a flopping debility well entitling it to
the name it bears.   Although the little dull green flower

is so small as to be almost microscopic, the frail stem is not equal even to such a featherweight, but droops and languishes in the most contemptible manner. Nor have I any very great love for *Cypripedium japonicum*, another, but far finer, woodland species, with a pair of plaited apple-green leaves (which end, like 'Arriet's toes, square, 'like a nangkerchif,' as if they had been bitten clean away), and large white and green flowers, with a fine pink infolded pouch. But we are now coming to the two sovereigns of the race, and at thoughts of them all minor species must retire into the background.

Cypripedium reginae is better known here by its other name, only less apt, of *Cypripedium spectabile*; and no one with a bog-garden can ignore this glorious plant, so thrifty and hardy, with its handsome tall leafy stems and its roundish flowers, generally two on a growth, of pure white and pure rose, in June and early July. It is a common peat-bog plant of North America, whence it is imported in the most alarming quantities, which would distress one more if the Queen-Slipper were not such a success in English gardens in well-drained, rich peaty loam, never allowed to parch.

But far away above *Cypripedium reginae* stands *Cypripedium ventricosum* as I collected it among coarse grasses on sunny hot slopes round Fuji-yama. This plant is a Japanese variety of *Cypripedium macranthon*, a Siberian species which, whenever I have seen it, has appeared rather lumpish in shape and dull in the tones of its purples. But *ventricosum* is quite another slipper, growing eighteen inches high, with the leafy stem of *reginae*, and flowers which are generally larger and of an equally noble build. With all their beauties, the blunted petals of *reginae* often give the flower rather too round and fat a look; whereas the petals of *ventricosum* are long and undulating and twisted as a commercial traveller's moustache—and,

despite the dreadful simile, give a solid brilliancy of grace
to the flower; while the dorsal, instead of being squatty,
is tall and waved and pointed, with a swollen pouch of
the right proportion and design, rather obese than
starved. And the colours rival those of *reginae*; for
the prevailing tone of *ventricosum* is a variable rose, dap-
pling and flushing over a cream-white ground, marbling
the lip, and streaking the petals and dorsal in dense,
effective lines. My feelings when I first espied this blushing treasure on the hillside can be imagined rather than
described—how I hurled myself from the caravan and
believed that I had discovered a new Cypripedium.
However, that pleasant vision soon faded, leaving me with
the finer certainty that I had got hold of as beautiful a
thing as Fuji-yama had ever brought forth. And so I
spent a happy afternoon all over the slopes behind Shoji,
for ever discovering great white Peonies, or the pinkness
of the Cypripedium, peering out at me from the long
grass or some light growth of copse. That importation,
however, failed; and my successful one is so recent that I
cannot speak decisively about the plant's culture, except
to say that it should surely be perfectly satisfactory in
any light soil and fair aspect. Hitherto it has been
impossible to procure, nurseries always sending out the
inferior *macranthon* instead; but now I rest secure in my
own goodly batch, whose fat noses are already beginning
to break up out of the soil as if they had not just
achieved a journey of twelve thousand miles.

The remainder of my orchideous tale is sorrow. The
Madeira Orchis I grow, but don't care much for; while
Epipactis palustris, and the American bog-species—
Calypso, *Arethusa*, *Calopogon*, and *Pogonia* (notorious
difficulties, I hasten to plead)—have never done anything
here but fail. I am beginning to doubt whether any
garden in England is so favoured as to have these North

CYPRIPEDIUM MACRANTHUM, VAR: VENTRICOSUM (THREE MONTHS AFTER ARRIVAL FROM JAPAN)

American lovelinesses flourishing in the open bog from year to year. And now, before leaving Orchidaceae, let me, for the benefit of others, make myself a *triste bidental*, and point out the dreadful insidiousness of this great Order. No one with a hot or unsteady head must ever look at an Orchid. For I myself was once an innocent and happy gardener, who always said the right thing about hothouse Orchids : ' Yes, very interesting; but rather morbid and monstrous, don't you think ? ' And then, one ominous day, I caught sight of *Cypripedium insigne Sanderae* — pure golden yellow, with white-tipped dorsal, and beautiful beyond the tongue of man to express. In that instant I understood Romeo and Juliet better than I ever had before. But my doom was sealed; as cruel engines draw in, first one's coat-tail, and then by degrees the whole body, so the Orchids have now enveloped me densely in their web. I am engulfed in Orchids and their dreadful bills ; nor do I see the slightest chance of ever tasting solvency or peace again. This is what it is to be too catholic an enthusiast. For I love the rock-garden no less than before ; I have simply added to my other enthusiasms the most ruinous enthusiasm in the world—and never again shall I be able to say the right thing about indoor Orchids. What a terrible thing to have a mind open to new beauties, and capable of accommodating in one shrine three or four equal enthusiasms !

Is there such a thing as an ugly Iris ? Less pretty ones there may be ; but uglies—perish the thought ! There are Irises for every soil and situation too—Spanish Irises and English for sunny borders, and German Irises for everywhere, even London, and Ochroleuca Irises for the bog, and Cristata Irises for the rockwork—and—and Oncocyclus Irises for the kingdom of Heaven ! Don't let any one tell me they are of any permanent real place on earth. I will not believe it ; I will make a point of not believing it. A high, proud race are the Oncocyclus Irises—a doomed, tragic line, in crapes and blacks and purples, sweeping by on their road to the grave. They belong to a bygone day, and none can marvel at their sombre glories without feeling that they are mourners at their own funeral—a sad, lonely group, royal to the last, but swiftly, sternly passing away from the world. And so (for my garden is a marriage-bed, not a burial-ground, if I can help it) I will have none of the Oncocyclus Irises; let others tend these agonising princesses, and enjoy what brief triumphs they can (a triumph that, of course, is longer and brighter where sun is hot and winters dry, than here where the sun at the best is only warm and the winters damp as Niobe); while, for my part, not liking sick-beds, I stand out against spoiling my garden by glass frames and fir-boughs and all the elaborate medicaments that must be ready for the need of the Oncocyclus. And, for the same reason, I will have no dealings with Calochortus. These I do not love as I love the Cushion Irids; and so my decision is easier and more painless. Let friends of the sun, and groove-choosing enthusiasts make a speciality of Calochortus; catholics like myself, and catholics afflicted with a cold wet climate, will do well to concentrate on what can reasonably be grown, rather than waste their time and money cosseting delicacies that have no intention of thriving except under conditions so artificial that they quite destroy the hypothesis of naturalness and ease which is the essential element of a garden's beauty. The moment glass frames and bells and fussments begin to cover your ground, gone is all the air of simple happiness that makes a garden joyful; and, instead, you have a constrained look, as of a kindergarten or a reformatory. And so I have not cared to pursue my culture of *Calochortus*, *Oncocyclus*, *Gerbera*, and *Lewisia Tweedyi*.

But, to leave this doubtful territory, the rock-garden owes most to the genuine dwarf Irids, of whom the true *Iris pumila* is the commonest and still the most unfailingly valuable. *Pumila* you will see along the Mediterranean coast, where I have found its almost invisible runners and its immense violet blossoms sitting apparently on the ground, among grass and rocks, round St. Raphael. In cultivation this little creature—which makes up in the awful length of its whip-like roots for any moderation it may show in the matter of foliage—likes a sunny place, bed or border, in any sound warm soil. There it runs about (all these German, Pumila, Pallida Irises—all the tuberous-rooted Irises, in fact—want planting with their tubers just showing on the surface, I fancy) making mats of neat foliage, and then bearing its colossal flowers abundantly in early summer. There is a white form, very rare, which I have not got; a most exquisite azure-blue one; an improved purple—Purple King, or something; and a pale grey one called *gracilis*, which is deliciously fragrant. And all these, and any others there may be, are worth collecting in the very highest degree.

Iris mellita is quite a new little person of the Pumila persuasion which I imported from Servia some seasons since, on the chance of his being good; and good he is, indeed, very remarkably so—a tiny dwarf plant, very floriferous and free-growing, with large *Pumila*-flowers, of a deep coppery-bronze colour, with blue and purple in the beard. He has, too, the rather uncommon peculiarity of bearing seed without human agency; and, altogether, makes me feel very satisfied with that particular importation. As far as cultivation goes, he follows *Pumila*; but is rather more sensitive, I find, to wet, rotting winters, although he is quite hardy and recovers as soon as he feels certain that spring is come.

Iris tectorum, in my eyes, stands far above all the other Irises, even above *lacustris* and *gracilipes*. But *tectorum* is supreme, absolutely, in his own class, which is that of the medium-sized Irises. He grows abundantly on the thatched roofs of Japanese cottages, and for some undiscoverable reason has always been treated with quite unreasonable distrust and care in England. Import your plants from the frost-ridden Tokio Plain, as I had the luck to do, and you will find that *Iris tectorum* is as incorruptibly hardy as any German Iris that ever throve in a London square. (This is the great secret of importing Japanese plants. Get them from the coldest districts, not from the South. This is how I have made such hardy perennial successes here of *Iris tectorum*, *Nandina*, and the Daphnes *odora* and *Genkwa*.) Another thing to remember is that he will thank you richly for rich feeding ; all Irises, although they look, like the Lilies, so superior to earthly matters, are yet, like the Lilies, dowered with a sturdy appetite for good old rotten manure. And, with this, *Iris tectorum* will go ahead for ever on any well-drained exposed corner of the rockery. The flowers are of an unusual beauty even among Irises ; the falls are broad and undulating, the standards large and spreading, so that the flower is freer and more graceful in build than the conventional Flower-de-luce form that you get in the German Irises. And the colour is of a wonderful soft crystal blue, dappled all over with a deeper shade ; and in consistency and tones has the same waved azure that you get in a healthy bloom, when you see it, of *Vanda coerulea* in a good variety. The Iris-flower, too, has a great jagged blue and white crest along each fall, which adds to the wild elegance of its design. The white variety is as beautiful as it is rare, and the deep-blue one is only a trifle less beautiful than the clear softness of the type. And now I am twittering with excitement, for it is just

possible that this year may coax a flower out of one or
two seedlings that I have raised, between *tectorum album*
and *florentina*. There is a whole batch all strong and
promising, and some so vigorous that really I almost
believe I may hope for flowers this second year of their
life. However, even if they continue to grow without
flowering, I shall be happy, still nursing my anticipations
of what may result from such an auspicious union. If
one can only couple the free habit and unquestioned
weedlike hardiness of *florentina* (to say nothing of its
beauty) with the fairylike loveliness of *tectorum album*,
both for shape and colour, a truly notable offspring
should result—as, for the matter of that, should also
develop from my other promising cross of the deep-blue
tectorum with the intense violet *Kochi*.

Iris cristata is quite dwarf and wonderfully beautiful,
with small rhizomes that like to run freely about over
sunny, stony soil, and then bless you with very large
flowers, delicately built, and of a lovely china-blue, with
a brilliant shaggy beard of gold. More brilliant even
than this is *Iris lacustris*, and also much rarer. *Lacustris*
is a miniature *cristata*, ideal for the choice rock-garden,
making tidy mats of rhizome, with big blue and gold
flowers, deeper in colour than those of *cristata*. I have
two splendid clumps of *lacustris* on the rockwork which
were put out rather in despair—for none of these Irises
are happy in pots, their roots being too hungry—but
which, as soon as they were thus emancipated, set to
work growing with the most prodigal generosity, and are
now only kept in check by the embittering affections
of slugs, to escape which they go flopping down over
the rock-faces, besides developing everywhere else as
well.

Of all my little Irises, though, and with every recognition of these two last delights, *Iris gracilipes* is queen—

a grassy-growing thing, forming a tuft, but never spreading along the ground, with three or four flowers carried on airy stems five inches high or so. And these flowers are, in shape, miniatures of the half-hardy *fimbriata*, with spreading bold falls and tiny standards. But in build and colouring they are more exquisite than most things seen outside a dream, cut from the filmiest soft pale-blue silk, crumpled into half a dozen different lights and tones, with a deeper eye surrounding the pale lined blotch, and following along the crest. I shall never forget my first real sight of this plant. I had often seen it for sale in Japanese gardens, but had no notion where it was to be found wild. However, we went northward, I and my friends, and alighted by the way to see the famous islands of Matsushima, above Sendai, on the western coast. It was about two in the morning when we arrived, and my friends immediately carried me off to sight-see, with the result that everybody slept so firmly that the sight-seeing was not a success. Ultimately, after a lunch of rice and Worcester sauce, I laid myself down to a sleep on the matted floor of the inn, while my friends departed insatiably to ramble about and do more sight-seeing. When I awoke I found myself less somnolent and heavy, and so went out and did a little shopping in the village until my friends should return, which they did at last, showing me two withered blossoms. One was an ordinary *Hemerocallis*, the other was *Iris gracilipes*. Instantly all desire to eat or cavil or slumber passed away from me, and with one of the explorers for my guide, I rushed off up the wooded hills to see whence he had plucked the Iris. And there at last I saw it; bursting through the thickets where Pyrolas were showing, I came out on a westerly clearing from which they had cut all the hazels and undergrowth, just as they clear it in England. And there, as Primroses grow in such a place in England, was

Iris gracilipes, abounding all down the slope in the soft rotten soil, but not to be seen anywhere else except on that one open bank. There are certain flowers that grip a hold of one even in excess of their vast intrinsic merits. Such a plant is *Lilium rubellum*, and such another was *Iris gracilipes*, whose fairylike, extraordinary daintiness of beauty as I saw it there it would be almost sacrilegious and quite impossible to describe. And, in cultivation, this darling is as good as he is beautiful. Believe not such as tell you that he is half-hardy. No such thing. Without protection of any kind he bears the coldest and the wettest winters here, in half a dozen different situations, without showing any sort of cowardice or ill-temper. Give him loose rich vegetable soil, light and well-drained, and he will teach you what beauty can be when it likes. Every autumn the growths die back to the stock, which develops into a fan of close-set rhizomes; but then, in spring, each shoot throws up its grassy leaves again, and soon the leaders are thinking about their frail exquisite flower-stems. And he is a good pot-plant, too—rarest quality in an Iris.

The shameful truth must now come out. I am utterly afraid of bulbs. With ordinary plants I have no such qualms, for they have no wish to disappear underground and keep you in the dark. The moment the plant feels poorly you can note its symptoms, and diagnose the disease, and heave up the whole thing with your trowel and give it repeated changes of soil and situation until you have either killed or cured. But how underhand and secretive a thing is a bulb! Your priceless Daffodil, your gracious Lily, blooms in glory; two months later there is nothing of them left above ground, perhaps, and you have not an idea what dreadful things may not be going on under the surface. In all probability a mouse or a slug is having a word with that bulb, and you may say a

last good-bye to your Lily and your money and your
happiness all at once. Therefore I maintain that there
is something ominous and terrible about bulbs. I am
slowly learning confidence, I will confess, and beginning
to feel some security that, if I plant a thing, I may, with
luck, hope to see it again next year. But still the old
terror grips me when it comes to things like the bulbous
Irises, that are full of fads and hate winter damps, and
all kinds of things that I cannot possibly guarantee them
against if they insist on sitting tight underground where
I cannot see what is the matter with them. If my soil
were sandy and my winters cold and sunny, then I might
be braver; but, as it is, I have so often planted bulbous
Irises with every care, and I have so very seldom seen
them again (and, even so, a slug has either eaten the
shoot of the flower, or a shower lashed it to ribbons and
splotched it all over with mud), that now I lie low when
bulbous Irises are talked of, and divert the conversation
to *Iris mellita* or *Iris gracilipes* as soon as I can.

But Crocus? Ah, there is a jewel-race for the rock-
garden! Far, far away, though, stand the profane crowd
of Dutch Crocuses—fat, bloated things that have lost all
the brilliant grace of the wild species. And of these my
best loves, among the autumn bloomers, are, of course,
the unequalled *speciosus*, with his variety *Aitchisoni*,
even larger and bluer; *pulchellus*, soft lavender; *zonatus*,
very early, of a vinous lilac; and *iridiflorus*, that rare
and lovely Crocus, deep purple, with reflexing outer
segments that make him look a little *Iris stylosa*.
There are, of course, innumerable others, but I have
never specialised on Crocus, much as I love the race, and
all I ask is glorification for my sad garden in autumn.
Then, of the Spring Crocuses, the first in esteem as in
date is *Imperati*, lilac-purple within, and nankeen without; next comes *etruscus*, beautiful soft blue; then the

dear old common *aureus*, a sheer blaze of gold ; *argenteus*,
really silver-white, with dark outer lines that enhance
his brilliancy ; and a stray plant, sent me two years ago
in a letter, of *Alexandri*—a great fatty from Servia, of
the deepest imperial purple with orange stigma. I should
like, of course, to have every Crocus, and every variety
of Crocus, under Heaven. But such an ambition is very
far yet from fulfilment, and though I dream of little
clumps of colour prying out at me from every bush as I
go, for the present the species I have mentioned make
up the pitiful number of my Crocuses (I will not say
Croci, nor will I meanly evade the difficulty ; Crocus,
by now, has become mere English, just as Narcissus is
beginning, thanks to the admirable sense of street-
vendors, to sink into the vernacular under the shape of
'Narciss'). Even as Snowdrops never look so beautiful
as when hanging their bells from some high place on the
rockery, even so the Crocuses never look so lovely as
when winking at the sun from under some light bush-
shelter on its slopes.

The Lilies are a high and haughty race, impatient of
cultivation and incalculable of temper. Nor are most of
them in place in the rock-garden, though, on shrubby
banks above the bog, *auratum* (never, never buy *auratum*,
when you can get *auratum platyphyllum*), *Hansoni*,
Henryi, *szovitzianum*, *monadelphum*, *pomponium*, *gigan-
teum*, and *Martagon* look nothing short of superb.
Lower down I have thickets now of *pardalinum*, *Grayi*,
and *Roezlii* ; while in the New Garden *Humboldti* is beginning to make itself at home, I think, as well as all the
others that I have quoted from the Old Garden. As for
the rockwork itself, nothing more effectively breaks its
horizontal lines than the upstanding grace of the smaller
Lilies. *Chalcedonicum* is superb in July in any rough
corner, while the scarlet little *tenuifolium* and *concolor* are

equally precious, though I have never found them equally
pleasant or trustworthy to deal with. For your Lilies
provide drainage as sharp as Katharina's tongue, then
fill in with light rich cool soil, and plenty of grit and
peat and chips. And then (I believe) feed, feed, feed.
Discreetly, and with refined stuff, but still feed, feed, feed.
These Lilies, one and all, are so stately and ethereal that
they seem to scout the very suggestion of food, and to
imply that they are of natures too fine to delight in anything more substantial than air or dew. Don't you
believe them. They are merely acting up to early
Victorian rules of female conduct. They are sisters to
those women of Thackeray's who pecked at their food
indifferently, to pretend as if, like Amina, a grain of rice
was enough for them; but one knew perfectly well that
they had previously had roast mutton and rice-pudding
with the children in the nursery. Even so, these dainty,
superb Lilies are rank, greedy feeders, gorging every
morsel of fatness that the soil contains, and then asking
for more. But their feeding must be done so that they
can pretend not to be feeding at all; old rich manure, well
mixed and dug in and laid far down in a bed a foot or
more beneath the bulbs. Another point on which I
would remark is that people usually fail to realise the
moment at which the Lilies are most thankful for surface
refreshment. This moment is not in late autumn or even
in spring, but just when the flowers are over, and the
plant's forces returning, exhausted with the strain of
bloom-bearing, back into the bulb. If you administer
a good tonic of cow-manure at that moment, the wearied
forces go back more invigorated than when they came up,
and set to work immediately building a finer bulb than
ever for next season. For a plant's lowest ebb of vitality
is always when the blossoming period is over, and, at that
instant, any help you can give it is more thankfully

received, and more generously repaid, than at any other time, though help never comes amiss.

Setting aside the bigger Lilies, and concentrating on the smaller growers, there are two besides *concolor*, its yellow form *Coridion, tenuifolium*, and *alutaceum*, that are splendid for the rock-garden. Of *Lilium Alexandrae* the greatest living grower of Lilies once went so far as to inform me, very irreverently, that she was 'a beast.' I am afraid, though, despite her euphemious ascription, that the unladylike epithet is well deserved. This Japanese Lily, whose prettiest name is the native one, Yuki-Yuri—Snow Lily—is a supposed natural hybrid between *longiflorum* and *auratum*, a low-growing species with immense pure-white flowers, that resemble *longiflorum* in colour, but have the wide starry shape of *auratum* and the Archelirion Lilies generally. I bloomed her last year well enough to see how splendid she was, but most of my plants have since departed, and I see clearly that *Lilium Alexandrae* has no notion of making herself cheap in English gardens. In the Old Garden I made a special paradise for her this season. I first took out every scrap of soil for two and a half feet down. Then at the bottom of this pit, which was about two feet across, I laid a bed of rough stones. On that four or five inches of old manure. On that a solid layer of rough, rich soil, with stone, and blocks of peat and leaves and loam and manure, and then filled in the rest with the most delicious velvety compost that any Lily ever throve in—leaf-mould, rich and dark and ancient; sand, loam, shredded peat, and abundance of crock, coarse and fine. Then, enshrined each in silver sand, I planted my Lilies—*Alexandrae* and the adored *rubellum*, so lovely and so prosperous—and then, on the top of them, a six-inch bed or more of the same soothing mixture, in which I planted a second choice of rare

T

treasures—*Omphalodes Luciliae* (who now looks as dead
as Queen Anne), *Primula Reini, Primula spectabilis,
Meconopsis aculeata, Meconopsis grandis, Meconopsis
simplicifolia, Meconopsis racemosa, Cypripedium ventricosum, Shortia uniflora, Schizocodon, Daphne arbuscula,
Cyclamen libanoticum, Sisyrinchium grandiflorum,* and
Crocus Imperati wherever there was a chink left. Now,
it will be very hard if all those delicacies refuse to thrive
after such care and consideration!

Of the Tulips I have all the lesser kinds descending
the rockwork into choice spaces, while up above, in
thickets of the dwarf mountain-pine, gleam the crimsons
of *gesneriana* and the saffron of *florentina*—which is
only a form, I fancy, of our own native *Tulipa sylvestris,*
so abundant in the few places where it is found, and yet
so shy of flowering. I have seen a whole orchard full of
it near Oxford, but not a sign of blossom. *Tulipa kol-
vakowskiana* is very early and very dwarf, of a creamy
pinky flush like *Lewisia Tweedyi*; then *Tulipa Orpha-
nidesi*, scarlet; *Greigi*, terrifying in its vermilion; *per-
sica*, little and rather delightful, with golden flowers,
coppery outside; *clusiana*, the Lady Tulip, tall, with
glaucous bluey leaves, and long flowers, striped, of rose
and white—the sweetest and most fascinating of painted
ladies, which is now so rare all over the Mediterranean
shores, that my surprise may be imagined when I once
found a whole olive-yard full of it right in the heart
of Cannes. No doubt that plot has long since been sold
for building, and the Tulip exterminated; when I saw
it those delicious rosy-white blossoms were shining everywhere among the coarse grasses and garlics, under the
gnarled old olives. Then comes the common Mediterranean
Tulip, *praecox*, large and fine, but inferior to the other
great scarlets and crimsons, to *gesneriana, spathulata,
Greigi, micheliana, Eichleri* and *fulgens*, in that the out-

side of his segments is comparatively dull and opaque, no match for the black-eyed brilliancy of their cup's lining. Next, *Tulipa Lownei*, a rare beautiful dwarf, with one or two pale whity-red goblets, with bluish ribs to the inner segments; and, to conclude, my two best beloveds are *Tulipa linifolia*, with crinkly, wavy, brown-edged leaves and flowers of an appalling scarlet, carried six inches or so above the ground; and *Tulipa Batalini*, about the same size, with large and very beautifully designed blossoms of a clear, gentle, butter yellow—no hard or golden shade, but a true, bland, canary colour—the right Chinese Imperial note, and harmonising most gloriously with the Imperial purple of *Edraianthus serpyllifolius major*.

And I must not forget to do justice here to the lesser cousins of Lilium—to the Solomon's Seals, of whom our native *officinale* has been treated in his own deserved place. But the big *Polygonatum multiflorum* is superb for a rough place near water; while the little pink-flowered Himâlyan, *roseum*, is a rare and easy treasure. *Maianthemum* is a dear little creature, too, with pairs of glossy heart-shaped leaves on a stem about six inches high, and then a tiny fluffy white spike like a miniature Spiraea. He grows wild all over the Alpine forests (and in one Yorkshire wood on the east coast), and makes a precious inhabitant for any dank, rather shaded, corner. I have often collected him abroad, and now the Old Garden has specially fine colonies of him, as he rambles all over the place, and wrestles amicably for supremacy with *Cystopteris montana*. *Paris quadrifolia* is another quaint person from our own woods, with four leaves in a cross-pattern, and, in the middle, a small green flower followed by a big black berry. Nor must I forget the smaller *Funkias*, who are precious, and a certain marvel that I found on the grassy down close to the seashore at

Victoria in British Columbia. It was an open common sloping towards a sea of incredible blueness, and beyond there were white snow mountains, and everywhere the glory of ·life. And there, among the grasses, was the loveliest dwarf thing—a *Brodiaea*, I believe, but anyhow a jewel—bearing, close to the ground, one or two great cup-shaped flowers of a deep intense blue-violet. I clamoured for a weapon immediately, and ruined my friend's best knife in getting up a bulb or two. And now these have grown and grown, but never flowered; this year, however, I have better hopes, for I turned them all out of their pots last season, and they have already shown their gratitude by spreading unbelievably, and already one leaf looks solid enough to promise flowers later on. (Oh me! it *has* flowered. Tall! And white!!)

And now, I think, the tale of these notes is full, and over me creeps a chilling conviction of their inadequacy. Fellow-enthusiasts, forgive me for all that I have left out (space compelling); non-enthusiasts, forgive me for all that I have put in; and so, to make no long apologies, I will only appeal for mercy to every true gardener's pleasure in talking about his plants, whether they be few or many, good or bad, blotched Odontoglossums or bedding Verbenas; I have spoken only as my opportunities have allowed, neither more nor less, and honestly, too, I hope and fear. Therefore, without presuming to offer help or advice, I hope this selection from my experiences may find sympathy with others who may have suffered better fates or worse. To all who have a fellow-feeling with this book and its heroes, I offer my thanks beforehand; to all who despise its enthusiasms, or scorn them because these mutilated notes pass over so many of their rarer treasures, I offer beforehand my disarming confession. Yes, I have had to leave out so much that this annotation of my favourites is far more partial and incomplete than I had meant. But, after all, no one need trouble to read my rhapsodies, nor to condemn them. Be pacified, mightier gardeners, and pass by on the other side. I have done my best within my limits; and I turn to those who recognise my difficulties. Wherefore, to borrow Parkinson's conclusion, 'let Momus bite his lips, and eat his heart' (though it seems a pity), 'and so, farewell.'

INDEX

295

THE END